THE COMPLETE IDIOT'S GUIDE® TO

Aquaponic Gardening

by Meg Stout

ALPHA

A member of Penguin Group (USA) Inc.

To my daughters and husband, who inspire me every day

ALPHA BOOKS

Published by Penguin Group (USA) Inc.

Penguin Group (USA) Inc., 375 Hudson Street, New York, New York 10014, USA • Penguin Group (Canada), 90 Eglinton Avenue East, Suite 700, Toronto, Ontario M4P 2Y3, Canada (a division of Pearson Penguin Canada Inc.) • Penguin Books Ltd., 80 Strand, London WC2R 0RL, England • Penguin Ireland, 25 St. Stephen's Green, Dublin 2, Ireland (a division of Penguin Books Ltd.) • Penguin Group (Australia), 250 Camberwell Road, Camberwell, Victoria 3124, Australia (a division of Pearson Australia Group Pty. Ltd.) • Penguin Books India Pvt. Ltd., 11 Community Centre, Panchsheel Park, New Delhi—110 017, India • Penguin Group (NZ), 67 Apollo Drive, Rosedale, North Shore, Auckland 1311, New Zealand (a division of Pearson New Zealand Ltd.) • Penguin Books (South Africa) (Pty.) Ltd., 24 Sturdee Avenue, Rosebank, Johannesburg 2196, South Africa • Penguin Books Ltd., Registered Offices: 80 Strand, London WC2R 0RL, England

International Standard Book Number: 978-1-61564-235-9
Library of Congress Catalog Card Number: 2012951749

15   14   8   7   6   5   4

Interpretation of the printing code: The rightmost number of the first series of numbers is the year of the book's printing; the rightmost number of the second series of numbers is the number of the book's printing. For example, a printing code of 13-1 shows that the first printing occurred in 2013.

Printed in the United States of America

Note: This publication contains the opinions and ideas of its author. It is intended to provide helpful and informative material on the subject matter covered. It is sold with the understanding that the author and publisher are not engaged in rendering professional services in the book. If the reader requires personal assistance or advice, a competent professional should be consulted.

The author and publisher specifically disclaim any responsibility for any liability, loss, or risk, personal or otherwise, which is incurred as a consequence, directly or indirectly, of the use and application of any of the contents of this book.

Most Alpha books are available at special quantity discounts for bulk purchases for sales promotions, premiums, fund-raising, or educational use. Special books, or book excerpts, can also be created to fit specific needs. For details, write: Special Markets, Alpha Books, 375 Hudson Street, New York, NY 10014.

Publisher: *Mike Sanders*

Executive Managing Editor: *Billy Fields*

Senior Acquisitions Editor: *Tom Stevens*

Development Editor: *Lynn Northrup*

Senior Production Editor: *Janette Lynn*

Copy Editor: *Jaime Julian Wagner*

Cover Designer: *Kurt Owens*

Book Designers: *William Thomas, Rebecca Batchelor*

Indexer: *Heather McNeil*

Layout: *Ayanna Lacey*

Proofreader: *Amy Borrelli*

Contents

Introduction

An aquaponic garden allows a gardener to avoid chemical fertilizers by using fish to provide nutrients for the plants. The plants grow in a soil-free environment, and the roots clean the water for the fish. Together, the fish and plants work together so the water can be recycled indefinitely. You only need to replace water that has evaporated, reducing your water bill.

Aquaponic gardens produce food naturally with much less water than a conventional garden. Aquaponics is becoming popular among people concerned about nutrition, avoiding artificial additives, and protecting the environment.

You can create an aquaponic garden almost anywhere you can bring together light and space using a footprint as small as a single square foot. And aquaponics is easy. Once you've created your system, you won't need to water or weed it, or even bend over. You will be able to grow more plants in less space than in a traditional garden, and your plants will grow faster and larger.

How I Stumbled Upon Aquaponics

I'm an engineer/physicist, and I love elegant systems. I discovered aquaponics in the spring of 2010 while surfing the web. I tumbled upon Britta Riley's Windowfarms, small hydroponic gardens grown in a tower of recycled bottles hanging in a window.

I loved the idea of these small gardens, but I didn't fancy the idea of bottles of chemical nutrients in my home. Dumping the nutrient solution every couple of weeks as recommended was something I knew I would forget to do. The search for better plant nutrients led me to aquaponics: the idea of using a fish tank as my nutrient reservoir. Within days I had created my aquaponic Windowfarm.

I loved my two aquaponic Windowfarms made out of their recycled bottles. Fun as they were, though, they weren't much more than edible conversation pieces.

When fall arrived, I decided to create a bigger aquaponic garden in my basement with 50- and 100-gallon stock tanks, heavy duty shelving, and fluorescent grow lights. With a bit more web research, I realized I could move my fish and plants outside.

Reduce Your Footprint

Aquaponic gardening gives you a chance to reduce your carbon footprint because your food doesn't have to travel hundreds of miles to get to your house. It reduces your water footprint because it recycles its own water. Aquaponics is also good for the environment because you aren't adding fertilizer and chemicals that can pollute local water.

Even if you don't care about going green and reducing your footprint, aquaponics is a great way to grow food. Economic and health concerns are excellent reasons to adopt aquaponics.

Do It Yourself—or Not

In this book you'll see a lot of DIY plans, but you can always decide that your time is worth more than the additional cost to buy a pre-made system. As aquaponics becomes more popular, I expect it will become possible to buy more and more components locally without having to pay for shipping. In the meantime, this book gives you enough information to create a system in a weekend using materials from local hardware and pet supply stores, if you want to.

How This Book Is Organized

This book has 24 chapters organized under five parts:

Part 1, Creating Your System, explains the planning, placement, and plumbing you need to create an aquaponic garden so it recycles its own water. This section also tells you about the light you need for growing your garden and the best water conditions for your fish and plants.

Part 2, Growing Options, discusses the different ways you can grow plants without soil by using either rocks that are alternately flooded and drained or by floating your plants over the surface of the water in rafts. This section also explains how to maximize the yield of your garden by taking advantage of vertical space to grow your plants.

Part 3, Nutrients and Plants, tells you how to create the natural process that transforms fish ammonia into fertilizer. This section also discusses what plants grow best, how to start your plants, and how to protect your plants from pests, and it gives you tips for increasing the quantity of produce your garden provides.

Part 4, Fish and Other Animals, talks about the fish you might want to consider raising in your garden and how to take care of them. This section covers how to catch, prepare, and cook edible fish. Finally, there are details on animals other than fish you might want to add to your garden ecosystem.

Part 5, Beyond the Basics, covers topics you might want to consider if you to take your garden outside or extend your growing season. This section also talks about how to automate your garden and eliminate dependence on municipal water and electricity. This section covers maintenance as well as integrating aquaponics into schools or communities, and includes a DIY section with plans for making a variety of the components mentioned in the book.

I also include two appendixes to help further your understanding of aquaponic gardening: a glossary of terms and a list of books, websites, and other resources.

Extras

Throughout the book you will find four different types of sidebars that provide tips, cautions, definitions, and other miscellaneous information to enhance your understanding of aquaponics. Look for these boxes:

GREEN TIP

Check these boxes for tips to help make your garden grow better or reduce the number of resources you need to devote to your garden.

SOUNDS FISHY

The information in these boxes clarifies misconceptions and cautions you against making costly or potentially dangerous mistakes.

DEFINITION

These boxes define terms used in aquaponic gardening that you might not be familiar with.

DID YOU KNOW …

Check these boxes for interesting tidbits that relate to aquaponic gardening.

Acknowledgments

I am forever grateful for the generosity of the gardeners who have shared their knowledge with me, either in presentations, videos, books, forums, or formal research. I am particularly grateful to those whose examples and photos are contained in the book. They have been overwhelmingly generous in sharing their wisdom so you can better understand this amazing technology.

I am also grateful for Marilyn Allen, who asked me to write this book, as well as Tom Stevens, Lynn Northrup, and the rest of the folks at Alpha Books who worked to transform my arcane text into understandable prose.

Finally, I must acknowledge the love, kindness, and patience my husband and daughters showed me throughout this process.

Trademarks

All terms mentioned in this book that are known to be or are suspected of being trademarks or service marks have been appropriately capitalized. Alpha Books and Penguin Group (USA) Inc. cannot attest to the accuracy of this information. Use of a term in this book should not be regarded as affecting the validity of any trademark or service mark.

Creating Your System

In this first part of the book, we cover a variety of things you will want to think about as you plan your aquaponic garden. The first chapter explores what you want in an aquaponic garden. Do you want a garden inside your home our outside? Do you want to buy a pre-made kit, or do you want to build it yourself? Chapter 2 helps you ensure your plants get enough of the right kind of light. Chapter 3 explains how to make water work for you on both a physical and chemical level. Chapter 4 covers various options for fish tanks. This chapter also discusses what to use for grow beds—and even includes instructions on how to make your own grow beds if you're handy with tools. Chapter 5 shows you how to plumb your system so you can pump water between your fish tank and grow beds properly.

What Is Your Vision?

In This Chapter

- How aquaponic gardens work
- Coming up with a plan
- Sample home-based systems
- Expanding into aquaponic micro-farming

Aquaponics is a way to garden by combining fish and plants in a garden with no soil. By combining fish and plants, the water in the garden can be constantly recycled. It's a great way to grow your own vegetables without chemicals in a relatively small space.

This first chapter is all about you and your goals for an aquaponic garden.

What Is an Aquaponic Garden?

You may have heard of *hydroponics*, where plants are grown without soil using water with chemical fertilizers. *Aquaponics* takes hydroponics and makes it green by using fish in the water tank to provide the plant nutrients. In an *aquaponic garden* you don't have soil. The roots of the plants are either in water directly or they are supported by some sort of rock material into which water ebbs and flows.

The three main components of an aquaponic system are the fish tank, watertight *grow beds*, and the pump that moves water from the fish tank into the grow beds. (See Chapter 4 for information on how to make or buy grow beds.) The plants cleanse the water, which then drains back into the fish tank. Because the grow beds are watertight, the water is constantly recycled.

DEFINITION

Hydroponics is a type of gardening where plants are grown without soil by adding nutrients to the water. **Aquaponics** is gardening where the plants are grown without soil and the nutrients come from fish kept in the water tank (aquaculture). **Aquaponic gardening** is gardening using an aquaponics system, where the water from your fish tank irrigates your plants and then drains back into your fish tank. A **grow bed** is a watertight planter or container that holds your plants.

It is the proportions that make aquaponic gardening different than simply connecting a hydroponic system to a fish tank. The secret to successful aquaponic gardening is achieving balance. The grow beds need to have roughly the same volume as the fish tank, and the entire volume of water needs to circulate through the system every hour.

You can use these basic components to create an elegant garden hanging in your window with a single goldfish or a multi-acre urban farm producing millions of pounds of fish and produce.

Creating Your Plan

You are the expert on what you want. Your desires and needs will shape the type of garden you buy or build. What are your hopes for your personal adventure in aquaponics? Do you want a garden that is exquisitely beautiful, with ornamental plants and koi? Are you trying to teach students about physics and biology and want all the components exposed to view?

How hectic is your schedule? Are you a jet-setter who needs a garden so automated it can be run from your cell phone, or are you willing and able to tend to your garden and fish in person each day?

What size of garden are you looking for? Do you want a garden that merely brightens a dreary corner? Are you trying to produce all the vegetables your family needs in a year, or are you trying to feed a community?

A clear goal can save you time and money. You will save you money as you avoid buying extra toys you don't need. You will save time as you focus on what works for you rather than trying to use designs that don't fit your situation.

Your Long-Term Goals

Why do you want to create an aquaponic garden? It may be that you want to grow tomatoes during the winter without artificial fertilizers, or you might simply want a decorative fishpond surrounded by lush plants.

You may be part of an organization with larger ambitions. Take a moment and write down a big goal and a few small goals that lead up to your big goal:

My big goal (complete in a few years):

_____

First small goal (complete in a month):

_____

Second small goal (complete in a couple months):

_____

Third small goal (complete in six months):

_____

Goals are stars to guide by, not whips to beat yourself up with. There are no goals too lofty or too modest. The important thing is that these goals reflect your hopes and dreams.

DID YOU KNOW ...

The Arc is a nonprofit serving individuals with developmental delays. It has 700 chapters in the United States. In 2012, the Arc organization in Meriden-Wallingford, Connecticut, created an aquaponic greenhouse that grows food for the Arc Eatery, a division of the nonprofit organization that trains and employs adults with developmental delays. For more information about the Arc, visit www.thearc.org.

Strengths and Limitations

Do you have any particular strengths going into your project? Do you or your friends have skill with tools, building talent, or gardening expertise?

Along the line of strengths, do you have any current or future resource opportunities? Maybe you have a pile of rugged plastic containers just sitting around. Perhaps there's a vacant lot or sunny alley in your area that neighbors agree should be "dealt with." Maybe you've relocated and have a bigger yard than before. Perhaps you can get funding for green initiatives or for addressing drought conditions common in your region, or maybe a nearby business has a greenhouse they're looking to sell or donate. You'll be surprised at the opportunities you find when you're looking.

Then there are your weaknesses. Are you short on cash or handyman skills? Have you strained the patience of family or roommates with past projects? Are you so busy you barely have time to consider a project, much less complete one? Are there laws in your area that will prevent you from collecting water or raising certain fish or plants? Writing weaknesses down makes them conquerable.

One of my weaknesses starting out was a lack of experience: I'd never gardened, and I'd only raised fish as a hobby. But my strengths were my ability to build things and my training in engineering.

Take a moment to write down your strengths and weaknesses:

My strengths and assets:

_____

_____

My limitations and liabilities:

_____

_____

Inside or Out?

Will you put your system inside or outside? If you can keep your garden inside, you have freedom to maintain your system temperature according to the needs of your fish and plants; however, if you locate your garden outside, you won't have to buy grow lights, which can be pricey. (I'll discuss grow lights and other indoor lighting options in Chapter 2.)

You should also find out how much load your floors can bear since water is heavy, weighing 62 pounds per cubic foot. Concrete floors in basements may be able to support as much as 100 to 200 pounds per square foot, but a standard residential wood floor may only be able to support 40 pounds per square foot. This doesn't mean you can't have an aquaponic garden inside a home or business, but you might have to keep the system small.

If you've never gardened outside because your soil isn't good, don't worry. An aquaponic garden doesn't need *any* soil. My outdoor garden exists on a brick patio, and I could fit it onto a bit of paved ground the size of a parking space, as long as that patch of ground got good light.

Another consideration is whether your outdoor location has access to water and electricity. It's possible to have an aquaponic garden in a remote location, but it's easier to add water to your garden and power your pumps if your garden is close to an electrical outlet and a hose.

A third consideration is pests. Will you need to build fences to keep out birds, squirrels, deer, or neighbors? Will you need to consider termites or mosquitoes? If you're new to gardening, you might want to ask someone who has a garden already what problems they've encountered.

Finally, if you're thinking of fish or plants that require warm water, are you prepared use heaters to keep the fish tank warm? Unless you live in a place that is warm year-round, this can get expensive, as I'll discuss in Chapter 19.

DIY or Kit?

If you find a kit system that fits your needs and your budget, buy it. There is great comfort in using a system from a reputable outfit with experience in aquaponics. Another option is to acquire good plans and build your system accordingly. Either way, make sure you are dealing with someone who has solid credentials.

If you feel you have the time and skills, DIY has some benefits. It can be significantly less expensive. You can customize your system to fit your space, and when you're done, you know exactly what each part does and how it works. If you decide to expand your system later on, you'll be better able to do so without worry that some company's product line has been discontinued.

The challenge of DIY is the time it takes. It's not just the time to construct a system; there's the time to find and buy parts and tools, and time you may spend on dead ends. And there is also expense involved in buying any tools you don't already own.

If you do have the tools, time, and skills, I've included DIY plans for components and systems throughout this book.

Plants and Fish

In Chapters 11 and 15 I'll discuss the different types of plants and fish you can consider. It's good at this point, though, to think about what kind of fish and plants appeal to you.

I strongly recommend you use freshwater fish, the kind of fish that live in landlocked lakes and rivers. If you use saltwater fish that come from the ocean, you will be severely limited in the types of plants you can use.

Ornamental fish like goldfish or koi are commonly treated with chemicals that could cause cancer in humans. If you plan to eat your fish, you'll want to use fish that are traditionally eaten, like trout, catfish, tilapia, and my favorite, bluegill. In Chapter 15 I talk more about fish and their needs.

Think about how much effort you're willing to expend to meet the needs of your fish. Some fish, like tilapia, require warm water. Others, like sunfish and goldfish, prefer warm water but can survive near-freezing temperatures. Others, like trout, really need cool water. And some fish, like catfish, grow long and need a tank that can hold at least a couple of hundred gallons.

GREEN TIP

Find out what regulations and laws govern the types of fish you're planning to use. Goldfish and koi are rarely regulated. Game fish often require a permit. And exotic food fish, like tilapia, are usually regulated and may even be illegal in your town. Even some plants may be illegal. Contact your state Department of Natural Resources to find out how they regulate fish and if there are additional plant regulations in the county or town where you live.

If you don't much care what kind of fish you use, consider your gardening goals. If you want to grow cool-weather plants like lettuce, spinach, and peas, you may want to avoid warm water fish. If you want to grow tomatoes year round, you'll want fish that can tolerate warm water.

If you want to grow crops in season, both warm-weather crops and cool-weather crops, you need fish that can endure a wide range of temperatures. (Chapter 11 goes into detail about warm-weather and cool-weather crops.) Fish and plant options are detailed in the following table.

Fish	Cool-Weather Plants	Warm-Weather Plants	Seasonal Plants
Koi and goldfish	Yes	Yes	Yes
Tilapia	No	Yes	OK in warm climates
Trout	Yes	No	OK in cool climates
Bluegill and catfish	Yes	Yes	Yes

Sample Home Systems

Now we're going to briefly touch on a few different types of aquaponic gardens, so you can hone in on the kinds of gardens that catch your interest. A home-based garden can be small enough to fit on a countertop or large enough to feed your family. Your garden can be inexpensive, using affordable and recycled components, or it can be an elegant addition to your yard.

Creating an Aquaponic Window Garden

A vertical window garden (or Windowfarm) is the smallest practical aquaponic garden. You won't be able to grow much, but it is fun. A window garden is too small for a traditional water pump; it is not much more than a simple fish tank with an under-gravel filter. The air pump that powers the under-gravel filter can also be used to lift droplets of water from the fish tank to the topmost bottle. It's a bit complex, but very energy efficient.

The steady stream of droplets is more than enough to keep a handful of plants irrigated. A single small goldfish will provide enough nutrients for mint or lettuce. You should not count on using this kind of garden for fruiting plants, though my daughters did enjoy the few strawberries we got from our window garden. Fruiting plants usually need more nutrients than you can get from just one or two fish.

Perhaps the most valuable products you'll get from an aquaponic window garden are experience and fun. If all goes well, in a few months you'll have gravel full of the bacteria that convert fish waste to plant food. That could come in handy if you want to create a larger system later.

I was so pleased when the strawberry plant in my aquaponic window garden actually blossomed.

Using a Water Pump in the Fish Tank

The simplest kind of aquaponic garden uses a water pump in the fish tank to push water into the grow beds. The size of this kind of garden can be as small as a plastic bin for your plants connected to a small aquarium or as large as several acres. If you are considering a medium-sized aquaponic garden to grow a few food crops in your home, this is the kind of system I recommend.

This small system uses plastic bins and metal shelves purchased at Ikea in Japan.
(Photo courtesy of Aragon St. Charles of Japan Aquaponics)

Using a Sump to Keep Your Fish Safe

Some people are nervous about putting a water pump in their fish tank. Little fish can get sucked into the water pump, and food, waste, and plants can clog the pump over time. Adding a second, lower tank, or *sump*, and putting the pump in the sump gives you several benefits:

- You don't need to clean your pump as frequently.

- Because your fish tank overflows into the sump, the water level in the fish tank stays constant.

- Assuming you prevent small fish from getting into the sump, you won't get small fish sucked up into the pump.

The pump in the sump sends water to the fish tank and the grow beds, which then drains back into the sump. This kind of system is sometimes called a *constant height, one pump (CHOP)* system.

Adding a sump low enough to accept drainage from the fish tank and grow beds may not be practical for all situations, but I highly recommend a CHOP configuration if you have the space and the budget.

DEFINITION

Sump means a low-lying place that receives drainage, from the old German word for a low-lying pit or swamp. Many aquaponic gardeners drain their grow beds and fish tanks into a central sump tank, then pump the water back out again. A **constant height, one pump (CHOP)** system is a configuration that has a pump in the sump such that the water in the fish tank stays at a constant height.

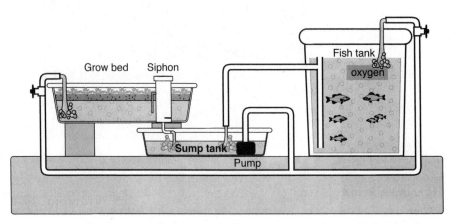

Adding a sump allows the fish tank to stay at a constant height. Water is pumped from the sump into the grow beds and fish tank, which then drain back into the sump.

(Adapted with permission from illustration created by EcoFilms Australia, ecofilms.com.au)

Sample Micro-Farms

Many people grow gardens to increase the amount of vegetables in their diet, since a diet rich in fresh fruits and vegetables can keep you healthy and slender. This is particularly true in so-called *food deserts*, areas where there is limited access to stores that sell fresh produce, protein, and milk.

Once you've mastered the basics of aquaponic gardening, it's possible to consider something larger, and sometimes the term *garden* simply isn't adequate. If your garden produces more than enough for you and your family, you might want to consider becoming a small-scale farm. A *micro-farm* is a bit like a microbrewery, where individual businesses produce their own beers.

Sahib Punjabi built this aquaponics system in a lane next to a shopping center.
(Photo courtesy of Pat Chiu)

Environmentally conscious folks and *locavores* may find the idea of micro-farming particularly appealing. If this is your dream, the full range of skills required to become a *micro-farmer* are beyond the scope of this book. But this book can help you develop a basic foundation in aquaponics so you can determine if aquaponic micro-farming is for you.

DEFINITION

A **food desert** is an area with limited access to affordable fresh food, resulting in malnutrition and obesity among residents. A **micro-farm** is an area approximately one acre where fresh food is grown for sale, and a **micro-farmer** is the person who grows food on a micro-farm. **Locavores** are people who make a point of eating locally grown food to promote sustainability and green businesses.

Aquaponics and rain catchment system between the kitchens at Main Event Caterers near Washington, D.C.

(Photo courtesy of Joel Thevoz of Main Event Caterers)

The Least You Need to Know

- There are as many individual system designs as there are aquaponic gardeners, but there are only a few fundamental types of systems.
- Write down your goals as well as your gardening-related strengths and limitations—you may be surprised by what you learn.
- You can learn a lot from a small starter garden—it's better to make your inevitable mistakes with only a few living things.
- Once you've learned how to garden with aquaponics, there may be ways to make a modest profit by expanding from a family-based system to a micro-farm.

Giving Your Plants the Right Light

In This Chapter

- Things a gardener should know about light
- Growing outdoors with natural light
- Growing indoors with artificial light
- Basic accessories for your indoor garden

Your plants need light to grow—for them, it's a matter of life or death. This chapter contains a lot of detail because it's so easy to fail before you begin by not planning for the light your plants need.

If you plan to garden indoors, you will need special grow lights, which are special lights and fixtures that produce large amounts of light in colors plants use (white, but with more red and blue than normal lights). These lights can cost more than $100 and use a lot of electricity.

As long as you plan to consult professionals who know about indoor gardening and buy what they recommend, you can skip this chapter. If you plan to garden outside, you can skip the parts of this chapter that deal with artificial light and read only the bits about how to make the most of the light the sun pours down on us all. But if you are tempted to save money on lights and design your own indoor solution, you need to read this chapter and understand it thoroughly.

What You Need to Know About Light

Your plants will use the energy from light to grow. It is critical that you give your plants enough of the right kind of light or your garden will not thrive. There are two particularly important concepts when it comes providing light to your plants: the first is the amount of light you'll need and the second is the color (or wavelength) of light your plants want.

Buckets of Sunlight

Grown inside, your plants will need as much light as they would normally get outside during the proper season for that plant. The measure of light quantity is the lumen. If you think of an individual particle of light being like an individual molecule of water, a lumen is like a gallon—a collection of individual bits of light.

Light, like water, is absolutely necessary if you want to grow plants. Your plant absorbs energy from light using chlorophyll, the molecule in plants that converts light into energy. Plants need a certain amount of light each day, and that light should be a specific color or wavelength.

How Much Light Do You Need per Square Foot?

When it comes to the quantity of light a plant needs, we express those needs in terms of lumens. But we also need to think about how many lumens plants need per square foot. The term *lux* is used to measure how much the light is spread out over an area. Lux is a number of lumens per square meter (roughly 11 square feet) and is similar to the term *inches of rain*, which refers to the quantity of rainwater spread over an area.

The output of light fixtures is usually reported in terms of light humans can see, but that isn't the same as the light plants need. The reddish, blueish light plants need is called *photosynthetically active radiation (PAR)*. If you are growing indoors under lights, you need to figure out the amount of PAR lighting a light fixture and bulb will provide to your plant, which is a calculated based on the lights you use and the distance that light is from your plants.

> **DEFINITION**
>
> **Photosynthetically active radiation (PAR)** is a term used to describe the light that plants convert to energy, which isn't the same as the light the human eye sees.

The following table shows the amount of lux (light per unit area) available in different lighting conditions. For fun, I added a column showing how much money this would be if lumens on the ground were like pennies in your wallet.

Lumens per Square Meter for Different Lighting Conditions

Light Conditions	Lux (Lumens per Square Meter)	Value if Lumens Were Pennies
Moonless night sky	0.002	$0.00
Full moon in the tropics	1.0	$0.01
Family living room	50	$0.50
Hallway lighting	80	$0.80
Office lighting	400	$4
Overcast day	1,000	$10
Clear day	20,000	$200
Direct sun (noon, no clouds)	100,000	$1,000

A plant needs the amount of light it could usually expect to get on an average day: 20,000 lux (or $200 if lux were pennies). That is a lot more than the 400 lux (or $4 if lumens were pennies) an indoor plant would get in a well-lit office. No wonder a plant indoors will grow pale and spindly. It's starving for light.

Growing Outdoors

If you are willing to grow only those plants that would naturally grow in your standard outdoor garden, then you can disregard all this talk of lumens, lux, and wavelengths. The sun will shine on your aquaponic garden in the same quantity and with the same array of colors as it does on your neighbors' gardens. However, there are a few things to consider even in an outdoor aquaponics garden. Attention to light is important in an aquaponic garden because you have much more flexibility than you would have simply growing in the ground.

Making Sure All Your Plants Get Sunlight

You need to design your garden so your tall plants aren't casting their shadows over shorter plants. To help your plants to get as much sunlight as possible from morning twilight to evening twilight, make any rows in your garden run from north to south—that way, light isn't blocked by adjacent plants.

Some aquaponic gardeners grow plants in vertical planters or grow tubes, which I cover in Chapter 8. These can be great, but always make sure you place these tall structures at the back of your garden, where they won't cast a shadow on your other plants.

Where You Live Makes a Difference

The farther you are from the equator, the less total light you will get on average. The earth is tilted, so in summer the days in these areas are longer. But far from the equator where summer days are really long, the actual length of the growing season gets shorter. In Chapter 18 I'll talk about how to extend your growing season.

If you garden outdoors, you need to know your local weather conditions. The website gaisma.com is a great source for information on average monthly sunlight, rainfall, and temperature.

Growing During Short Winter Days

As the days get shorter, your plants will no longer get as much sunlight as they might want. You have two options:

- Grow plants that don't need much light. Cool-weather plants are already adapted to grow during short days. Therefore, growing plants in season is an easy way to continue getting a harvest as the days get shorter.

- Add artificial lighting to extend the length of time your plants are lit. You'll want some kind of structure to support the lights and protect them from rain and wind.

You can also use reflective foil to bounce the available light back onto your plants.

The north wall of this greenhouse is covered with insulation material that reflects light coming from the south.
(Photo courtesy of Pat Chiu)

Growing Indoors

After Thomas Edison invented a method to produce light with electricity, it was only a matter of time before artificial lights were able to produce enough lumens to support serious indoor growing. Today, growing under artificial lights is not only possible, some feel it is the preferred way to ensure that plants enjoy optimal conditions. Even people who have greenhouses sometimes add artificial lights. If you're interested in growing indoors, let's talk a bit about artificial light options.

Not All Lights Are Equal

As I've discussed, your indoor plants will want an amount of light similar to what they'd naturally get each day. But you can't just compare the wattage of the lights you use. Some light sources provide much more useful light to your plants per watt than others. The following table shows the number of light bulbs of different kinds you would need to light a 4×4-foot area.

Source	Bulbs Required for 4×4-Foot Area	Total Wattage
Standard white light bulbs (60-watt incandescents)	84	5040
Standard T-12 fluorescent bulbs (40 watts)	42	1640
Compact fluorescent grow lights (125 watts)	5	630
T-5 high-output fluorescent bulbs (54 watts)	10	540
High-intensity discharge HPS bulb (400 watts)	1	400

If you're thinking of growing indoors, you will want to compare prices for the fixtures and bulbs you would need to light your planned garden because any of these options can cost hundreds of dollars. But before you buy, read on. There are factors other than price you may want to consider.

Fluorescents

Fluorescent grow lights were the solution I picked when I created my first indoor garden. I liked the relatively low price of the fixtures and bulbs, I liked how cool they ran, and I liked the efficiency of the lights. But fluorescents aren't the perfect replacements for sunlight. First and foremost, sunlight is free. No artificial light source is free, no matter how efficient. That's one reason I eventually decided to move my garden outdoors.

Fluorescent lights used for growing plants are usually available in *T-5* sizes—tubes that are ⅝ inch in diameter. T-5 lights are large enough to produce serious light but small enough to allow many to be packed into a small space. You could use standard T-8 or T-12 bulbs that are an inch or more in diameter, but you'd need many more bulbs burning a lot more energy. An alternative is using *compact fluorescent lights (CFLs)* that can use standard light fixtures.

> **DEFINITION**
>
> **Fluorescent** bulbs produce light by making gas bounce off metal powder inside the bulb. **T-5** refers to straight fluorescent bulbs with a diameter of ⅝ inch. **Compact fluorescent lights (CFLs)** use a twisted bulb to reduce the size of the bulb for the same light output.

A disadvantage of fluorescent grow lights is that they go bad after only 6 months. The bulbs still produce light, but you will no longer get the quantity of PAR illumination your plants need. Unless you're proactive about replacing your lights on a set schedule, your indoor garden will simply stop thriving after six months.

The sunlight your plants want to receive penetrates deeply into a leafy canopy. Unfortunately, the way fluorescents use electricity and mercury to produce light results in extraordinarily uniform energy levels. This uniform energy light can't penetrate a leafy canopy, stopping after the first leaf or so it encounters. If you are growing simple plants, like lettuce, the inferior light penetration won't be an issue. But taller plants with lots of leaves, like tomatoes or peppers, will require additional lighting. Depending on the design of your garden, you may be able to light your plants from the side as well as from above to provide the required light.

> **SOUNDS FISHY**
>
> The 620 million fluorescent bulbs discarded in the United States every year release an estimated 2 to 4 tons of mercury, a heavy metal that can cause numerous health problems. Never intentionally break a fluorescent bulb. If a bulb does break, turn off fans and heaters, open a window, and evacuate the room. After 10 to 15 minutes, return to the room and carefully sweep up the debris. Use tape to pick up the last fragments, and put the broken pieces in a sealed bag outside. Your local government may have special disposal restrictions. The Environmental Protection Agency (EPA) has more info at www.epa.gov/cfl/cflcleanup.html.

Fluorescent lights are good for short plants. Notice the reflective enclosure, which maximizes the light being delivered to the plant.

(Photo courtesy of Jesse Hull of Imagine Aquaponics)

High-Intensity Discharge (HID) Bulbs and Ballasts

Most indoor growers use *high-intensity discharge (HID)* lighting. It is hard to beat HID lighting for powerful, deep-penetrating, plant-appropriate lighting.

You'll see the most popular bulbs labeled with HPS and/or MH. High-pressure sodium (HPS) HID bulbs produce reddish light and are used for flowering plants. Metal halide (MH) HID bulbs produce bluish light, perfect for green leafy plants. HID lights shoot high-voltage electricity into the bulb, making the gas spark. These sparks produce a mixed spectrum of light and mimic the different energy levels in sunlight.

HID lighting does have its disadvantages. HID bulbs and fixtures are expensive. HID bulbs can cost more than $100 each—even discount bulbs run $20. Each fixture also requires an expensive *ballast*, an electrical device that supplies and controls the light's voltage. Fixtures, ballasts, and bulbs are typically not interchangeable across manufacturers, so if you decide you aren't happy with the brand you started with, you have to buy all-new equipment to switch brands.

DEFINITION

High-intensity discharge (HID) lights are like standard light bulbs, except they operate at much higher voltages.

HID bulbs also use a lot of energy, with individual bulbs consuming anywhere from 250 to over 1,000 watts, and all that sparking gas produces a lot of heat. If you go with HID lighting, you will almost certainly have to put venting and air conditioning in place as well. Despite their initial cost and high heat production, HID lights are the best way to produce sunlight-like conditions indoors. You can find the required cooling fans and ducting at any store that sells HID lighting.

The HID lights in this indoor garden are water-cooled. The waste heat from the lights is used to heat the fish tank.

(Photo courtesy of Jesse Hull of Imagine Aquaponics)

Light-Emitting Diodes (LEDs)

Light-emitting diodes or *LEDs* don't have filaments that can burn out and they don't generate much heat. Recently LED lights have started to become affordable, and good LED lights for growing plants may soon be affordable as well.

DEFINITION

Light-emitting diodes (LEDs) convert electricity to light and don't use mercury or high voltage. LED technology is not yet mature but may be adequate for some plants.

Although LED grow light technology hasn't matured yet, it promises to be less costly than HID lighting and more environmentally safe and efficient than fluorescents. You may be able to use regular LED lights in a few situations, like growing micro-greens, which are shoots of standard salad plants that are unusually rich in flavor and vitamins.

These LED lights are used to grow micro-greens at Main Event Caterers in Northern Virginia.
(Photo courtesy of Joel Thevoz of Main Event Caterers)

Basic Accessories

Here are the key accessories I recommend you start with:

- **Timer.** Your timer can be a simple unit that automatically turns your lights on and off to get the number of hours of light desired. Standard timers allow you to turn your devices on or off in 30-minute increments, which is perfectly adequate.

- **Reflective film.** You will use this film to bounce light from walls back onto your plants. Mylar film is commonly used for this purpose and can be purchased from hydroponic supply stores. I've even seen folks use Mylar emergency blankets for this purpose.

- **Fan.** A fan will provide ventilation to exhaust excess moisture and heat from the room. It will circulate oxygen and carbon dioxide, and it will provide some movement to help pollinate plants in the absence of the insects you'd naturally have outside to do the job.

- **Calendar or log.** Use this to remind you when to buy replacement bulbs, particularly if you go with fluorescents.

The Least You Need to Know

- Your plants need good light to thrive. Ensuring adequate light should be one of your primary considerations as you design your aquaponic garden.
- If you garden outdoors, know your local conditions.
- If you decide to garden indoors, modern technology can help you succeed. You will need to use specialized grow lights rather than the typical lights sold for offices and homes.
- There are a lot of accessories on the market, but the basics you'll need for an indoor garden are a timer, reflective film, a fan, and a calendar or log.

Water: Vital to All Forms of Life

In This Chapter

* Important properties of water
* How water temperature impacts your garden
* The best water conditions for your fish
* How water interacts with plants

Without water, plants will not grow. Without water, fish simply cannot function. In an aquaponic garden, you will no longer have the chore of watering. Instead you have a near-constant resource that, properly managed, will ensure a healthy environment for your plants and fish independent of the torrential rains or crushing drought your soil-gardening neighbors may face.

I write this chapter expecting that some of you will decide to design a system unique to your particular property and situation. You DIY designers will need to understand how water works in more detail. Even if you are buying a system from someone else, it helps to know how your water affects other parts of your aquaponic garden.

How to Make Water Do What You Want

I have spent decades designing things to operate in the ocean, but I encountered a few surprises when I started gardening using aquaponics. Those surprises tended to involve either coming back to my garden to find water all over the floor or returning home to find a garden full of crispy plants when my "automatic" watering system failed. Even if you are planning to buy a system, you might want to scan this section to understand (and avoid) potential problems.

Water Will Move to Lower Pressure

Water will always try to leave a high-pressure area and retreat to a place with lower pressure. A pump works by creating an artificial high pressure through some mechanical means. Whether you use electricity, person power, wind power, or gravity, you will need something to make water the water in your fish tank flow into your grow beds.

Water molecules will create pressure on other water molecules beneath them—much more pressure than gas molecules in air exert. So even with a pump, you may not be able to force the water very far uphill. Many pump catalogs and packages show you how high the pump will push water above pond level and what flow rate you'll see at those higher levels.

If your grow beds are substantially higher than the water the pump is in, you'll waste a lot of energy trying to overcome the weight of the water in the piping leading up to the grow beds. However, you need your grow beds to be high enough to drain into the tank where you have your pump, letting gravity do the work for you. It's a balancing act.

There are additional ways to control where water goes and stays. To prevent water from flowing backwards through a pipe, you can install a *check valve*, which allows water to flow in only one direction.

To keep water in a grow bed, you can install a *standpipe*, an open-ended vertical pipe in the inlet or drain that forces the water to stay in your grow bed unless it can flow out over the open top of the pipe.

If a drain or pipe leading out of a grow bed or tank gets clogged, water will continue to rise until it flows over the edges of the grow bed or tank. It's important to design your system up front so water can't accidentally empty your fish tank or flood your floors. Periodically inspect your system for loose pipes and clogs.

DEFINITION

A **check valve** is a fixture you attach between two tubes or pipes to ensure that flow goes only one way—it's like a one-way street for water. A **standpipe** is a vertical pipe in a tank or grow bed that prevents water from draining out of the tank until it reaches the open end on top of the standpipe.

Because water always seeks low pressure, you can get water to do amazing things. In Chapter 7 I cover several ways you can "trick" water into automatically draining from your grow beds, drawing oxygen down into the root zone to supercharge growth.

The Universal Solvent

Water is often called the universal solvent because most substances will dissolve in water over time. You need to make sure anything you put in your system won't leach harmful substances into the water in which your fish and plants live. For example, if you had your fish in a lead tank, you would expect some lead to get into the water, even though the tank itself didn't dissolve.

Because water is such a good solvent, it can uniformly distribute nutrients throughout your grow beds. In soil gardening you have to worry about the pH and nutrients in different parts of your garden. But with aquaponics, the water chemistry will stay fairly consistent throughout your system. As you assemble your system or buy components from vendors, make sure that everything is food grade or safe for drinking water.

Acid Water, Neutral Water, and Alkaline Water

As different substances dissolve in water, the water can become acidic or alkaline. pH is the measure of how acid or alkaline water is. Acids break down complex organic molecules due to high hydrogen content. Alkaline solutions are corrosive liquids that contain high levels of salts, metals, and earth metals. Pure distilled water is completely neutral and has a pH of 7.0.

When water becomes more acidic, the pH drops below 7.0. Acids you may be familiar with are urine (pH = 6), coffee (pH = 5), tomato juice (pH = 4), orange or lemon juice (pH = 2-3), and stomach acid (pH = 1).

When water becomes more alkaline, the pH rises above 7.0. Alkalis you may be familiar with include baking soda (pH = 9), milk of magnesia (pH = 10), soapy water (pH = 12), and bleach (pH = 13).

Both acid and alkaline substances can damage surfaces they touch. Most plants thrive at a pH between 6.0 and 7.0, for reasons I'll discuss in Chapter 10. That chapter also talks about how to measure pH and how to adjust the pH in your system if it gets too low or too high. For now, all you need to know is that it is easier to keep your pH stable if you have a system with at least 250 gallons of water.

The pH levels in municipal water systems are usually kept higher than 7.0. The high levels of dissolved salts and metals in alkaline water prevent older metal pipes from leaching harmful amounts of copper and lead into the water.

The pH of the water in your garden will need to be 6.0 to 7.0 for the combined health of your fish and plants. The surface of lead and copper pipes will dissolve in water at those acidic pH levels—so don't use lead and copper pipes in your garden, even though they may be used for drinking water in your home.

Weight of Water

Water is heavy. A gallon of water weighs 8 pounds, and a cubic foot of water weighs 62 pounds. If you're designing your own system, you need to respect this weight. The ground in your yard can support about 200 pounds per square foot, a concrete basement floor can support at least 100 pounds per square foot, and a wooden floor or deck should be able to support about 40 pounds per square foot.

> **GREEN TIP**
>
> The weight of water isn't all bad. You'll often see pavilions tied down with 55-gallon drums filled with water; it's a great way to anchor a structure when you can't drive piles into the ground like in a parking lot. You can use the weight of your tanks and grow beds to anchor a temporary greenhouse or other structure in your garden.

Temperature and Water

Water has a wonderful ability to absorb and retain thermal energy. Water also has a powerful ability to cool. And since water is the way your plants and your fish will get their oxygen, it's important you understand how to get oxygen to dissolve in water and the effect temperature has on dissolved oxygen.

Thermal Mass

Water is able to absorb large amounts of energy without getting terribly hot. It takes a 300-watt submersible heater almost an hour to increase the temperature of 100 gallons of water by a single degree Fahrenheit. This is terrible if you are trying to maintain warm water for your fish, but this stability is wonderful if you're using your water tank to help moderate the temperature of your garden.

As water circulates through your pipes, tanks, and any rocks in your system, it will absorb heat from these parts during the day as the sun warms them. An inexpensive digital water thermometer will allow you to check water temperature easily whenever you visit your garden. You can find these online or in pet stores for about $10.

I was surprised to find that my garden didn't freeze during the winter even when the outside temperatures dropped well below freezing. Cold air killed my summer plants, but my fish and cool weather plants survived the long, cold, dark days of winter simply because of the solar energy captured by my simple plastic greenhouse.

If you have an outdoor garden where nighttime temperatures dip below freezing in winter, see Chapter 19 for more information about heating and cooling. In the meantime, these simple measures can help keep your water temperature above freezing:

- Turn the water pump off a couple of hours after dusk and on a couple of hours after sunrise. This holds water in the tank, where it will tend to lose heat more slowly during the hours when air temperature drops.

- Insulate pipes, grow beds, and tanks on surfaces that don't get warmed by sunlight during the day.

- Put a temporary greenhouse over your garden.

- Keep an air pump running full time to keep the surface of your fish tank from freezing. This will also add oxygen to the water, which is good for your fish.

Water Evaporates When Air Is Warm

Water evaporates when the air is dry or hot, and the amount of evaporation will increase if you expose more water to the open air. Warm, dry air is like a sponge, pulling water up into itself. The way to reduce your water loss through evaporation is to keep that "sponge" away from your water. First, minimize the surface area of exposed water in your tanks. Second, install some kind of cover over your tanks. Third, make sure the water in your grow beds is covered, either by the floating raft material or by an extra 1 to 2 inches of rock, if growing in rock.

Even if you perfectly covered the water in your system, your plants transpire or "sweat moisture" from their leaves as a necessary part of drawing water and nutrients through the plant. The leaves of your plants have small pores in them through which water evaporates and cools the plant.

DID YOU KNOW ...

If you've ever enjoyed the cool air in the wooded mountains on a hot summer day, transpiration is part of why it is so pleasant. The leaves of the trees provide shade, and transpiration from the leaves actively cools the air. In the height of summer, shade cloth over your garden will mimic the shade provided by a leafy canopy, and evaporation from your plants will further cool your plants.

During the height of summer you will need to top off your system more frequently. Even so, the amount of water you'll need to add to replace evaporation will be a small fraction of what you'd need to add to a traditional garden, where the water is also seeping away underground.

Water Condenses on Cool Surfaces

When moist warm air encounters a cool surface, the air becomes cool. Cold air can't hold as much water as warm air, so the extra water vapor "falls" out of the air and sticks to the cool surface. This is why a cold glass mug gets frosty when you pull it out of the freezer.

If you have an indoor garden that is warmer than the rest of your house, you'll find that moisture from your garden will condense on walls and windows in your home. On the other hand, if you keep your garden cooler than the rest of your house, moisture in the air will condense on the surfaces of your garden. At temperatures of 68 degrees and above you should be okay as long as you keep the relative humidity below 50 percent. Thermometers that also measure humidity are inexpensive and widely available.

If you have an outdoor garden and put up a winter greenhouse, you can expect water to condense on the roof and walls of the greenhouse as it gets cold inside. It can be a surprise to find it "raining" the first few times you walk into your greenhouse. But since that "rain" is falling back onto the grow beds, fish tanks, and ground inside the greenhouse, it will all remain in your aquaponic garden ecosystem. I discuss greenhouses in Chapter 18.

Dissolved Oxygen

Your fish need oxygen to live, and they get that oxygen from the water in your system. It turns out your plants need oxygen, too. And if you have worms in your system (a good thing!), they will usually absorb the oxygen they need from the water in your system.

It's almost impossible to put too much oxygen into your water. If you don't know how much dissolved oxygen your water holds, you can get expensive gear from an aquarium store to test the water—or you can simply look at your fish. If they are swimming near the top of the tank, skimming the surface with their mouths, they probably need more oxygen. Otherwise, they're probably good. Chapter 10 talks about testing oxygen levels.

Hot water can't hold much oxygen. To increase the amount of oxygen in your water, use a combination of these methods:

- Keep the water from getting hot.

- Add oxygen to the fish tank with an air pump and air stone (see Chapter 5).

- Add oxygen to your grow beds by using flood and drain (Chapter 6) or putting air stones in floating grow beds (Chapter 9).

- Spray water over the surface of your fish tank so oxygen can mix where the water splashes.

SOUNDS FISHY

Fish in a sun-warmed barrel can die quickly if you don't add oxygen to their water. This can happen when you are transporting your fish home or if you don't have your tank ready when you buy your fish. The heat drives oxygen out of the water and the fish suffocate. Even if your fish don't all die, their gills will be damaged. The easiest way to add oxygen to a barrel is using an air pump with an air stone.

Fish Need Water to Live

Water provides oxygen to your fish, gives them the ability to move elegantly and efficiently, and controls their body temperatures. A fish in nature has the ability to migrate to a location with the food, temperature, light, clarity, and population density they need. But when you raise fish in a tank, they cannot escape the conditions you provide.

Know the temperature range your fish need, and keep your tanks in that zone. If your fish are too hot or too cold, they will stop eating and could die. If your tank temperature goes outside the comfortable zone for the fish, stop adding food to the fish tank. Uneaten food will decompose and create toxic conditions for your fish.

While some fish like light, most fish are happier when they are sheltered from sunlight. The fish that survived to produce more generations of fish were the ones that avoided becoming a meal—and being visible to overhead predators is a good way to become a meal. If in doubt about whether your fish like to have their tank shielded, you can try this experiment: cover half the tank with an opaque board, then watch to see if the number of fish in the shady part of the tank and the sunny part of the tank are similar. If you find most your fish huddling in the shady part of the tank, your fish have evolved to hate open space overhead. Make them happy and provide a tank cover.

Finally, you can only sustain a certain amount of fish in a tank. One rule of thumb is to put no more than 1 pound of fish in your tank for every square foot of grow bed volume (roughly 7.5 gallons). A 100-gallon tank connected to a 100-gallon grow bed could support 12 to 15 pounds of fish.

Plants and Water

When a tree grows on a patch of ground, it doesn't consume the dirt to fuel its growth. If anything, the ground will mound up around a plant as the roots displace soil and rock. So where does the mass of that plant come from? Plants are formed from carbon from the air and nitrogen from water in the soil, and they are spun into an elegant form by nature given sufficient water and sunlight. If a plant has reliable access to light, air, and water, it will have the building blocks required for strong growth.

The Least You Need to Know

- Water is heavy. Make sure your design is strong enough to support the water in your system.
- Water will evaporate into hot, dry air and then condense on cool surfaces.
- You can turn your water pumps off at night to reduce massive temperature drops in cool weather.
- You can keep a pound of fish per cubic foot of grow bed volume if you circulate the entire volume of water through your system every hour.
- Your plants and fish will both be happiest if you make sure the water contains plenty of oxygen and has a pH between 6 and 7.

Fish Tanks, Grow Beds, and Plumbing

In This Chapter

- Container options for fish tanks
- Container options for grow beds
- Creating gutters and towers for additional plant growth
- Plumbing the system together
- Do-it-yourself plans for building a grow bed

Fish tanks, grow beds, and plumbing are the skeleton of your system—the structure without which the living organisms cannot properly function. In this chapter I'll tell you about the various options from which you can construct a system and their pros and cons. First I'll talk about the tank options for your fish, followed by options you can consider for growing your plants. Finally, I'll cover the variety of ways you can plumb the two together.

Fish Tanks

You'll need at least one fish tank and you may have a sump tank. Many aquaponic gardeners also like having a separate tank for *fingerlings* to grow in until they're large enough to avoid becoming food for their bigger siblings.

Your first instinct might be to swing by the pet shop and pick up an aquarium or two. That's fine if you're creating a small system with a 10- or 20-gallon aquarium. For a large system, however, you'll want something that can hold hundreds of gallons. Aquariums that can hold hundreds of gallons can cost thousands of dollars.

Whether or not you choose to raise edible fish, you probably expect to eat the plants grown in your system. You'll want to make sure your components are food grade and/or drinking-water safe. If you are building your system with used tanks or barrels, find out what the tanks had in them. If they were used for food, you're good. Otherwise, you'll want to do some research to make sure there is no toxic residue in the tanks or barrels. If you can't find out what was in the barrel or tank, I'd recommend you don't use it for an aquaponic garden.

Finally, make sure any sealants, glues, or paints in your system are both watertight and drinking-water safe.

Now on to our options!

Aquariums May Not Be the Best Fish Tanks

Aquariums are designed to house fish. But they are designed to display fish with the assumption that you will use a traditional aquarium filter. Aquariums are often kept clear by adding chemicals.

Your plants will filter water, but that water will be full of nutrients. When you combine a clear aquarium with light, water, and abundant nitrate, you will get algae. Algae can use up the oxygen your fish and plants need.

You should also think about whether your fish will be comfortable in an aquarium. If you're raising koi or goldfish, they've been bred to be on display and don't mind light. But if you're raising food fish, they have evolved to be shy of light and overhead predators. A clear aquarium will make them feel exposed and vulnerable. You can make food fish more comfortable by giving them hiding places such as sections of large-diameter polyvinyl chloride (PVC) pipe or flowerpots placed on their sides.

As I've mentioned, another consideration is cost. However, if you can get an inexpensive aquarium in a size that matches your needs, you know you're dealing with a safe, watertight tank for your fish.

Plastic Barrels

A popular, low-cost option many early aquaponic gardeners have used is the 55-gallon plastic barrel. These are used to transport any number of products, including agave syrup, soda concentrate, and honey, to name a few. The barrels are made of the same kind of material often used for milk jugs.

These barrels come in four standard colors: white, blue, green, and black. Most aquaponic gardeners who use barrels use blue barrels. Black is often used for chemicals that are not food safe, so you rarely see black barrels used in aquaponic systems. However, a barrel is not toxic just because it is black. White barrels may not block light sufficiently to prevent algae growth, and you may need to paint them on the outside.

In order to use 55-gallon barrels for your system, you'll need to cut them. These barrels are thick, so you would need a jigsaw or other power saw to cut them. Grow beds are usually created by cutting the barrels in half lengthwise. Fish tanks can be created by cutting out the end containing the bungholes, leaving the sturdy ring in place to provide structural integrity.

Once you've cut the barrel, you may find the plastic begins to sag and deform. It is common to support the base of the barrel with boards. You can also screw the cut edge to something (like the half-barrel next to it) to prevent sagging.

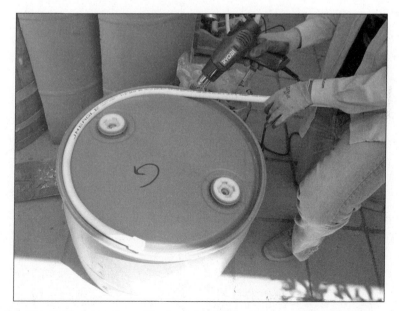

Bending PVC pipe to shape. The bent pipe will be used to prevent the open barrel from sagging.
(Photo courtesy of Ron Maggi)

Most plastic will break down over time if it is exposed to sunlight. These barrels are thick enough that you'd probably get several years of life out of them, but you may still want to either paint or cover the barrels to shield them from ultraviolet rays.

> **DID YOU KNOW ...**
>
> Re-using barrels is a sustainable practice. A decade ago food companies would sometimes give these barrels to anyone willing to cart them away. Even now it's often possible to get these barrels for less than $50 apiece. It's not a lovely look, but the price is hard to beat.

Intermediate Bulk Containers (IBCs)

The *intermediate bulk container (IBC)* is the big brother of the 55-gallon drum. These are very large containers, so you'll probably need a truck to transport an IBC from point of purchase to your intended garden site.

IBCs are rounded plastic cubes in metal cages and can hold 275 gallons or more. Like 55-gallon drums, they are designed to hold liquids and usually come with a spigot at the base of the metal cage. As with the 55-gallon barrels, you'll want to make sure the previous contents of the IBC can't have left a toxic residue.

One backyard gardener assembles materials for his system. The barrels will be used for grow beds and the white intermediate bulk container (IBC) will hold his fish.
(Photo courtesy of Ron Maggi)

The garden plan, created in Google SketchUp, a free 3D modeling system.
(Photo courtesy of Ron Maggi)

The finished garden.
(Photo courtesy of Ron Maggi)

The metal cages surrounding the plastic cubes are designed so that IBCs full of liquid can be lifted with forklifts and stacked on top of one another. And even though the metal cages are designed to sustain most of the load, the plastic tank itself has impressively thick walls.

You'll need some serious tools to convert an IBC into a fish tank. At the very least you'll need a hole saw and jigsaw to cut a panel out of the top of the plastic IBC cube. For those wanting to lop off the top foot or more (to reuse the top as either a sump or grow bed), you'll also need an angle grinder to cut the metal cage as well as the jigsaw to cut around the plastic cube.

As with the 55-gallon barrels, cover or paint your IBC system to prevent ultraviolet damage. The fish tank you'll get by using an IBC tote can be pretty tall—as high as 48 inches in some cases. Some gardeners even fill whole IBC totes with gravel and use them as grow beds.

GREEN TIP

Several good resources are available to help you design an aquaponic garden around IBC containers. A free manual called "The IBCs of Aquaponics" is available on the Backyard Aquaponics website, backyardaquaponics.com. This manual gives a thorough and concise description of aquaponics and showcases dozens of different IBC installations from aquaponic gardeners throughout the world. If you prefer video or kits, Murray Hallam of Practical Aquaponics has created a video showing how to create a constant height, one pump (CHOP) system using three IBC totes. IBC tote kits are also available for sale in the United States from the Aquaponic Store. See Appendix B for more information.

Stock Tanks

Stock tanks are designed to feed, water, and wash livestock. If you decide to use stock tanks in your system, I recommend the sturdy plastic tanks instead of either the galvanized metal tanks or the flimsy plastic tanks. The galvanized metal is coated with zinc, which will dissolve in the slightly acidic water in an aquaponic garden.

Stock tanks are available from plastic manufacturers and agricultural stores such as Southern States and Tractor Supply Co. Some have even had luck finding stock tanks from national chain stores like Ace Hardware. If you don't have a nearby agricultural supply store, though, you may have a hard time finding these locally, and shipping costs can be more than the cost of the stock tank itself, so you may want to investigate other options.

Stock tanks have several benefits:

- They are inexpensive. A 300-gallon stock tank can be purchased for under $300, compared to over $3,000 for a 300-gallon aquarium.

- Because they are meant for use with animals, there is no worry about toxic residue.

- They may be purchased locally and transported in a normal minivan (the 50-, 100-, and 150-gallon sizes).

- The 25-inch height is short enough that grow beds can be placed above the tanks and garden comfortably.

- There is no need to cut or grind—all that's needed is a drill bit to create a hole in the base for the drain plumbing.

- They are easier to work with than either IBCs or 55-gallon barrels.

The 50-gallon stock tanks are usually about 12 inches high, which is the recommended depth for an aquaponic grow bed. The larger sizes are all about 2 feet tall, which is a comfortable working height. The rounded shape of the tanks means the water can circulate without the dead spots you can get in a rectangular tank.

SOUNDS FISHY

A tank cover will help your fish feel protected, and it will also keep your fish in the tank. There are few things as distressing as coming out to your garden to find a dead fish on the ground next to the tank. Tank covers also keep people and animals out of your fish tank. You don't want birds or raccoons snacking on your fish—and you absolutely don't want a curious child to be able to fall into your fish tank. Check if there are local laws about requirements for covers and fences around fish tanks, ponds, or pools.

In 2011 I created a stock-tank aquaponic system for demonstration and auction at the inaugural Aquaponics Association Conference. I created a series of blog posts and YouTube videos showing how I created the system, which are available online at my blog, 365aquaponics.blogspot.com.

Stock tanks may be available locally and may be used in landscaping as well as for watering livestock.

Specialty Fiberglass and Plastic Tanks

If you are able to invest a bit more money and have the space, you can consider fiberglass or plastic tanks that are specifically designed for aquaculture and aquaponics. These tanks are designed to hold 1,000 gallons or more and can be outfitted with windows that let you view your fish. If you are looking into an investment of this magnitude, I recommend you do a bit of market research to determine what size and brand best suits your needs.

Not all the options are huge. The aquaponics industry in Australia is mature enough to have multiple vendors catering to the backyard aquaponic gardener. These vendors sell systems that are ready to go. Two of the leading vendors in this market are Backyard Aquaponics (backyardaquaponicsshop.com) and Practical Aquaponics (practicalaquaponics.shopfactory.com). In America, there isn't yet a nationwide chain that caters to aquaponic gardeners. The Colorado-based Aquaponic Store (www. theaquaponicstore.com) is a good resource for aquaponic tanks and components, and you may be able to find local businesses that carry tanks.

The downside to tanks specifically designed for aquaculture and aquaponics is they do not have a large customer base. Therefore the components will tend to be a bit pricey and shipping costs, where applicable, can be as significant. Complete systems tend to start around $2,000, not including shipping and handling. On the other hand, these specialty tanks are designed for the job, which can be reassuring. And if you can get these products delivered to a business address, your shipping costs can be drastically lower than residential delivery.

If you want to sell your produce or fish, aquaponics supply stores can help guide you to the materials, requirements, and training to support that goal. See Appendix B for some resources.

Bathtubs

Used bathtubs are an interesting option that you can consider for your fish tank, sump, or grow bed. They are definitely designed to be watertight and can be inexpensive or even free.

A bathtub usually holds only 80 gallons of water, so a bathtub system will not be as stable as one that holds the recommended 250 gallons. Most used bathtubs are built in, so they aren't designed to look lovely on their own—but a bathtub system definitely sends a message about reuse and sustainability. And with a bit of trim and ingenuity, you may be able to transform a bathtub-based system into a striking design element.

Enough people use bathtubs for their aquaponic systems that several aquaponics businesses have created kits specifically for converting bathtubs into aquaponic grow beds. I suggest doing an online search for "bathtub aquaponics" to see what is out there.

Even if you're not immediately drawn to the idea of an entire system created from used bathtubs, a sump created from a bathtub is definitely an option to consider. You're likely to have your sump tucked away somewhere inconspicuous, where it won't matter whether it's a fancy tank or an old bathtub. (I discuss sumps in detail in Chapter 5.)

GREEN TIP

Before you put an old bathtub into service, I recommend you clean it out using a fish-friendly method. Rubbing the surface with a paste of water and sea salt will clean the tub and be safe for fish, but residue from alkaline cleansers like soap, bleach, and baking soda can harm your fish, so those should not be used.

Liners and Sealants

A final option is to construct your own fishpond that is lined or sealed with food- and drinking-water-safe products. Appendix B includes some resources for understanding pond construction. If you decide this is the right path for you, make sure you follow the latest guidance regarding creation of a safe water feature by checking with your local government code office.

Concrete is a durable option for lining a fish pond. Douglas Hoover has built hundreds of custom ponds and waterfalls. In Appendix B I include a link to Doug's article on how to build a concrete koi pond. But you may not have space for a traditional in-ground fish pond as part of your aquaponic garden.

You can also use synthetic rubber or plastic to line a fish tank constructed from wood or dug into the ground. The most common pond liner is EPDM (ethylene propylene diene monomer), which can be fish and food safe. I recommend you use virgin EPDM if you want to use this material. Other kinds of EPDM may be made from the scrap left over from manufacturing virgin EPDM, leaving the possibility of contaminants in the rubber. You may use PVC pond liners, but PVC liners tend to be more brittle than EPDM over time.

Another liner used by organic gardeners is Dura-Skrim. This liner is made up of multiple layers that provide great strength and UV protection. Dura-Skrim isn't as widely available as EPDM or PVC, but it is meets organic certification requirements.

To install the liner, drape a nonwoven fabric or pond underlayment inside your tank, if recommended by the liner manufacturer, to protect the liner from sharp objects. Next drape the liner over the underlayment. Take care to ensure that the liner has been pushed securely into all the corners and angles or the liner may rupture in those locations when the pond is filled with water.

A third option is to construct a tank using concrete blocks held together with surface bond cement and painted with a drinking-water-safe sealer like ThoroSeal. This is the construction technique used for municipal water towers and has been used by some for koi ponds.

Use of cement and concrete blocks opens up a world of geometric design options. While the fundamental plumbing is the same as any system constructed of plastic barrels, you are free to incorporate decorative elements that could be a truly beautiful accent to a home or a business. Think of the most beautiful koi pond installation you've ever seen, but instead of a structure hiding all the filters and pumps, you have a series of grow beds filled with an array of decorative or edible trees and plants.

Surprisingly, a concrete block tank might be one of the most affordable options if you are creating a large system. If you're not sure about the safety of an applied sealer, you could also construct a tank of rigid plastic sheet (¼ inch) and pour a concrete shell around the plastic to provide structural strength.

Grow Beds

A grow bed is any tray, tube, or tank in which your plants grow. However, deep grow beds will produce more vigorous plants, yielding harvests roughly 20 percent larger than shallow trays.

Anything from which you can make a tank is an option for a grow bed. But grow beds deserve special attention because they must be able to drain into your tank or sump.

Depth You Need to Grow in Rocks or Water

Aquaponic grow beds should be about 12 inches deep. This gives adequate room for almost any root system. In a grow bed filled with rocks, this depth provides enough volume to support a truly robust colony of bacteria to convert ammonia to nitrate. And in a grow bed filled with only water, this depth ensures that temperatures in the grow bed stay stable.

You can use a container that's shallower than 12 inches—I've created grow beds from concrete mixing tubs and other plastic bins—but 12 inches is the gold standard.

Some people use deeper containers for their grow beds. Aleece Landis, known on the aquaponics forums as TC Lynx, likes to use 100-gallon stock tanks, which are 24 inches deep. She is using these grow beds for large plants and trees, though smaller plants like lettuce and basil can be grown there, too. Pat Chiu of Utahponics used heavy-duty storage totes for grow beds, connecting them at the bottom with 2-inch plumbing to allow her to use siphons designed for larger grow beds.

*These 18-inch-deep bins were plumbed together to create 60 gallons' worth of grow
bed filtration volume. Not only are these parts inexpensive and widely available,
this gardener already had these bins in her possession.*
(Photo courtesy of Pat Chiu)

Width and Volume

You'll want a grow bed that allows you to reach all your plants. If you only have
access from one side of the grow bed, you'll want a grow bed that is 32 inches
across at the most. If you can get to the plants from both sides, 48 inches is a good
dimension.

For a home gardener, I recommend each grow bed be no more than 96 inches long.
An empty grow bed that is 48 inches by 96 inches could be carried by two people
and might fit reasonably in a personal truck or van that can carry sheets of plywood.
However I personally wouldn't try to have a grow bed that is bigger than approximately 16 square feet (4 feet by 4 feet or 3 feet by 5 feet).

You can always add more grow beds in your garden if you want to expand in the
future.

Support

Whether you are simply filling your grow bed with water (62 pounds per cubic foot) or with rocks and water (up to 105 pounds per cubic foot), your grow beds will be heavy. Luckily, standard cuts of lumber are designed to support these kinds of loads. If you aren't sure, you can calculate whether your intended shelf or plank will sag too much under your planned load using the Sagulator tool at www.woodbin.com/calcs/sagulator.htm.

I like using 2×6 or 2×8 planks supported on concrete blocks every 24 to 36 inches. Concrete blocks are designed to support large compressive loads and a pair of 2×8 planks under your grow bed will be strong enough to bear the weight without sagging (or breaking). If you are using small tubs or bins, you may be able to get away with standard shelving.

SOUNDS FISHY

Always check to make sure the weight of your grow bed can be safely supported by whatever shelf you're looking at. The last thing you want is to wake up to a flooded floor covered in mangled plants because your shelf failed.

Draining

You will not want to try to suck the water out of your grow beds. Gravity is your friend and will happily drain your grow beds for you. You just need to position your grow beds higher than the tank that contains your pump.

If you are blessed with a sloped yard or greenhouse, you can let gravity do even more. In some systems, several banks of grow beds are arranged so that the highest bank of beds empties into the next bank and so forth until the water eventually reaches the lowest bank of grow beds. Water draining from the final bank of grow beds is collected in a sump, then pumped back to the fish tank to circulate through the system yet again.

Grow Beds That Are Narrow or Vertical

In addition to the flat containers implied by the term *grow bed*, there are ways to grow in either vertical structures or in horizontal gutters if your garden has extra space and you want to grow more plants than will fit into your grow beds.

You will want to place vertical grow towers where they won't block light to the rest of your garden. Horizontal gutters, on the other hand, could be placed anywhere you have a bit of space and sun. Chapter 8 goes into more detail about vertical towers.

Plumbing Tanks and Grow Beds Together

So how do you connect all this stuff? First I want to explain the bulkhead fitting and standpipe design that forms the basis for getting water out of all grow beds. Then I will talk about the options for plumbing your pump to your grow beds.

Bulkhead Fittings and Standpipes

When it comes to water, a bulkhead is a wall-like partition that forms a watertight compartment. In this sense, the sides and bottom of your grow beds are bulkheads. A bulkhead fitting is used to allow you to pass water through one of these watertight walls or bulkheads. A standard fitting has three parts:

- A threaded male part that projects through a hole cut in a bulkhead

- A gasket or O-ring

- A threaded female part or collar that is screwed onto the male bulkhead, pressurizing the gasket to form a watertight seal to prevent water from leaking

With the bulkhead fitting in place, you next insert a vertical pipe into the bulkhead fitting. When the water in your grow bed reaches the top of the standpipe, it will flow over the top of the pipe and drain out of the grow bed.

An alternative to standard bulkhead fittings is the Uniseal, an O-shaped rubber gasket you can fit into a hole in your grow bed or tank. When you slide the appropriate diameter pipe into the Uniseal, it creates a watertight seal with both the grow bed or tank and the pipe.

You can also create a bulkhead fitting using electrical conduit connections and an O-ring. Since aquaponics systems are relatively low pressure, the square lip of the electrical conduit fittings pressing on the O-ring is enough to form a watertight seal. The components are inexpensive and available at hardware stores. The downside is that manufacturers don't consider drinking water and food safety when they make PVC electrical conduit fittings. Standard PCV pipe is white, but there shouldn't be a problem with gray or black PVC pipe. However, if standard PVC worries you, you'll want to pass on this inexpensive way to create a low-pressure bulkhead fitting.

Uniseals form a watertight bulkhead fitting and don't require complicated plumbing. Simply drill a hole of the proper dimension in the side of your tank and insert a pipe of the proper diameter.

GREEN TIP

When water drains out a standpipe in a grow beds, it can make a lot of noise. To reduce that noise, cut the top of the standpipe at an angle. Pipes with larger diameters are less likely to be noisy. Durso standpipes and aqua silencers are other ways to quiet a noisy standpipe that have been developed by saltwater aquarium enthusiasts.

Plumbing with PVC Pipes

Most aquaponic gardeners use PVC pipe to connect their grow beds as it is one of the least expensive ways to plumb an aquaponic garden. It is the best option for draining water from grow beds and the fish tank into a sump.

Many people also like to use PVC for transporting water from the pump to their grow beds. Pumped water has higher pressure than drainage. Let me tell you why I'm ambivalent about using PVC for this part of a system:

- The plumbing taking your water to the grow beds is more likely to be exposed to sunlight. Unpainted PVC becomes brittle in sunlight.

- The valve fittings cost about $10 to $20 and are designed to be hidden and adjusted rarely, if ever; therefore, these fittings are stiff and kind of ugly.

- The elbows create sharp bends in fluid flow. The turbulence in a single 90-degree elbow will reduce flow rates and invite blockages.

However, PVC will work just fine if that's what you feel comfortable with. In fact, some consider working with PVC pipe and fittings to provide great enjoyment. If you want to be able to find a part immediately in a local hardware store at 6 A.M. or 9:45 P.M., PVC is a great choice.

Irrigation Poly-Tubing

Whether your local community enjoys frequent rain or must cope with crushing drought, it's likely that well-groomed yards in your neighborhood maintain their look with the aid of irrigation.

Irrigation supplies are not as readily available as PVC plumbing. An average handy-man might take on a plumbing project once a year because there are so many different plumbing fixtures in a home. A home irrigation system is usually just for one lawn and is not usually a DIY project. But if you're comfortable working with irrigation tubing, this can be a great option for getting water from your pump to your grow beds. Irrigation fittings are designed to reliably transport water over years, so they are less likely to clog than the miniature fittings used in hydroponic systems.

> **DID YOU KNOW …**
>
> Some irrigation fittings are specifically labeled *nonpotable*, which means they aren't drinking-water safe. If you're not sure about a piece, don't use it.

Traditional irrigation systems presume water simply seeps into the ground, so you won't usually find good piping options for returning water from grow beds back to the sump or fish tank. But it never hurts to look through the catalogs to see what new products might have been added. Search the web for "irrigation supplies" or "sprinkler warehouse" to see what is available. Once you know what to look for, it may turn out that these kinds of components are available in your local hardware store.

Garden Hose

Standard garden hoses are not drinking-water safe. If you read the fine print on the label, a regular green garden hose will leach lead. This makes me wonder why anyone buys green garden hoses at all, much less for aquaponics.

There are hoses that are drinking-water safe. In fact, in warm-weather states, it is illegal to use anything other than drinking-water-safe hoses with motor homes and campers. It's probably illegal elsewhere, but people just don't know about it.

I can loop a hose around to dump water to exactly the right spot of my grow bed. Depending on how I fasten the hose, I might be able to use it to directly water a particular plant, block it with my thumb to create a spray to dislodge bugs, shift it to fill up a bucket (useful when I'm taking a miniature system on the road for demonstration), or easily fill up my pH and nitrate test vials. I can create sinuous curves with my hose so there are no local problem spots (as long as I avoid kinking the hose).

I recommend buying the $\frac{5}{8}$-inch diameter hose if you can find it. This size is compatible with all the plastic hose fittings, allowing you to take a single long hose and turn it into multiple shorter lengths that can screw into manifolds and other standard hose accessories. I can use inexpensive garden hose manifolds to split the flow from my pump into several different streams, and each stream has a built-in valve to regulate flow.

The following photo shows how you can use three manifolds to separate flow from the pump into four separate streams. Each of these manifolds costs less than $10 and comes with an integrated valve for adjusting flow.

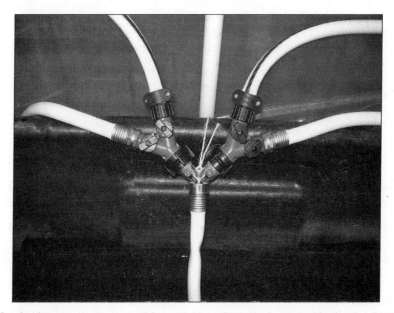

Garden hose accessories are widely available and may be less intimidating that PVC piping. These hose splitters have built-in valves to regulate flow.

Vinyl Tubing

Vinyl tubing is readily available at local hardware stores and is a great option for transporting the water from your pump if you have a small system. Vinyl tubing is usually available in clear and black. Always use the black tubing, as this will prevent algae growth in your tubes.

Small pumps usually come with a barbed fitting that is perfectly suited to vinyl tubing. If you can, take the pump with you to the store to make sure you buy the right diameter tube to fit your pump.

The biggest problem with vinyl tubing is keeping it where you want it. Fasten it securely to eliminate the possibility of having your vinyl tubing shift and pour water onto the floor. This doesn't need to be fancy. I've seen people use twine and binder clips or specific barbed fittings that mount into the top edge of the grow bed.

Vinyl tubing is usually sold in rolls of 10 feet, though you might be able to find a store that sells it by the foot. If you are creating a large number of systems, you can get rolls hundreds of feet long, making the cost per foot drop to well below a dollar.

GREEN TIP

If you have a local hydroponic store, they will likely have not only vinyl tubing but also a dazzling assortment of barbed fittings and other cool gardening tools you never knew you wanted to buy. Not sure where to find a hydroponics store? Go to the wholesale website hydrofarm.com and click on "Where to Buy."

Corrugated Tubing

Corrugated tubing is vinyl tubing all grown up and is usually used for ponds. A plastic coil is incorporated into the wall of the tubing, which prevents the walls of the tube from bulging out and makes it almost impossible to kink the tube.

Corrugated tubing is always glossy black. It comes in ¾-inch and 1-inch diameter sizes and is usually sold in 20-foot or 100-foot lengths when you can't purchase it by the foot.

Installing ponds is a favorite homeowner DIY project, so you will almost certainly be able to find corrugated tubing and accessories at your local hardware store. The downside is that people who are installing ponds are usually willing to drop a pretty penny, so you might find the prices for accessories, like pumps and valves, adjusted to the target market.

A great thing about corrugated tubing is that it looks very nice. If looks matter to you, shop around. You might be able to purchase what you need for not much more than you'd pay for PVC or garden hose.

DIY Plan for Grow Beds

In this section is a plan for a grow bed you can make out of plywood, lumber, and liner. It can be created from a single sheet of plywood with a minimum of waste. This bed is designed to be supported on cinderblock posts to keep it away from garden-variety termites. If you live in an area with aggressive termites, you should not make your grow beds out of wood.

The recommended liner material is Dura-Skrim, which is amazingly tough and is certified safe for organic food production. EPDM is also acceptable, but you will have to make sure the liner won't be stretched when the grow bed is filled or EPDM will tear under the load. Plastic sheeting available at local hardware stores will break down in sunlight, so is not recommended.

If you also want to make your own fish tank or pond, I suggest you consult a reputable source for fish-safe pond or tank construction. Given the popularity of koi, you should be able to find instructions that fit your space and budget.

3×5-foot Grow Bed

A 3×5 foot grow bed is a convenient size if you will only be able to reach the bed from one side. This size will also hold about 100 gallons of media and water if you fill it to the brim. A 4×4 foot grow bed can be made with these same parts and holds about the same volume, but will require that you can access the grow bed from both sides.

You can assemble the structure for a grow bed in an afternoon using materials available at your local hardware store. You might have to purchase the bulkhead and liner online, however.

Supplies:

(1) 4×8 plywood (½" or thicker)

(4) 2×4 boards, each 8' long

(1) 2×8 plank at least 10' long

1 liner (6'×8'), either white Dura-Skrim (20 mil thick) or fish-safe EPDM (45 mil thick)

¾" *S×S* bulkhead fitting

1 box 2" deck screws

1 box 3½" deck screws

1 box heavy-duty staples

8 cinderblocks

> **DEFINITION**
>
> **S×S** is a plumbing term that tells you what kind of piping you can attach on either side of a fitting.

Tools:

Saw

Drill

Hole saw, sized for bulkhead (probably 1¼")

Measuring tape

Staple gun

Box cutter

Assemble the grow bed base:

1. Cut a 1'-wide strip off the long edge of your plywood. You will end up with a 12"×8' piece and a 3'×8' piece.

2. Cut the 3'×8' piece into a 3'×5' (60") piece and a 3'×3' (36") piece.

3. Cut the 3'×3' piece into three, so you have three boards that are 12" wide and 3' long.

4. Cut the four boards so you have four 5'-long pieces. Set aside the short boards.

5. Screw two of the 5'-long boards to the long edges of the 3'×5' plywood piece using 2" screws, making sure the short side of the board is touching the plywood and an edge of each board runs along a long edge of the plywood.

6. Measure the distance between the two boards at each end. The distance should be about 33".

7. Cut two of the short boards from Step 4 so they will fit between the two boards you've screwed to the plywood.

8. Screw the two short boards to the two short ends of the plywood using 2" screws.

9. Screw the long boards to the short boards at each corner using 3½" screws. You've now completed the grow bed base.

Assemble the grow bed sides:

10. Measure the distance between the two short boards. The distance should be about 57".

11. Cut the 12"×8' plywood piece so it will fit between the two short boards (57" long). Set aside the short piece you cut off for use in Step 13.

12. Place one of the 3' plywood pieces on the long plywood piece you've just cut. Measure how much extra you'll need to make up the whole length. This distance should be about 21".

13. Use the short piece left over from Step 11 and cut it down to the size you need based on the measurement in Step 12.

14. Screw the long piece of plywood into the inside of one long edge of the grow bed base using 2" screws every foot or so. Screw through the plywood piece into the board.

15. Screw the 3' plywood piece and the short piece you created in Step 13 to the other long edge of the grow bed base using 2" screws every foot or so.

16. Measure the distance between the two plywood sides. This distance should be about 32".

17. Cut the remaining two 3' lengths of plywood to the size you measured in Step 16.

18. Screw the two lengths of plywood you cut in Step 17 to the short edges of the grow bed base using 2" inch screws.

Frame the top of the grow bed:

19. Screw the remaining two 5' long boards to the top of the long plywood edges, making sure you leave equal amounts extending past the long edges on each side.

20. Confirm the length you'll need for each short board you'll need to screw at the top to complete the grow bed. This distance should be 33".

21. Cut the remaining short boards to the proper length.

22. Screw the short boards to the short ends of the grow bed along the top using 2" screws.

23. Screw the top corners together using $3\frac{1}{2}$" screws.

Install the liner:

24. Staple the long edge of the liner to the bottom of a long board framing the grow bed. Place a staple roughly every 4", preferably at an angle relative to the edge of the grow bed.

25. Drape the liner into the bottom of the bed and up the far side. If you are using EPDM, make sure you have enough slack so the liner won't stretch (and tear) when you fill the bed.

26. Staple the long free edge of the liner to the underside of the long top board framing the other side of the grow bed.

27. Staple the middle of each short edge of the liner to the underside of the short boards framing the top of the grow bed, again making sure there is enough slack so the liner won't stretch and tear when filled.

28. Fold the liner at the corners so the liner fits neatly into the corners. Staple the remaining edges of the liner to the underside of the boards framing the top of the grow bed.

29. Trim the excess with a box cutter.

Install the bulkhead for the drain:

30. Place a large scrap of plywood under the location in the grow bed where you want the drain—I suggest you either pick a corner or the middle of one of the short sides. Leave about 6" between the center of the hole and the edges of the grow bed.

31. Place one of the smaller scraps of plywood on the liner over the location where you want to drill the hole for the drain.

32. Holding the scrap down, drill through the scrap, the liner, and the plywood bottom of the grow bed. The scraps will prevent the liner and grow bed bottom from ripping as you screw the hole.

33. Insert the bulkhead into the drain. Screw the plastic nut onto the bulkhead from the bottom.

Assemble the support for the grow bed:

34. Cut the 2×8 board into two 5' lengths. If possible, angle the edge so these support boards won't be as noticeable.

35. Place the cinderblocks in four stacks to form the legs of your grow bed. Make sure your cinderblock legs are placed so none of them is in the same location as your drain.

36. Place the two 2×8 planks on the cinderblock stacks.

37. Place the grow bed on the planks.

The Least You Need to Know

- Make sure you use components that are safe for your fish, your plants, and you. If it isn't labeled as food safe or drinking-water safe, ask an expert.
- Avoid clear tanks and tubing, since algae will grow wherever light consistently reaches the water.
- The optimal grow bed depth is 12 inches. This provides enough space for most root systems and will keep temperatures stable in your grow beds.

- Bulkhead fittings can be purchased online from hydroponic and aquaponic stores, or you can create your own from electrical conduit connectors.
- PVC is the best kind of plumbing to use for your drains. For the plumbing carrying water from your pump to the grow beds, you can use PVC, drinking-water hose, or other plastic tubing.

Making Water Move: Pumps and Standpipes

In This Chapter

- Air pumps to add oxygen and circulate water
- Water pumps to move water
- Adding water to your fish tank
- Solids lifting overflow (SLO) systems
- Do-it-yourself plans for standpipes and overflows

An air pump is like the lungs of your aquaponic garden, the thing that puts oxygen into your garden for your fish and plants. In Chapter 7 I talk about additional ways to add oxygen to your system, but an air pump ensures that your fish and plants can get the oxygen they need even if other parts of the system stop working properly.

If an air pump is like lungs, a water pump is the heart of your system. Your water pump moves the life-giving fluid through all the other parts of the system.

Almost all aquaponic systems need a standpipe, a length of pipe that makes the water fill your grow bed and deeply nourish the plants. It's an unsung marvel that makes sure your plants get the fluid and nutrition they need.

Finally, unless you have your water pump in your fish tank, you will also want a standpipe to keep the water level constant in your fish tank. A solids lifting overflow is a special kind of standpipe that keeps the water at a constant level in the fish tank and sends out the dirty water from the bottom of the tank as fresh water enters the tank. A good solids lifting overflow can clean the fish tank so you don't have to.

Air Pumps

In Chapter 3 you learned why it's critical for your fish and plants to have water that has a lot of oxygen. In nature, oxygen gets into the water when waterfalls, waves, and rain disturb the surface. In your aquaponic garden, you are creating a concentration of natural processes. Your fish tank has limited surface area to disturb, so fish and plants might not get enough oxygen.

An air pump is your oxygen insurance policy. Not only will your air pump add oxygen to the water, the movement of that air will help the water circulate, which the fish like. Air pumps use very little power—about as much power as a night light. If your system is tiny, an air pump may even be able to lift water to your plants.

Capacity

Air pumps are usually sold for aquariums, so they typically tell you the aquarium size for which a pump model is supposed to be adequate. But what you want is a pump that produces the air volume you need, which may be different from the water capacity in your fish tank.

The following table shows the approximate relationship between watts, air volume pumped (in liters per minute), and fish tank size. You can use this table to estimate how much air you'll need to provide sufficient oxygen to the fish in your tank.

Fish Tank Size (in Gallons)	Outlets	Watts	Liters per Minute
10	1	1.5	2
20	1	2.5	5
40	1	3.0	7
60	2	4.0	10
100	2	5.0	12
175	4	6.0	15
250	8	12.0	25

The number of outlets a pump has is important. An air pump outlet is a port on the side of the air pump from which high-pressure air is pushed. In your aquaponics system you will want to have a line going to your fish tank, but you may also want a line going to your sump and lines going to your deep water culture grow beds, if you're using them (see Chapter 9). It's also handy to have a separate line you can pull out and insert into a separate tank for sick fish or fingerlings. To allow the air from an outlet to feed more than a single air line, you can use a T-fitting, which is a plastic connector shaped like a T for joining three lines. However, an air pump with multiple outlets pumps a lot more air and is a better solution.

Diffusers

An air pump will put volume out, but it's not enough to have a simple stream of bubbles coming out of the end of the tube. *Diffusers* break up the air volume into small bubbles, increasing the surface area between the air bubbles and the water. A crowd of tiny bubbles will be much more effective in creating water movement because the water is dragged along by the air bubbles.

> **DEFINITION**
>
> A **diffuser** breaks up the airflow in an air line so that you get a cloud of tiny bubbles instead of large individual bubbles.

There are different sorts of diffusers:

- Air stones usually slide onto the end of an air line, forcing the air to come out in little individual bubbles as it streams through the small pores in the stone. An air stone can be particularly useful to force water to rise in a tube, but they can be used for all applications.

- Line diffusers put air out along the length of a tube. This is potentially handy if you are trying to aerate the water under a floating raft or trying to create rolling circulation of water in a tank.

- Disc and circle diffusers expand the area over which the air escapes, moving water across a larger area than possible with a simple air stone.

Diffusers will clog or break apart over time, so I like to keep a couple of inexpensive air stones on hand to replace my diffusers in a pinch, even if the ones I prefer to use are more expensive.

Preventing Water from Getting Into Air Pumps

A check valve is a little device that will only let air (or water) travel one way through a tube. The check valve is placed between the air pump and the tubing leading to the air stone. You'll need to take care to install it in the right direction or the check valve will prevent air from coming out of your pump.

Since water could short out your air pump and possibly trip off electricity to your entire system, an inexpensive check valve is always wise. If your air pump is higher than your water tanks, water might not get sucked back up the air tube and enter your pump. But if your air pump is lower than the surface of your water, a check valve is vital.

Using Air to Pump Water

In 2009, artists Britta Riley and Rebecca Bray started the Windowfarms project (windowfarms.org) to grow food in urban windows, inspired by Britta's desire to have a garden in her fifth-story Brooklyn apartment. The project inspired a vibrant group to conduct what they called R&DIY: hands-on research into how to make these window gardens more efficient and productive. One of the early successes was showing how an air pump could be used to lift water from the tank to the bottles containing plants.

My first aquaponic system was a 5-gallon tank connected to a tower of water-bottle planters. I used a plastic T-fitting in the air line near the bottom of my tank to allow water to drip into the stream of air rushing through the air line. As long as the water in the tank is at least a foot higher than the T-fitting, the *air lift* can carry water up to 6 feet higher than the top of the water tank.

> **DEFINITION**
>
> An **air lift** is when air bubbles lift water so it can rise from the fish tank into the grow bed or vertical tower where you are growing your plants.

On a larger scale, Glenn Martinez uses pumped air rather than traditional water pumps to move water through his aquaponic gardens. It's a clever, if complex, pumping scheme. In one installation in the Philippines, Glenn was able to use a 40-watt air pump to move water in a garden that feeds an entire school.

If you are attempting to create a solar-powered system, air pumps may meet your needs. I talk more about solar power in Chapter 21.

Water Pumps

For this discussion, we'll focus on submersible water pumps powered by electricity. If you are in an area where electricity isn't readily available, I cover a few other pumping options in Chapter 21.

Water pumps are simple to operate—plug them in, and water flows. So unless you have an unusual situation, I would recommend you pump your water with a traditional water pump.

Capacity and Head

You'll want a pump that can circulate the entire volume of water in your system every hour. The problem is that you can't just go by the gallons-per-hour rating on the box, because that rating assumes you're only pushing the water a foot or so uphill. It also assumes you have no significant pressure losses in the tubing through which the water flows. Plumbing in aquaponic gardens often has lots of sharp bends—thus, pressure losses.

A good rule of thumb is to get a pump that is rated to at least twice the flow rate you need to circulate your entire water volume every hour. In some cases you will want an even more powerful pump for unique circumstances, like a garden on a slope or complex plumbing.

People might try to charge you a lot for a pump. My first pump cost $50 for something that was only rated to pump 100 gallons. Once I knew where to shop, I was able to get a pump for $60 that can pump 1,000 gallons.

GREEN TIP

Buy pumps offered by either aquaponic or hydroponic supply outlets. Pumps sold for ponds, aquariums, and fountains are usually more expensive even when they are the same model.

Filters

Your pump may put out less than the advertised flow rate due to the filter inside your pump. Pumps usually come with a block of mesh that catches debris right before it reaches the rotating blades of the impeller. You have to take your pump apart to clean this mesh filter, which is a messy hassle that risks breaking the brittle plastic shell of your pump.

I remove the mesh filter from my pumps. If you don't think the plastic grate on the outside of the pump is adequate to keep debris out of your pump's impeller, I'd recommend a mesh bag around the outside of the pump.

You mainly want to keep chunks away that are so large they could gum up the works—like small fish or wads of roots or leaves. One way to keep these things out of your pump is to keep your pump in a covered sump where there are no fish, roots, or leaves.

There are two more ways worth noting to reduce the debris reaching your pump. One is to elevate your pump slightly. This will keep the pump from simply sucking in gunk from the bottom of the fish tank or sump. A second measure is to keep a few goldfish in your sump. The goldfish will nibble away at the stuff, keeping your sump relatively clean.

Filling Up Your Fish Tank

During cool weather, water levels will stay fairly constant in your system. But during the height of summer you'll find that a lot of water evaporates, making it a challenge to keep your fish tank full.

There are a few options you can consider to keep your fish tank or sump topped up:

- Top up using a hose
- Use a "water cooler" reservoir
- Use a float valve

Let's look at each of these methods in more detail.

Fill Up with a Hose

You can always just drag over the hose and turn on the spigot when you find your water is getting low. Better than that, you can run a hose from your spigot to your garden, and simply turn on the spigot whenever the water is looking low.

You can also hook up an automatic water timer—a mechanical timer that lets water flow until the timer reaches zero. This is great if you are in a hurry and don't want to stick around for as long as it will take for the fish tank to get topped up.

The downside of refilling your garden from a hose connected to city water is the chlorine and other chemicals in city water. These chemicals are designed to discourage plants from growing in city water pipes—they will discourage your plants and fish from thriving as well. If you are replacing more than 10 percent of your water, this will be a concern.

Use a Water Cooler Design

Most people have seen a water cooler—you put an inverted water bottle on top of the cooler. You can use a water bottle reservoir to add water while you're away. As water evaporates out of your garden, the water from the reservoir will replace the losses.

A 5-gallon water bottle can replace water losses from a 200-gallon system for a whole week in spring or fall, but may need to be filled every couple of days during the summer.

A 5-gallon bottle works to keep my garden topped up for about a week in cooler weather, but in summer I have to refill it every couple of days. It's a bother dragging around the 40 pounds of water a 5-gallon bottle holds.

If you're trying to scientifically document the amount of water you're using, a reservoir like this lets you precisely measure how much water your garden is using—useful if you're trying to prove something about water use.

DID YOU KNOW ...

The rule of thumb in traditional dirt gardening is to give your garden an inch of water every 3 to 4 days. An inch twice a week works out to 100 gallons per week for a 40-square-foot garden. My 40-square-foot aquaponic garden was only using 10 to 20 gallons per week.

Use a Float Valve to Add Water

Float valves are devices that open to let water flow when the float drops. Most toilets use a specialized sort of float valves to refill their tanks, for example.

Float valves are used in farms to keep water tanks full for animals like cattle and sheep. You can use these agricultural float valves to keep the water level topped up in your aquaponic garden. You can find float valves sold in agriculture supply stores (where you would also find stock tanks). These float valves are inexpensive, simple, and robust since they are designed for use around livestock.

If you live in a dry climate, you have probably seen a swamp cooler, also known as an evaporative cooler. You can use a float valve designed for a swamp cooler to keep your water levels topped up.

There are also electronic devices that do the same thing, such as the AquaFill electronic water leveling system (aquafill.com). The beauty of any of these float valves or water-leveling systems is you never have to think about adding water at all. But if your system develops a leak, your water bills could go through the roof.

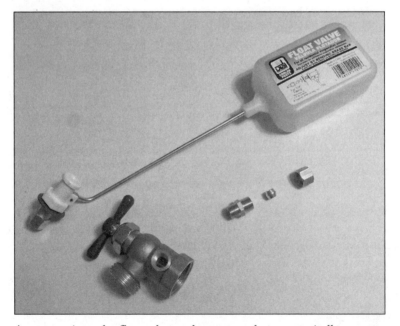

An evaporative cooler float valve can be repurposed to automatically top up an aquaponics tank.

Solids Lifting Overflow in Fish Tanks

If you've got your pump in a sump, you won't have to worry about accidentally draining your fish tank dry. But if your pump isn't in your fish tank, it won't suck up the
organic debris at the bottom of your fish tank and send it out to your grow beds.
Rather than have your fish tank merely overflow into your sump, you want pull water
from the bottom of your fish tank and sent to your sump.

A *solids lifting overflow (SLO)* forces the water from the bottom of the fish tank to be
pulled out without draining your fish tank. There are three basic configurations that
will lift solids from the bottom of your tank while preventing your tank from emptying. I call these variations the soda straw, the bottom drain standpipe, and the side
drain standpipe.

DEFINITION

A **solids lifting overflow (SLO)** is a special kind of standpipe that will suck the
organic gunk off the bottom of your fish tank while keeping the water in your
fish tank at a constant level.

The Soda Straw

If the drain for your fish tank will be at the top of the tank, this is the kind of SLO
you want. A pipe extends down into the fish tank so that the water that leaves the fish
tank must come in at the bottom of the pipe, the way a straw lets you suck soda from
the bottom of your glass.

I recommend installing two of these overflows so you don't have a problem if one of
them gets clogged. I've also found that when the pipe is at an angle, water flows up
the pipe more easily. A grate on the top inlet to the pipe will prevent debris or floating fish food from getting sucked out of the fish tank into the sump.

The Bottom Drain Standpipe

If you have a drain in the bottom of your fish tank, the bottom drain standpipe will
work great. You'll have two pipes: a simple standpipe fitted into the drain and a second, larger-diameter pipe around the standpipe with holes in the bottom.

Just like with the soda straw design, water will have to enter at the bottom of the
tank to get out through the standpipe. A benefit of having a drain in the bottom of
your fish tank is the ability to reduce the water level in your tank if you need to. This

could come in handy when it comes time to harvest your fish. Unfortunately, not everyone has enough room for a fish tank with a drain located in the base of the tank.

The Side Drain Standpipe

This last option is similar to the bottom drain, except you can place the drainpipe through the side of the fish tank near the bottom without having to actually plumb through the base of the tank.

In this variation, the standpipe has an elbow, and the outer pipe is cut so it fits over the elbow and the length of pipe connecting the standpipe to the drain in the side of the tank. This would be a particularly attractive option if your fish tank were already fitted with a drain or spigot in the side of the tank near the bottom.

The following figure shows the three different designs for SLOs.

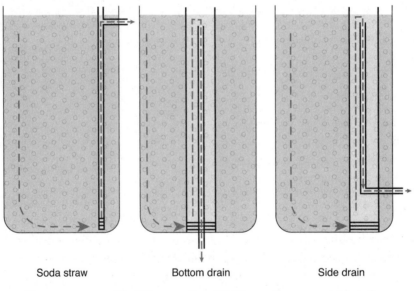

Soda straw   Bottom drain   Side drain

You can create a solids lifting overflow (SLO) to pull water and debris from the bottom of your tank whether your drain is at the top, bottom, or side of your fish tank.

DIY Plans for Standpipes and Overflows

The plumbing to create standpipes and overflows is very simple. Here are some basic plans for components that you can create from parts available at your local hardware store.

PVC Media Guard

Most people use 4-inch or even 6-inch polyvinyl chloride (PVC) pipe so they have room to reach into the media guard if they need to adjust something in the system. If you have to buy a longer pipe than you need, you can make several additional media guards and share them with other aquaponic gardeners.

Supplies: (1) 4" schedule-40 PVC pipe

Tools:

Permanent marker

Miter saw

1. Mark the PVC pipe to the height of your grow bed.
2. Starting 1" from the end of the pipe, cut a slot in the pipe a little less than halfway through the pipe.
3. Shift the pipe 1" and rotate the pipe so the edge of the prior cut is at the top of the pipe.
4. Cut another slot.
5. Shift, rotate, and cut until you are no closer than 1" from the top you've marked on the pipe.
6. Cut the PVC pipe to length.

Inexpensive Bulkhead Fitting

If you are using a plastic grow bed, you can use plastic conduit connectors to make an adequate bulkhead fitting. If your grow bed is made out of wood or some other thick material, you should buy standard bulkhead fittings from an online supplier like Aquatic Eco-Systems (aquaticeco.com).

Supplies:

(1) ¾" PVC conduit connector with male threads

(1) ¾" PVC conduit connector with female threads

(1) #18 O-ring (sold in boxes of 10 in the plumbing section)

Tools: None, but you'll need to have drilled a 1" hole in the base of your grow bed.

1. Push the PVC connector with the male threads through the 1"-diameter hole in your grow bed.

2. Push the #18 O-ring over the male threads of the connector until it is tight against the underside of the grow bed.

3. Thread the PVC connector with the female threads onto the bottom of the connector sticking through the bottom of the grow bed.

4. Tighten the connection until the O-ring is compressed between the bottom of the grow bed and the PVC connector threaded onto the bottom.

PVC Standpipe and Drain

The standpipe is simplicity itself. If you find the straight-cut standpipe makes noise, you can reduce the noise by cutting the top at an angle.

The drain in these instructions is designed to empty straight into the fish tank or sump. If you need to plumb the drain any distance from the grow bed, make sure there is a slight downward slope in the pipe between the drain from the grow bed and the outlet into the tank.

If you are using a simple standpipe in a 100-gallon grow bed, you should increase the pipe diameter to $1\frac{1}{2}$ inches in diameter and use a standard bulkhead fitting.

Supplies: (1) ¾" PVC pipe (2' length)

Tools:

Permanent marker

Miter saw

Drill

¼" drill bit

1. Determine how high you want your standpipe to be.

2. Cut the PVC pipe to length.

3. Push the PVC pipe into your bulkhead fitting. Mark the pipe where it comes out of the bulkhead fitting. Remove the pipe.

4. Drill a ¼" hole in the bottom of the bulkhead fitting just above your mark. This allows the grow bed to drain when the pump shuts off. After you've watched your grow bed fill and drain, you may want to drill additional drain holes in the base of the standpipe.

5. Push the standpipe back into the bulkhead fitting.

6. Cut another length of PVC pipe.

7. Push this second length of PVC pipe into the bottom of the bulkhead fitting.

Solids Lifting Overflow for Drain in Bottom of Fish Tank

Experienced professionals who raise fish recommend round fish tanks with drains in the center of the tank. If your tank is already plumbed with a drain in the center, adjust your pipe diameters accordingly. In these instructions, I presume a 2-inch PVC pipe will fit snugly into the drain in the bottom of your tank.

Supplies:

(1) 2" diameter PVC pipe, sold in 10' lengths

(1) 6" diameter PVC pipe, sold in 10' lengths

Tools:

Permanent marker

Miter saw

Hacksaw

1. Determine how high you want the water to remain in your fish tank. Leave a few inches of space between the top of the water and the edge of your tank to reduce how much you get splashed at feeding time and how often fish jump out of the tank when it is not covered. You can always cut these pipes shorter if you decide to reduce the height of water in your tank later on.

2. Cut the 2" pipe about ½" longer than the desired height of your water, since about ½" will probably be sticking into the drain. Insert the 2" pipe into the drain.

3. Cut the 6" pipe so it is 3" taller than the desired height of your water.

4. Cut three shallow slots around the bottom of the 6" pipe, about ¼" from the end.

5. Use the hacksaw to cut through the bottom to the edges of the slots. You should end up with what looks like three legs coming out of the bottom of the pipe.

6. Optionally, cut a few more slots into the base of the pipe. This will increase the flow rate that can go up the pipe without creating large holes through which little fish can get sucked.

7. Slide the 6" pipe over the 2" pipe so it rests on the three legs and is roughly centered on the 2" drainpipe.

Solids Lifting Overflow for Drain in Side of Fish Tank

This works best if the walls of your tank are vertical or nearly vertical or if you already have a drain in the side of your tank. If at all possible, you will want this overflow to be in the center of your tank. In these instructions, I presume a 2-inch PVC pipe will fit snugly into a drain already plumbed into the side of your tank. This isn't as simple as the overflow for a tank with a bottom drain, but is great when you simply can't drain your tank through the bottom.

Supplies:

(1) 2" diameter PVC pipe, sold in 10' lengths

(1) 6" diameter PVC pipe, sold in 10" lengths

(1) 2" 90-degree PVC elbow connector

Tools:

Permanent marker

Miter saw

Hacksaw

Drill

2½" hole saw

Cut your pipes to length:

1. Measure the distance from the side drain to the center of your tank.

2. Cut a length of 2" PVC pipe 1" shorter than the distance between the side of the tank and the center. This is the horizontal leg of your drainpipe.

3. Measure how high the top of your drain is above the bottom of the tank. Write this measurement down.

4. Determine how high you want the water to remain in your fish tank. Leave a few inches of space between the top of the water and the edge of your tank to reduce how much you get splashed at feeding time and how often fish jump out of the tank when it is not covered. You can always cut these pipes shorter if you decide to reduce the height of water in your tank later on.

5. Take the desire height of water you measured in Step 4 and subtract the height you measured in Step 3. Cut a section of 2" pipe to the number of inches you got from that subtraction. This will be the vertical leg of your drainpipe. If in doubt, cut long. You can always trim it back later on.

6. Cut the 6" pipe so it is 3" taller than the desired height of your water.

Cut and drill the outer sleeve:

7. Measure how high the center of your drain is from the bottom of your tank.

8. Make a mark near the bottom of your 6" pipe based on the measurement you made in Step 7.

9. Drill a $2\frac{1}{2}$" hole in the side of your 6" pipe, centered on the mark you made in Step 8.

10. Cut three shallow slots around the bottom of the 6" pipe, about $\frac{1}{4}$" from the end.

11. Use the hacksaw to cut through the bottom to the edges of the slots. You should end up with what looks like three legs coming out of the bottom of the pipe.

12. Optionally, cut a few more slots into the base of the pipe. This will increase the flow rate that can go up the pipe without creating large holes through which little fish can get sucked.

Assemble the solids lifting overflow:

13. Insert the vertical leg of your drainpipe into the 90-degree elbow.

14. Slide the leg/elbow section into the 6" pipe so the elbow is near the hole at the base of the 6" pipe.

15. Insert the horizontal leg of your drainpipe into the hole in the 6" pipe and into the 90-degree elbow.

16. Set the assembly on the bottom of the tank so the 6" pipe is resting on its three short legs.

17. Fit the free end of the horizontal leg of the drainpipe into the drain in the side of the tank. Push as required on the 6" pipe to ensure the connections at either end of the horizontal drainpipe are secure.

18. Holding the horizontal drainpipe in place, slide the 6" pipe away from the drain a bit so the 6" pipe is centered around the 2" drainpipe.

The Least You Need to Know

- An air pump with a good diffuser is an inexpensive way to put oxygen in the water for your fish and plants.
- A properly installed check valve will prevent your air pump from shorting out (and shorting out your entire system).
- You need to circulate the entire volume of water in your system every hour. A rule of thumb is to get a pump rated for three to four times the actual capacity of your system.
- Use an external mesh bag, keep your pump off the floor of your tank, and take other precautions to reduce maintenance and prevent debris from reaching the pump.
- A float valve can eliminate the chore of topping up your system.
- A solids lifting overflow in your fish tank can ensure fish emulsion gets sucked out of your fish tank without risk of accidentally draining your fish tank.

Growing Options

Part 2 goes into detail about the options you have for growing plants in your grow beds. Chapters 6 and 7 discuss media beds: grow beds filled with gravel, river rock, or expanded clay or stone. Media beds are recommended for home gardeners because they allow you to grow almost any plant without needing to fuss with filtering out fish waste. Chapter 7 particularly talks about how to get your system to flood and drain, ensuring your plants and fish get plenty of oxygen to remain healthy. Chapter 8 talks about taking advantage of vertical space with stacking containers, trellises, and arbors and includes directions for building a pergola next to your garden. Chapter 9 covers how you could also grow plants by just floating them in water or letting water drain past their roots.

Growing in Gravel: Using Media Beds

In This Chapter

- Reasons to use media beds
- Challenges of using media beds
- Different kinds of recommended media

If you're planning to simply grow in water, you might be tempted to skip this chapter and go right to Chapter 9. However, I urge you to read this chapter to find out why most aquaponics experts recommend media beds for home hobbyists. Media beds offer many benefits to beginning aquaponic gardeners. Even commercial aquaponic farmers are increasingly adding media beds to their systems.

Benefits of Using Media Beds

Media beds are grow beds that are filled with some kind of rock or gravel. The term *media* is a fancy word for anything used to support plants in a soil-less garden setting. Some of these media include rocks, sand, perlite, Styrofoam, mineral wool, and clay beads. (Since most aquaponic gardeners use gravel, expanded shale, or clay beads, I'll use the term *rocks* to refer to media in the rest of the book.)

Media beds are almost always heavier than grow beds that just contain water, since even the lightest rocks are heavier than water. But the benefits a media bed provides make it well worth your effort. You'll be able to confidently fill your bed with media recommended by centuries of combined experience. In addition, you'll learn how to reliably create the ebb and flow action that keeps your roots supplied with both water and oxygen.

> **DEFINITION**
>
> A **media bed** is a grow bed filled with an inert substance or medium to support the plants that grow in the bed. In aquaponics, the most common media are rocks, expanded clay pellets, and expanded shale. These materials are ideally larger than ¾ inch in diameter to allow for good drainage.

Plant Varieties

Filling your grow beds with media gives your plants something to grab onto. When you're using media, you can grow small bushes, root vegetables, and even trees. I wouldn't recommend you start your aquaponic adventure by attempting to grow a grove of papaya and banana trees. Nevertheless, filling grow beds with gravel gives you the support you need to attempt a wider array of plants than could be grown in water alone.

*When you use media in your grow beds, you can grow tall,
heavy plants, like this banana tree.*

There is almost nothing you can't grow in a media bed. In aquaponics, your only limitation is growing plants that thrive in the pH range that is acceptable for your fish (6.0 to 7.0).

Mineralization

Mineralization refers to the decomposition or oxidation of chemical compounds in organic matter so they become accessible to plants. The surfaces of your media provide a huge area that is constantly being bathed in oxygenated water and organic waste from the fish tank. These are the perfect conditions for transforming fish waste into plant nutrients.

When you have to remove fish waste from the system, you are removing nutrients you originally introduced to your system as part of the fish feed. Allowing the media to naturally transform this waste into nutrition will increase the vitamin content of your plants and will even allow you to grow plants that a water-based system is too dilute to nourish. In Chapter 11 I talk more about the broad range of plants you can grow in a media-based system.

Protecting Roots from Light and Solids

Light will damage roots and prevent them from absorbing the moisture and nutrients your plants need. Light burns the tender hairs that roots use to absorb water. Algae will grow on surfaces exposed to light, and some roots may turn green in an attempt to perform photosynthesis.

In a bed filled with media, the roots of the plant are below the layer of media, preventing root burn. Algae may grow on the surface of moist media and surfaces exposed to light, but this surface algae is nothing like the algae blooms you can get in grow beds filled merely with water.

The water coming out of your fish tank is filled with tiny particles of organic waste. In a grow bed simply filled with water, waste remaining in the water collects on the roots, clogging their ability to absorb water and nutrients. For this reason, systems with grow beds that don't have media must use elaborate filtration systems to remove these particles. In a media bed, those particles of fish waste collect on the surface of your media, so the plant roots stay clean, in most cases eliminating the need for additional filtration.

SOUNDS FISHY

I recommend you use rocks or clay pellets instead of sand, pea gravel, or other small particles. Fish solids will tend to clog the sand or pea gravel, preventing oxygen from reaching the roots. Experienced aquaponic gardeners recommend media at least ¾ inch (19 millimeters) in size for beginning gardeners.

Flood and Drain Your Grow Bed

One of the best things about media beds is you can drain the water out without leaving the plants high and dry. You don't want to leave the grow beds drained, but you do want to pull air and oxygen deep into the root zone for your plants. By allowing the media beds to flood and then drain every hour, the roots of your plants have constant access to both water and oxygen. This oxygen supports rapid vigorous growth in your plants. I'll talk about the mechanics of flooding and draining the media beds in Chapter 7.

Worms

Worms are garden gold. They consume decaying matter and transform it into worm castings, which make fabulous fertilizer. A grow bed full of media gives the worms lots of room to exist and puts nature's perfect fertilizer right where your plants take up their nutrients.

You may wonder how the worms can survive if the grow bed is constantly being flooded. Worms absorb oxygen through their skin, so water doesn't drown a worm the way it would you or me. Worms only suffocate if there is no oxygen. If the water is full of oxygen, worms are perfectly happy to live in water.

Great for Landscaping

We almost always talk about using aquaponics for growing food. But there is no reason you can't use aquaponics to landscape your property. By integrating a fishpond with trees and plants grown in decorative grow beds, growing in media allows your plants to thrive without expensive irrigation systems. This works best if you live in a climate that doesn't freeze over or if your landscape is protected in a building of some sort.

Drawbacks of Using Media Beds

Few things are perfect. There are some drawbacks to putting media in your grow beds: these media almost always increase the weight of the grow bed compared to simply growing in water, the media can get clogged, and the media can change the water chemistry of your system.

Supporting a Rock-Filled Grow Bed

Any aquaponic grow bed filled with water a foot deep requires substantial support. Adding media that are heavier than water will increase the weight from 62 pounds per cubic foot to as much as 105 pounds. But a small system can easily fit into any space strong enough to support the weight of a person.

A 4×8 foot grow bed filled to a depth of 12 inches with wet gravel weighs 3,350 pounds. Add the weight of water and the grow bed itself and the weight of a 4×8 foot grow bed can be as high as 4,000 pounds—or 2 tons. This is about the size of a pickup truck, so you should put such a garden somewhere you would feel comfortable parking a truck.

A flat backyard should be an acceptable location—dirt can support 200 pounds per square foot. Concrete slab foundations, like you might have supporting the lowest level of your home, can usually support at least 100 pounds per square foot. The typical rating for a residential floor in the United States is 40 pounds per square foot.

One of the most inexpensive ways to support your grow beds is to use stacked cinderblocks. Termites won't bother cinderblocks and are unlikely to bother lumber that is raised more than 18 inches off the ground. Span a couple of stacks of cinderblocks with 2×8 boards and you'll have adequate support for most grow beds. If you are supporting a long grow bed with either cinderblocks or wooden legs, it's wise to position supports every 3 to 4 feet. If you are concerned about movement of these blocks, you can bind stacks together using surface bond cement. In addition to preventing the blocks from shifting relative to one another, this will give a nice smooth appearance to your support columns.

You could also support your grow beds is a wooden structure with 4×4 legs. One concern with the wooden legs is the possibility of insect damage or water damage to the wooden legs where they come in contact with the ground. But if the idea of a wooden stand is otherwise attractive, you can minimize insect and water damage by sealing the ends of the wooden legs with epoxy.

Finally, you can purchase metal stands or shelves that are designed to support hundreds of pounds. Many hardware stores stock heavy-duty shelving for home hobbyists—these shelving solutions can usually support up to 300 pounds per shelf. I know from experience that the Rubbermaid oval stock tanks (50- and 100-gallon capacities) will fit inside the supports of a heavy-duty 2×4 foot shelving unit. Finally, there are commercial shelving solutions that would provide more than enough load-bearing capacity.

GREEN TIP

Raising your grow bed to waist height helps in several ways. A raised grow bed is easy to work with, will drain more easily, and is above the ground to prevent termite damage, important if you make the grow bed out of wood.

System Clogging

Grow bed filters can clog over time, even if you use ¾-inch rock. When grow beds clog, oxygen can't get to the plant roots. Without oxygen, the roots begin to decay, rot, and stink. Ironically, the most common cause of clogging in media beds is dense root balls—the roots are cutting off their own oxygen.

There are two symptoms that point to a clogged grow bed even before you start smelling a problem. First is a rapid increase in pH, which indicates that some portion of the bed is no longer getting enough oxygen. We'll talk about how to test your pH in Chapter 10.

Second, you may notice a reduction in the amount of flow that can pass through the bed that you can't solve simply by clearing out the drain. Chapter 22 discusses what you can do if an entire grow bed is significantly clogged.

pH Properties of Your Media

In Chapter 3 I talked a little about pH, the measure of whether your water is acid, neutral, or alkaline. Sometimes media affects the pH of your system. Your media can impact your system's chemistry in two ways.

I've already discussed how the pH of your grow bed can increase rapidly if a portion of the bed becomes clogged. A large, mature plant can cause this, as the roots lock themselves around the media so tightly that water and oxygen can't get to the center of the ball of roots. Tomato plants that have been growing for more than nine months are famous for producing these kinds of large, dense root balls. Luckily, pH swings related to root balls are easily fixed by removing the plants that are most likely to have caused the problem. And if you accidently pull up something that wasn't causing problems, it can easily be replanted in most media beds.

The media itself might not be pH neutral. This is most likely if you are using gravel or river rocks. Soft rocks like limestone and marble will dissolve in water and keep the pH high. If you are purchasing your rocks, your vendor should be able to confirm whether the rocks are pH neutral. But even if the rocks themselves are pH neutral, they may be covered with sand or dust that will buffer the pH.

I recommend rinsing your rocks in a water bath before pouring them into your grow bed. You can re-use the same water bath for multiple loads of rock. Washing these rocks can also reduce the amount of silt and sand that gets into your grow bed and prevent your grow bed from getting clogged.

Media Options

Your choice of media is important. Once you've selected a particular kind of rock, you will likely be keeping those rocks for decades to come. Your options vary widely in weight and price. You can ask someone else to do the work and simply take delivery of lightweight media particularly suited for aquaponics, or you can buy inexpensive but heavy, sharp rocks to keep your costs low. The most common media choices are as follows:

- Gravel
- River rock
- Expanded clay pellets
- Expanded shale
- Volcanic rock

Gravel

Gravel is often your least expensive option, as inexpensive as $0.20 per gallon or $1.50 per cubic foot. It's readily available, and it can be attractive. A grow bed filled with granite chips, for example, would be striking. Unfortunately, wet gravel is almost certainly your heaviest option, at 105 pounds per cubic foot.

Gravel also has sharp edges that can tear your skin. Its weight and the sharp edges make gravel difficult to work with, so you probably won't be moving your plants around, like you can in a lighter media like expanded clay pellets.

Local hardware stores are a convenient source for gravel, but if you can locate a store that specializes in rocks and stone, you can pay only dollars for tons of the stuff. You can buy your rocks in bulk and have large bags of gravel delivered to your location. But even if the gravel is sold "washed," you'll want to wash it again yourself.

River Rock

River rock is gravel with the edges worn off by being tumbled over years in streams, rivers, or oceans. River rock is about as heavy as gravel, at 105 pounds per cubic foot when wet. The weight makes it difficult to work with even though the smooth edges won't rip your skin. But river rock's low price ($1.50 per cubic foot) and rounded corners make it an attractive option.

I used river rock for my first large system. I loaded a 50-gallon tank into the back of my van, drove to the rock store, and shoveled river rocks into the tank. The store weighed my car before and after and charged me for the difference. I paid less than $11 for 50 gallons of rock.

After working with it for a few months, I was willing to pay a higher price for something lighter and easier to work. But heavy rocks can be a benefit in a grow bed where you plan to raise trees or tall crops.

Expanded Clay Pellets

Lightweight expanded clay pellets are specially created for use in hydroponics. The rounded clay balls are so light that they sometimes float in water when they are dry. When wet, they only weight 75 pounds per cubic foot.

You will often see references to Hydroton, a type of expanded clay pellets made in Germany. But the Hydroton brand of clay pellets was discontinued around the summer of 2012.

Because these expanded clay pellets are so specialized, you can usually only find it in stores that cater to the hydroponic market. When I was building my backyard system, a 50-liter bag retailed for roughly $60. That works out to $35 per cubic foot compared to the $1.50 per cubic foot I paid for river rock.

Prices for expanded clay pellets will also fluctuate depending on where you live. In 2011 I found clay balls available in Florida for less than $30 for the 50-liter bags—still expensive, but not quite as bad as what I originally paid.

> **GREEN TIP**
>
> Pay attention to the cost of shipping if you're not buying at a local hydroponics store. As expensive as clay balls will be at retail stores, it can be far more expensive to have them shipped to your door. As aquaponics becomes more popular, you may be able to special order clay balls for local pick-up from big-box stores, such as Lowe's, Home Depot, and Walmart. It never hurts to ask!

Expanded Shale

Expanded shale is a lightweight aggregate invented in the early 1900s. Shale or slate is baked in a rotating kiln, making it puff up much the way heated popcorn kernels do. Brand names for expanded shale and expanded slate include Haydite, Stalite, and Utalite. Expanded shale looks a bit like gravel, but the manufacturing process tends to knock off the sharp edges. Expanded shale isn't quite as light as expanded clay pellets, but it's still only 85 pounds per cubic foot.

Expanded shale has been used widely in the construction industry for decades to create lightweight concrete structures and to improve drainage in landscaping. If you're lucky enough to have a local aggregate company that sells expanded shale, you can get it for pennies. My mother was able to load 250 gallons of expanded shale in her pickup at a local quarry for only $50 back in 2011. That works out to about $1.50 per cubic foot.

The hydroponics industry has started marketing expanded shale. One brand name is simply Rocks. The selling point is that the expanded shale is made in the United States, which is appealing to folks who are concerned about sustainability and reducing their carbon footprint. Expanded shale that is marketed to the niche hydroponics and aquaponics markets have been carefully graded and evaluated for pH stability. You will pay prices comparable to expanded clay pellets for expanded shale marketed to gardeners. An alternative is to check your local network of aquaponics enthusiasts. You might find someone who will go in with you for a bulk purchase, reducing your costs.

Volcanic Rock

Volcanic scoria (also called cinders) is formed when dissolved gases expand as magma cools. Scoria typically forms at the surface of volcanic flows. Scoria just barely sinks in water when dry and is filled with tiny fissures, making it highly appropriate for use in aquaponic systems. Scoria weighs about 85 pounds per cubic foot.

The price of scoria or cinders will depend on how close you live to a volcanic source. In Hawaii, which is famous for its volcanoes, scoria is very inexpensive.

The Least You Need to Know

- Media beds are grow beds filled with rocks or some other inert medium to support the plants.
- Media-based grow beds can greatly increase the range of plants you can successfully cultivate because nutrients mineralize in the grow beds themselves.
- Even with light rocks, media-filled beds will be heavy. Make sure your garden is located and supported accordingly.
- Do not use sand or media smaller than ¾ inch in diameter. Sift out smaller rocks and sand that can clog your system.
- You can purchase gravel and river rocks inexpensively. If you want light rocks or want someone else to prepare the rocks, you can expect to pay for your convenience.

Flooding and Draining a Media Bed

Chapter 7

In This Chapter

- The benefits of flood and drain for plant health
- Using a timer to flood and drain media beds
- How an indexing valve can send water to different garden zones
- Using auto-siphons to automatically drain media beds
- Do-it-yourself plans to flood and drain your media beds

You want your grow beds to enjoy plenty of water and plenty of oxygen. Flooding your grow bed with water and then allowing it to drain every hour or so during the day will make your plants happy, filter the water for your fish, and encourage a robust population of the friendly bacteria that convert fish waste into plant fertilizer.

There are several ways to flood and drain your grow bed, which I'll talk about in this chapter. Each method for flooding and draining your media-filled grow beds is presented separately. In your garden, though, you can mix and match these methods if you want to experiment to see what works best for you.

Why Flood and Drain Your Media Beds?

Your plant roots need water and nutrients, but they also need oxygen. When you flood your media bed—fill the bed with water—the nutrient-rich water from your fish tank bathes the roots and your rocks. But if you leave your plant roots constantly submerged in water, they will attempt to adapt, and that effort takes energy away from food production.

When you drain your media bed—suck out the water—air will rush into the spaces between the rocks in your grow bed. Air is 21 percent oxygen, and that oxygen will dissolve in the water remaining on the surfaces of the rocks and roots and can be absorbed by the living things in your grow bed. These will include your plant roots and the bacteria that convert ammonia into nitrate. This could also include worms, if you added them to your system.

When you flood and drain your media beds, the constant ebb and flow of water and oxygen produces ideal growing conditions for your plants. It also increases the ability of the grow bed to effectively filter the fish water.

A key downside to flooding and draining your grow beds is the changing water level in your fish tank or sump. However, it only takes about a quart of water to flood a gallon of media in your grow bed, so this change is not large.

In order to flood and drain your grow beds, you will need to use either a timer or a *siphon*. A timer will turn off the flow into your media bed, allowing it to drain using gravity. A siphon will suck the water out of the media bed.

No matter how you plumb a media bed to flood and drain, I recommend you install a *media guard* around your drain to keep rocks away from your plumbing so you can adjust and clean the drain as necessary.

> **DEFINITION**
>
> A **siphon** is plumbing that sucks water out of a container, such as a media bed. A **media guard** is a shield around your drain or siphon to keep rocks out and allow you to inspect or clean your drain plumbing.

Methods for Flooding and Draining a Media Bed

There are several different ways to get your media beds to flood and drain. An easy, reliable method is using a timer to turn the pump on and off. When the pump is on, the media bed floods. When the pump is off, the bed drains.

Gardeners with a large number of grow beds may want to combine a timer with an indexing valve to flood their grow beds in turns. This is more complicated, but it allows the pump to stay on almost continually.

Many first-time aquaponic gardeners have used a flood tank with a flood valve because it is simple, doesn't require electricity, and allows the pump to stay on continually. The plans for this kind of system are available online for free, so the price is right.

Finally, increasing numbers of gardeners are using auto-siphons to drain their media beds. An auto-siphon doesn't have moving parts so it doesn't need electricity. The pump never has to stop (that's a good thing) and there is no need for a flood tank. But an auto-siphon won't start if the flow rate is too low. If the flow rate is too high, the siphon won't stop to allow the grow bed to flood again. Some gardeners feel timers are easier to deal with than fussing with siphons.

Timers Turn Pumps On and Off

The simplest way to get your grow beds to fill and drain is to use a timer. This device turns power on and off and can be used to alternately flood and drain an aquaponic grow bed. When the timer is on, the pump sends water from the sump or fish tank to your grow beds. When the timer is off, your grow bed drains. Easy.

You'll need a media guard to keep rocks out of the plumbing. Then you'll need a standpipe as tall as the highest level you want the water to reach. You'll want to have a small hole in the base of that standpipe so the media bed can drain when the pump is off, but not so large that your media bed drains faster than it can fill up. A ¼-inch hole is usually sufficient.

There are a few reasons to go with a timer. First, it is truly easy. Second, you can get by with a simple standpipe, so the media guard can be pretty small as well. There is a price to pay for simple and easy, though. In order to circulate the total volume of water every hour (on average), you need a pump that can push that much water in the limited time the pump is on. Folks who use timers typically set the system to fill for 15 minutes and drain for 45 minutes, so you need a pump that can push all the water in your system through your grow beds in a quarter of the time.

If you have 100 gallons of water in your system, for example, your pump must be able to push 400 gallons per hour (GPH) under perfect conditions. You'll likely need to buy a pump rated at 800 GPH to cycle 100 gallons each hour since your garden will likely have things like pipe bends that reduce the number of gallons your pump will actually push each hour.

You can buy 24-hour timers with pins that let you turn electricity on and off in 15-minute increments (96 pins per timer). These usually have time and day/night indications, so you can easily see what time of day you're setting your system to be on and off. If you can't find 15-minute timers, you can combine two 30-minute timers to get your pump to turn on for 15 minutes every hour or so. Instructions for doing this are found at the end of this chapter.

You can also buy repeat cycle timers that repeat a pattern of on and off actions. Repeat cycle timers or programmable timers are specialty items you'll only find online or in aquaponic or hydroponic stores.

A manual repeat cycle timer often used in hydroponics repeats every 40 minutes with 48 pins that represent about 50-second increments. You can also purchase programmable electronic timers that allow you to specify the ebb and flow times very precisely.

Indexing Valve to Shunt Flow Between Grow Beds

An *indexing valve* is another way to turn flow to individual media beds on and off. This is useful if you have four or more media beds in your system. An indexing valve has one inlet and multiple outlets, but only one outlet is active at any given time. The valve switches between outlets when water pressure is turned off using a mechanism like the one in a retractable ballpoint pen. People who use indexing valves install either a repeat cycle timer or a *solenoid* upstream of the indexing valve to turn off the flow.

DEFINITION

An **indexing valve** moves the flow from one inlet to any of several outlets. An indexing valve requires some other device, like a repeat cycle timer, to interrupt the water flow briefly to trigger the mechanical shift between outlets. A **solenoid valve** opens and shuts based on electricity and is a way of interrupting flow to an indexing valve without forcing the pump to stop. Stopping the pump frequently can burn out the pump more quickly.

Indexing valves adapted for the low pressures in an aquaponic garden can cost $75 or more. But some gardeners with larger gardens like using indexing valves because they allow you to increase the number of grow beds you can support and provide constant filtration for the fish water.

Indexing valves allow you to cycle water to different zones over the course of an hour or so.

(Photo courtesy of Eric Maundu of Kijani Grows Aquaponics)

Even though an indexing valve system involves a lot of mechanical and electrical complexity, the pump feeds the grow beds almost continually, so there is no need to buy an oversized pump. On the other hand, since you'll need at least a 1,000-GPH pump to run the indexing valve, an indexing valve setup is not recommended for a small aquaponics system.

Flood Tanks and Mechanical Flood Valves

Travis Hughey designed a robust and affordable ebb-and-flow aquaponic system that uses plastic 55-gallon drums. This Barrel-Ponics system is one of the key technologies for his Christian ministry, Faith and Sustainable Technologies, or F.A.S.T. Travis's goal was to develop a low-cost system that is appropriate for parts of the world where complicated timers and valves are not available. Travis's Barrel-Ponics design uses a unique flood tank (a reservoir located above the media beds that holds water to flood the media beds) and flood valve (a flapper valve that opens when the flood tank is full). After the water floods his media beds, gravity drains the beds while the pump fills up the flood tank again. The Barrel-Ponics design is affordable to make and easy to understand, and Travis has posted the plans online where anyone can download them for free. Go to his website (fastonline.org) and look under Technology and Aquaponics for more information.

Auto-Siphons Have No Moving Parts

An *auto-siphon* is an automatic way to quickly drain a grow bed once the water level has reached the desired level. Auto-siphons don't have any moving parts, so they don't need electricity. The benefit of using a siphon rather than timers is the ability to use a smaller pump that can circulate the amount of water desired per hour and without needing the extra mechanical gear required for either an indexing valve or flood tank design.

The downside to an auto-siphon is the need to keep the flow rate coming into a media bed fast enough to trigger the auto-siphon but slow enough to allow the auto-siphon to stop siphoning once the grow bed has drained.

> **DEFINITION**
>
> An **auto-siphon** automatically drains a container when the fluid level rises above the lip of the siphon. Auto-siphons require no electricity or moving parts.

There are two fundamental auto-siphon configurations, the loop siphon and the bell siphon.

Loop Siphon. In a loop siphon, you install a loop of tubing or piping that runs from the bottom of your media bed to the height you want your media bed to flood and then down below the media bed towards the drain. The water in your container or grow bed rises until the water reaches the top of the loop. When this kind of siphon is made from piping, it is sometimes called a U-siphon.

If the flow rate is great enough, water will sweep through the top of the loop and continue down the tube, priming the siphon. When the water level in the grow bed near the siphon drains low enough to allow air to be sucked into the siphon, the siphon will break, allowing the grow bed to fill again.

A loop siphon is understandable, particularly if you have clear tubing that allows you to see the water moving in the loop. There are a few problems with loop siphons, however. They are usually external to the grow bed, making them vulnerable to being knocked loose. The tubing can crimp, stopping the flow of water and causing the media bed to overflow. Loop siphons can look clunky, and if you do use clear tubing, algae can grow in the loop. But if one of your aims is to educate, a loop siphon is a wonderful teaching tool.

Bell Siphon. In a bell siphon or bell auto-siphon, a bell or jar is placed over a standpipe to quickly drain water from the media bed when the water level reaches the top of the standpipe. The bell siphon is my favorite way to let a media bed to fill and drain. A bell siphon is a standpipe covered by a watertight bell.

Like the loop siphon, a bell siphon lets you leave your pump on continuously fill your grow beds. The standpipe is sized so the top is right at the desired fill level. Once the water reaches the top of the standpipe, a siphon will form, draining the bed until air enters from the bottom of the bell, breaking the siphon.

A bell siphon is almost always inside the grow bed. Since there are no bits extending outside the grow bed, bell siphons have a cleaner look and less chance of accidental damage. There's also no chance the bell siphon will crimp.

Early bell siphon designs used complicated tubes and epoxy to make sure the siphon broke and required continual tweaking. Two recent innovations improve the reliability of bell siphons.

The first is the invention of an Affnan bell siphon. In an Affnan bell siphon, the standpipe has a funnel-like top to increase the amount of water priming the siphon when the water begins flowing over the top of the standpipe. Affnan Ramli, an aquaponics enthusiast in Malaysia, popularized use of the funnel, which makes the siphon trigger more reliably. The metric parts Affnan uses are not available in the United States, but a ¾- to 1-inch reducer at the top of a ¾-inch standpipe creates the required funnel proportions.

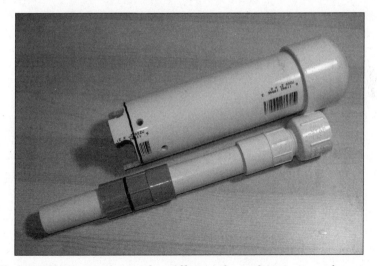

The large diameter at the top of an Affnan-style standpipe increases the range of flow rates that allow a bell siphon to function properly. This version of the Affnan-style standpipe uses parts commonly available in the United States.

The second innovation is a Coanda drain, which connects the lowest leg using 45-degree connector in the drain section instead of a 90-degree connector. The gentle 45-degree bend causes the water to mound up inside the connector, starting the siphon action. Since the water is still headed in a downward direction, the fluid velocity stays high, reducing clogs and washing away build-up.

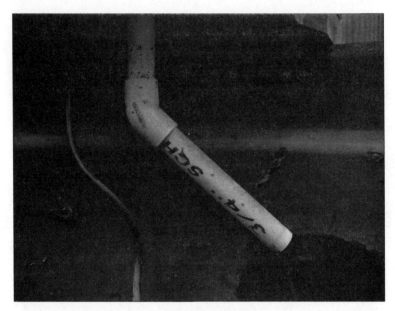

A Coanda drain beneath a grow bed. The 45-degree angle aids in forming a hydrodynamic plug to start the siphoning action for a bell siphon or internal loop siphon. The dust is an indication of how long it's worked without needing adjustment.

In media beds that are larger than 20 cubic feet, gardeners have found they need to add additional bells and whistles to get the bell siphon to operate properly. Rob Torcellini of Bigelow Brook Farm in Connecticut has developed a siphon variation that ensures the siphon will break reliably in a large grow bed. Rob uses a bend in the drainpipe to make sure the siphon starts and a cap around the base of a tube leading to the top of the bell to make sure the siphon breaks. This Torcellini siphon break makes a bell siphon extremely reliable and is useful in media beds larger than 20 cubic feet.

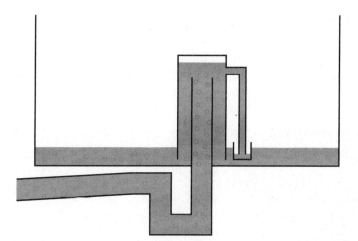

A Torcellini siphon break allows a bell siphon to work even in media beds that are larger than 20 cubic feet.
(Photo courtesy of Rob Torcellini)

GREEN TIP

If you find your media bed isn't filling up even though water is going in, the problem is likely a siphon that won't break. Try reducing the amount of water coming into the media bed and listen for the burp when the siphon stops sucking water out of the grow bed. If your media bed is always flooded, the siphon isn't starting. Try increasing (yes, increasing) the amount of water coming into the media bed. You should soon hear the gush of water as the siphon starts to drain the grow bed.

Combining Flood and Drain Methods

You may have plants that need a lot of oxygen in the root zone. People may say these are plants that like to have dry feet. To increase the amount of oxygen in the root zone, you can combine using a timer with using an auto-siphon. When the pump is on, the auto-siphon will empty the bed periodically. This will allow the upper portion of your grow bed to empty each time water fills the media bed instead of staying flooded to the top of your standpipe.

If you are growing plants that have different oxygen needs, feel free to use different flood and drain techniques in different media beds.

DIY Plans for Flood and Drain

Here are two sets of plans to help you make your media beds flood and drain on a budget. The first set of plans shows you how to use two inexpensive 30-minute timers to make your pump turn on for 15 minutes every hour or so. The second set of plans explains how to make a Affnan-style bell siphon and Coanda drain.

Making an Inexpensive 15-Minute Timer

It can be hard to find a 15-minute timer, but 30-minute timers are widely available. Here's a way to use two inexpensive 30-minute timers to achieve a 15-minute flood time about every hour.

Supplies:

(2) 24-hour timers with built-in pins to turn electricity on or off every 30 minutes (usually available at local hardware or home stores for under $5)

Extension cord

Tools: None

1. Push the pins on each timer so it will alternate between on and off every 30 minutes.

2. Plug in the first timer. Plug in a light to see if the timer is on or off. Turn the dial on the timer until the light switches off, then keep turning the dial until the light just barely switches on.

3. Disconnect the lamp. Connect the second timer to the first with an extension cord.

4. Plug in the lamp again. Turn the dial on the second timer until the light switches off, then keep turning it until the light just barely switches on.

5. Wait 15 minutes.

6. Turn the dial on the second timer until the light just barely switches off.

7. Unplug the lamp and connect your pump to the timers. Your pump will turn on for 15 minutes every hour or so.

8. Optional: To turn your pump off at night, move the pins on the first timer so no electricity goes to the second timer during the night.

Making an Affnan Bell Siphon and Coanda Drain Pipe

Here are plans for making a super-reliable auto-siphon out of PVC plumbing parts you can find at any hardware store. If you're not familiar with plumbing terms, just take this list to the store with you. The folks in the plumbing section will be happy to help you find everything.

Supplies:

(1) 1" slip to ¾" female pipe thread (FPT) connector

(1) ¾" male pipe thread (MPT) to ¾" slip connector

2' of ¾" polyvinyl chloride (PVC) pipe

9" of 2" PVC pipe

(1) 2" PVC pipe cap

11" of 3" PVC pipe (can use 4" pipe if desired)

(1) ¾" bulkhead fitting, if not already in grow bed (Chapter 5)

(1) ¾" 45-degree connector

(1) media guard made from 3" PVC pipe (Chapter 5)

Tools:

Miter saw

Drill with ¼" drill bit

Permanent marker

1. Install the bulkhead fitting in your grow bed if it isn't already installed.

2. Cut the ¾" pipe into three 5½" lengths.

3. Push one of the 5½" lengths of ¾" PVC into the slip end of the ¾" MPT to ¾" slip connector.

4. Screw the 1" slip to ¾" FPT connector onto the ¾" MPT to ¾" slip connector. This creates the Affnan-style standpipe as shown in the picture found earlier in this chapter.

5. Push the Affnan-style standpipe into the ¾" bulkhead fitting inside your grow bed. Mark the location near the base of the standpipe where you want to drill the drain hole.

6. Remove the standpipe and drill a ¼" hole near the base at your mark. Replace the standpipe in the bulkhead fitting.

7. Connect the two remaining lengths of 5½" lengths of ¾" PVC pipe into either end of the 45-degree connector. This is the Coanda drainpipe.

8. Push the Coanda drain pipe into the ¾" bulkhead fitting on the bottom side of your grow bed.

9. Cut three slots on either side of the bottom of the 2" PVC pipe, about 1" from one end. The slots should be very close together, so there is only a slender bit of PVC between the slots.

10. Put the 2" PVC cap on the end of the 2" PVC pipe on the far end from the slots. This is your bell.

11. Place the bell over your Affnan-style standpipe.

12. Cut slots spaced about 1" apart in the 3" PVC pipe. You can cut the slots on opposite sides, on just one side, or you can rotate the pipe after each slot so the slots spiral around the outside of the 3" PVC pipe. This is your media guard.

13. Place the media guard around the bell, making sure everything is centered over your bulkhead fitting.

14. Fill your grow bed with your media, making sure to hold the media guard so rocks don't get wedged underneath.

The Least You Need to Know

- There are several low-cost, ingenious ways to get media-filled grow beds to flood and drain. Each method has pros and cons—choose the method that appeals to you.

- A simple timer can turn your pump on to flood your media bed for only 15 minutes each hour, but this will require a larger pump.

- Indexing valves allow you to flood different zones in your garden in turn but can require a 1,000-gallon-per-hour pump.

- A flood tank/flood valve system is inexpensive and can be adapted to primitive conditions, such as wind-powered or human-powered water pumping.

- Auto-siphons have no mechanical or electrical parts and allow you to flood and drain your media bed without having to turn your pump off.

Taking Advantage of Vertical Space

In This Chapter

- Using towers and stacked planters
- Using layered beds
- Utilizing trellises and arbors
- Do-it-yourself plans for creating vertical space

Using vertical components in your garden will increase the amount of food you can grow in limited spaces. You can stack your plants on themselves or just let your plants climb above your grow beds. Several vertical planting systems were specifically created for hydroponics and aquaponics, while other methods are widely used in traditional soil gardens.

Growing Columns of Plants

One of the easiest vertical elements you can install is a vertical tower planter. This can be as simple as a length of polyvinyl chloride (PVC) pipe filled with gravel or as elaborate as rotating grow towers with dozens of plants in little more than a square foot. These kinds of planters were created with hydroponics in mind but can be adapted to aquaponics.

Commercial Tower Systems

A commercial tower can be a good choice if you want a design that works well and looks good. Commercial systems are designed by industrial designers to maximize functional and style. Commercial towers will come with detailed instructions complete with support networks to help you via phone, e-mail, or chat.

GREEN TIP

For more information on using vertical space in your garden, I recommend *Vertical Vegetable Gardening: A Living Free Guide* by Chris McLaughlin (see Appendix B).

Tower Garden is a design featured in a vertical vegetable garden display in Chicago O'Hare International Airport. Each tower segment is designed to be sprinkled from above, so that the water moistens the roots of the plants. The water collects at the base of the segment, where it rains down on the plants in the segment below. The Tower Garden is sold as a hydroponic system, it but can be easily adapted for use in an aquaponic system. You just need to pump your fish water to the top of the tower and drain the base segment into your fish tank.

These large-diameter towers are usually used to grow greens and herbs that grow well without soil. They should have lights installed on all sides. If used in greenhouses under sunlight, they should be rotated so all sides of the tower gets light. You can purchase a small Tower Garden designed for hydroponics at towergarden.com.

These commercial towers at Green Sky Growers are irrigated with water from a tank containing koi. The towers travel around the greenhouse on a track, which also rotates the towers.

(Photo courtesy of Pat Chiu)

Another vertical option is ZipGrow. With the ZipGrow system, you lay your plant roots onto open-cell plastic material, which is pulled up into a square tower. Water is plumbed to the top of the square tower and flows down through the plastic, evenly distributing the nutrient water. You can buy ZipGrow towers online at brightagrotech.com or from some online aquaponic stores.

There is also a commercial version of Britta Riley's Windowfarms. This is perfect if you have a bright window and just want a small garden for leafy vegetables or herbs. These are available for purchase online at windowfarms.org.

DID YOU KNOW ...

Britta Riley raised money to create the commercial version of her Windowfarms using the website Kickstarter in 2011. Her goal was $50,000, but supporters were so enthusiastic they donated over $250,000. The extra money went to creating the ability to manufacture these towers in the United States using sustainable techniques.

Making Your Own Towers

Commercial towers are great, but they can be expensive. Many gardeners make their own towers out of PVC pipe (see the DIY plan later in this chapter). A common technique for making PVC grow towers involves cutting and heating PVC pipe. The pipe is sliced every 12 inches on each side. The upper edge of each slot is heated to make the PVC soft. Before the PVC cools, you can use sticks and clamps to form pockets where the plants will grow. The pockets are filled with media to support the plant roots and serve as a biological filter.

PVC produces volatile organic compounds (VOCs) when heated. Heat PVC only in well-ventilated spaces and use a breathing mask designed to protect against VOCs.

You can also use plumbing joints to add planters to a central PVC trunk. The variations on this idea are only limited by your budget and the parts stocked at your local plumbing supply store. Filling this PVC piping with media will help reduce the probability of dry spots in the pipe, which could happen if the water merely streams into empty space.

When designing a DIY tower, make sure you support your tower securely, particularly if the tower is filled with media. Towers can be supported from below and fastened to a pole. They can also be hung from a sturdy beam overhead using metal hooks, chains, and cables rated to support the load.

Stacked Planters

Stacked planters combine economy and can look elegant. There are a few brands of stackable planters that can be adapted to an aquaponic system. You can buy stackable planters for as little as $10 per planter.

First is the Verti-Gro VG-1, a stack of cube-shaped planters made of polystyrene. The cubes stack neatly inside one another for shipping, then for use are rotated 45 degrees so the corners rest on the edges of the cube below. Because the container is made of expanded polystyrene, these containers insulate the plant roots. The plants grow in the corners of each cube, so you can grow four plants per container. The Verti-Gro website is vertigro.com.

AgroTower containers are made from sturdy black plastic. Each AgroTower container is designed with six planting sites and you can stack as many as six containers. These containers can be used with a variety of growing methods, including traditional soil gardening. You can buy AgroTower containers online at agrotower.com.

Sahib Punjabi's aquaponic garden in Florida includes homemade PVC containers, Verti-Gro containers, and AgroTowers.

Several stacking planter systems designed for the casual gardener have shown up on the market. I came across one version called Nancy Jane's Stacking Planters at the Philadelphia Flower Show in 2012. But a search of the internet for "stacking planter" produces a variety of designs. These stacking planters can be adapted to aquaponics if you're willing to modify the product.

GREEN TIP

When buying a commercial item online from a chain, you can sometimes get free shipping if you have the item shipped to a local store. Many smaller vendors also offer free shipping on popular sites like eBay or Amazon.com, an important factor when comparison shopping.

Stacking Grow Beds

In a large greenhouse or converted warehouse you may have a large amount of vertical space. Some aquaponic gardeners have developed multi-tiered gardens to use this extra space. With layered beds, water from the fish tank is often pumped to grow beds on the top level. Water from the top grow bed drains onto the beds below and so on, until the drain empties back into the fish tank.

You can go vertical with each bed emptying into the bed below it as long as the number of fish you have is balanced with the volume of your grow beds and your plants get sufficient light.

Designing a Stacked Grow Bed System

You will see stacked grow beds in photos, but I am not aware of a website that contains actual plans for building stacked grow beds. Possibly the most famous use of stacked grow beds is at Growing Power (growingpower.org), a 3-acre urban farm in Milwaukee, Wisconsin.

If you are going to stack grow beds, make sure your pump is powerful enough to push the water from your fish tank to the top level of grow beds. Also make sure your grow beds are far enough apart vertically that you can still harvest each one.

Many of these stacked grow bed designs locate the fish tank in the ground under the stacked grow beds. This gives the fish tank insulation against temperature extremes, but it makes it hard to clean the fish tank and harvest the fish.

*Will Allen of Milwaukee-based Growing Power uses stacked grow beds to maximize
the amount of food he can grow on his 3-acre urban farm.*
(Photo courtesy of Ryan Griffis)

If your grow beds are outside or get light from the sun, orient the beds from east to
west. The sun will shine onto both the top bed and the bottom bed during fall, winter, and spring. In summer the sun will be bright and the top grow bed can partially
shade the lower grow bed.

Supporting Stacked Grow Beds

An important consideration in designing a stacked grow bed system is supporting
the upper grow bed. The upper grow bed must be supported and secured so that it
cannot fall.

Professionals creating large gardens inside warehouses sometimes use the heavy-duty
metal shelving supports found in stores like Home Depot, Lowe's, or Costco. These
metal supports are probably not within your price range if you are creating a garden
for your home.

Wood columns made from 4×4 lumber can be an adequate alternative. Use untreated
lumber and apply a nontoxic, water-soluble treatment to resist rot and insect damage.

The toxic chemicals used in pressure-treated lumber can leach into your system over time if you use it in your structure.

You will need strong columns to support the grow beds. You will want to install cross braces on these columns so they can't fall over. I also recommend you bury your posts in the ground if you are in a soil environment using concrete or metal footings. Consult the folks at your local hardware store if in doubt.

SOUNDS FISHY

Pressure-treated lumber lasts a long time because it is treated with copper to keep insects away and chemical fungicides to prevent rot. The copper can be toxic to your fish, and there is enough concern about these chemicals that organic food cannot be grown in soil that has been in contact with pressure-treated lumber.

Helping Plants Climb Upward

Some plants love to climb and vine. Trellises and arbors let you move the vines, leaves, and fruit up above your grow bed. A trellis is usually a vertical lattice of twine or wood used to support vining plants. A pergola is a horizontal frame of wood or metal that supports plants. There's a plan at the end of this chapter for a pergola you can make yourself.

Trellises

The term *trellis* comes from the Latin word for three threads, and it can be as simple as a piece of dangling twine. Climbing plants like grapes or peas will send out *tendrils* that reflexively bend around anything they touch. As the tendrils coil, they pull the plant upward. Growth at the top of the plant produces new tendrils seeking ever-higher cords and branches to grab.

DEFINITION

A **trellis** is a vertical structure that supports plants that climb or produce long vines. **Tendrils** are special thread-like stems that climbing plants send out that curl and coil around anything they touch, lifting a plant upward.

Vining plants don't have tendrils. These can be trained upward along a vertical structure to hold the plant up off the ground.

You need a sturdy structure to support the twine or lattice of the trellis. A popular trellis used in traditional gardens is simple a grouping of three or four long sticks that are tied together at the top. A rectangular frame can be used to support strings of twine, mesh netting, or wooden latticework. You can even think of the circular wire cages used for tomato plants as a sort of trellis.

Using a trellis with your plants increases the airflow between your plants and minimizes damage to fruit from pests that live near the ground. In addition, the vertical space the plant takes up is space that plant doesn't have to cover on the surface of your grow bed.

Pergolas

Pergola comes from the Latin term for projecting eaves. When I hear the term *pergola*, I think of romantic Renaissance patios and pathways covered in masses of leaves and fragrant flowers. But a pergola can be created using any sturdy material that can provide a horizontal platform for the vines, leaves, and fruits of plants.

> **DEFINITION**
>
> A **pergola** is an open, roof-like structure, usually supported by four posts. Vining plants like tomatoes can be trained so stems and leaves spread over the surface of a pergola, allowing fruit to ripen overhead, within arm's reach.

With a pergola, the roots are usually at the base of one of the vertical posts supporting the horizontal roof of the pergola. The stem of the plant travels up to the open platform and the leaves, flowers, and fruit are allowed to spread over the top of the platform.

You don't want to put a pergola over your garden itself, since the leaves could shade your garden too much. But a pergola next to your garden on the side away from the sun can support the leaves and fruit of a plant with roots in your aquaponic grow bed.

A pergola keeps fruit out of reach of ground pests and can put your vegetables at a convenient height for harvest. The weight of medium fruits like tomatoes, grapes, cucumbers, and small squash will lead them to hang below the pergola roof. Larger fruit would need to be supported by some kind of net or hammock.

A pergola can even be used to support the vines of rooting vegetables like sweet pota-toes. A pot filled with dirt is tied up under a portion of the vine, allowing potatoes to grow. The potatoes are harvested by releasing the pot, allowing the dirt to simply fall off the potatoes.

Growing Up and Down

You can take advantage of vertical space even if you don't have any sort of structure. Some plants will naturally grow high above your grow beds. Corn, sunflowers, and fruit trees are examples of plants that can take advantage of sunlight several feet above the surface of the grow bed. With careful positioning and pruning, you will still have enough sunlight falling on the grow bed itself to sustain shorter plants.

Another option is allowing plants to trail over the edge of your grow beds. Chives and sage, for example, can trail over the edge of the grow bed to take advantage of sunlight that shines in the area between your grow beds.

DIY Plans for Creating Vertical Space

Here are a couple of easy projects that will allow you to take advantage of vertical space in your garden.

PVC Tower

These instructions are for a 4-foot-tall tower, but you can make the tower any height you want. I don't give instructions for how to plumb the flow from your pump so it reaches the top of the tower, because that will depend on your particular pump and garden design.

Supplies:

4' of 4" diameter PVC pipe (use thin-wall pipe if available)

2 S-hooks

(1) 4" PVC cap

12" of sturdy chain

1 hook to screw in wall (optional)

1' of 1" diameter dowel rod or similar stick

2 self-tapping screws to fasten cap onto pipe (optional)

Aluminum foil

Tools:

Miter saw

Heat gun

Drill with $\frac{1}{4}$" drill bit

Safety glasses and ear plugs for whenever you are using power tools

Mask to protect from VOC fumes when you are heating up the PVC

Cut the PVC pipe:

1. Put on safety glasses and ear plugs. Cut the dowel or stick at an angle on either side of one end so it looks like a large screwdriver.

2. Slice the PVC pipe on alternating sides every 6". The slots should be a bit less than halfway through the pipe.

3. Drill two $\frac{1}{4}$" holes about $\frac{1}{2}$" from the top edge of your pipe. These are for the S-hooks you will use to hang your tower.

Form the planter pockets in the pipe:

The next steps must be performed in a well-ventilated area and you should wear a mask to block VOC fumes. You can take off the safety glasses and ear plugs if you want.

4. Cover the pipe with aluminum foil below the slots.

5. Using a heat gun, heat up the PVC above a slot. You only need to heat a triangular area above the slot.

6. Wedge the angled stick into the slot, pushing the softened PVC inward. Hold until cooled.

7. Repeat Steps 5 and 6 until all the slots have been shaped so there is space for a plant's stem to grow out of the pipe.

Get the tower ready for plants:

8. Drill drain holes in the cap. If this will drain directly into a tank below, you can just drill several ¼" holes. Otherwise, adapt this step to install the particular piping you need to direct the flow to a drain.

9. Screw the cap onto the bottom of the pipe.

10. Install the S-hooks in the holes at the top of the pipe.

11. Connect the chain to the S-hooks. If the chain will hang your tower from a length of pipe or tubing, skip the next step.

12. Install a hook in the wall where you are hanging your tower.

13. Hang the tower and connect the inflow so it drizzles into the tower.

14. Fill the tower with your grow medium. If you have your plants ready, place the roots into the tube while you are filling the tower.

Pergola

This plan is for a simple pergola for supporting your plants. It's a very basic structure, but you can put an angle on the top boards to make it more decorative or add other details so it fits better with the architecture of your garden or yard. Remember to put this pergola on the side of your garden away from the sun, so it won't block the sun falling on your other plants.

Supplies:

(4) 4×4 lumber, 8' long

(3) 2×6 lumber, 8' long

(1) ½" diameter electrical metallic tubing (EMT) conduit, 10' long

(3) 2×4 lumber, 8' long

1 box 3" deck screws

1 can nontoxic paint or sealer

(4) 4×4 post anchors appropriate for your surface

Tools:

Drill

⅞" spade bit

Hex adapter

Saw

Pipe cutter

Spirit level

Measuring tape

Pencil or marker

Establish your foundation:

1. Determine the location of your pergola. The posts will be positioned so they fit just inside a 4'×6' rectangle.

2. Install the post anchors so the outside corners are at the corners of the 4'×6' rectangle. Alternately, you could dig holes for concrete footings, but the rest of these instructions presume you are using post anchors.

3. For uneven ground, determine the height difference between the anchors. Place a board across the tallest anchor. Move the other end of the board to each of the other anchors and raise the board until it is perfectly level as measured with a spirit level. Note how many inches you need to raise the board over each of the other anchors.

Install your posts:

4. Cut your posts to the desired height. If your ground is uneven, cut the posts so the tops will be level with one another once installed.

5. Place the 4×4 posts into the anchors. Fasten according to manufacturer's instructions.

Create three edges of the top frame:

6. Cut one of the 2×6s in half to create two 4" lengths.

7. Screw the 4" lengths to the posts to form the short edges of the trellis.

8. Optional: Cut the ends of the remaining 2×6s at a 45-degree angle to add a decorative touch to the pergola.

9. Screw one of the 2×6s to the posts to form a long edge of the trellis.

Create the grid inside the top frame:

10. Measure the distance between the posts along the long edge. This distance should be about 67".

11. Cut two of the 2×4s so they will fit inside the long edge between the posts.

12. Cut the last 2×4 so it will fit between the two short 4×6 boards at the top of the pergola. This distance should be 72" (6').

13. Stack the 2×4s on top of each other, with the longest board on top. Make sure the boards are centered so the long board sticks out the same amount on each side of the stack.

14. Mark the center of the long board on top of the pile at 2' and 4'.

15. Drill holes through the entire stack of boards with the $7/8$" spade bit on the marks you made in Step 14.

16. Screw one of the shorter drilled boards to the inside of the long board at the top of the pergola.

17. Screw the long board in between the short 2×6 boards at the top of the pergola.

18. Using the pipe cutter, cut the EMT to create two 4'-long pipes.

19. Slide the 4'-long pipes into the holes in the two 2×4s at the top of the pergola.

Finish off the fourth side of the top frame:

20. Slide the remaining 2×4 onto the pipes, pushing it to the middle so it touches the long 2×4.

21. Screw the final 2×6 board onto the posts. Before screwing in the last side, make sure the posts aren't closer together than the length of the short 2×4.

22. Slide the loose 2×4 to the edge between the posts so it touches the long 2×6.

23. Screw the loose 2×4 to the 2×6.

24. Paint your pergola with nontoxic paint or sealer.

The Least You Need to Know

- Careful use of vertical space will increase the amount you can grow.
- Vertical towers and stacking containers are widely available, and many are specifically designed for growing without soil.
- Stacking grow beds can expand your growing area, but you need to be careful to support the grow beds and design the system so the lower grow bed gets enough light.
- Pergolas and trellises let your vining plants grow up and away from the surface of your grow bed to maximize productivity.

Growing in Water

In This Chapter

- Pros and cons of growing in water
- Different ways to grow in water
- Removing excess fish waste
- Do-it-yourself plans for growing in water

Even though media beds are highly recommended for home growers, there are situations where it is useful to simply grow in water. Water is lighter than wet rocks, and several fast-growing, leafy plants can thrive grown just in water.

There are two major ways to grow with water in aquaponics: nutrient film technique (also called growing in channels), and deep water culture. We'll take a closer look at both methods in this chapter.

Benefits and Challenges of Growing in Water

A grow bed filled with just water will always be lighter than the same grow bed filled with waterlogged rocks. This may mean you can put a water-filled aquaponic garden in a location that couldn't support grow beds full of gravel. When you grow in water, you don't want to drain your grow beds. Because your grow beds aren't flooding and draining, you don't have to worry about your water levels going up and down.

On the downside, you won't be able to grow as many varieties of plants. You'll need to filter fish solids out of the water, and you'll need special pots filled with a little bit of grow media to hold your plants. The following sections discuss some specific things you'll need to think about if you want to grow in water.

Filtering Out Fish Solids

When you grow in gravel, the rocks filter your water. But when you simply grow in water, the solids in your water will mostly end up sticking to your roots. If you don't filter out the fish solids, your plant roots will become coated with a slimy layer of organic stuff, preventing the roots from absorbing oxygen and nutrients.

A filter can remove the fish solids. But when you remove those fish solids, you also remove the nutrition that was in those solids. The filter is also one more piece of gear you need to find space for, and removing the accumulated solids from the filter is a chore you don't have with a media bed system.

Net Pots and Media

You'll need to support your seedlings in the water. Typically, you'll be using net pots filled with some kind of media. Net pots are available online and through hydroponic and aquaponic stores. They are made from food-safe, inert plastic and are designed to allow the water to fully immerse the roots of your plant.

Net pots hold plants while allowing water to flow freely to the roots.

If you can't get net pots, you could use plastic food containers, like plastic drinking cups or used yogurt cups. You will need to punch or drill enough holes to allow free flow of water into the container.

In addition to the rocks you would use in a media bed, you have the option of using other inert materials in your containers, like rock wool and vermiculite. I recommend expanded clay beads or expanded shale as the best materials to use for filling your net pots.

Aeration

When you're growing in media, the flood and drain action naturally bathes the plant roots in oxygen. But when you grow just in water, your plants might not get enough oxygen to their roots. This is particularly true if your plants are floating on top of a deep grow bed filled with water.

To add oxygen you will need to install air lines with diffusers in the water beneath your plants. You'll probably notice that the plants closest to the diffusers will grow faster.

Nutrient Film Technique

In *nutrient film technique (NFT)* your plants are suspended in air while a thin stream of water runs along the bottom of your container. Your plant roots dangle in the water, absorbing moisture and nutrients.

> **DEFINITION**
>
> **Nutrient film technique (NFT)** is the growing of plants with their roots in pipes or gutters with a small amount of water flowing along the bottom.

Containers for Nutrient Film Technique

Since you only have a shallow stream of water flowing through the bottom of your container, you can use a wide variety of grow beds, pipes, and gutters for nutrient film technique. Many people use 4-inch-diameter PVC pipe and drill holes along the top for the net pots. Academics argue that round pipes create a small stream, not a film, but most folks refer to the horizontal PVC tube systems as NFT.

Another popular option is PVC fence post, which is square instead of round. An issue with the square fence post is getting the caps to be watertight. A bit of silicon or epoxy can eliminate leaks around the caps, and many find it easier to insert drains into the flat sides of the hollow fence posts.

You can also use gutters, but they are not as sturdy. Plastic gutters will have to be supported along their length to prevent sagging. You will also need some kind of cover for the gutter to prevent algae growth.

Temperature

NFT works well when the water is the same temperature as the growing area, like inside a home or in a temperature-controlled greenhouse.

When NFT is used outside, the water inside the pipes will get hot on summer days. Plants like lettuce need their roots to stay cool, so an outdoor NFT system will not be able to successfully grow lettuce in summer heat. On cold winter days, the water in the pipes will become chilled and could even freeze.

Plants Floating in Deep Water

In *deep water culture (DWC)*, you keep your grow beds flooded all the time. Water comes into the bed, which pushes water out the standpipe. A foam raft floats on the surface of the water, and net pots hang in holes drilled into the raft. Research performed by Dr. Wilson Lennard indicates that plants grown using deep water culture (and deep media beds) produce larger harvests than plants grown using nutrient film technique.

Some people will drill holes in the lid of a sturdy container filled with water and use that to support the net pots that hold the plants. However, most people who grow using deep water culture use the floating raft concept.

DEFINITION

Deep water culture (DWC) is a technique in hydroponics and aquaponics in which the plants are supported over grow beds filled with water. The grow beds should ideally be 12 inches deep.

My first deep water culture system used a foam raft to support my plants in a concrete mixing tub If I had to do this again, I'd drill my holes in straight rows.

Floating Rafts

You can make your raft from any combination of materials that float, but the recommended material is *extruded polystyrene (XPS)* foam. Sheets of this foam are widely available in climates where the weather gets cold. XPS foam sheets are sturdy and they should be nontoxic.

Since XPS foam is used in home construction, some manufacturers in the past added chemicals to prevent termite damage and rot. I recommend that you buy new XPS sheeting rather than re-using old foam. When in doubt about a particular type of foam, consult the online aquaponic forums listed in Appendix B.

Many individuals paint their rafts with white latex paint. White latex interior paint is nontoxic once dry. The white also reflects sunlight back toward the plant, reduces UV damage to the foam, and keeps the raft cool under the summer sun.

Expanded polystyrene foam (EPS) is cheaper than the extruded foam and is made up of individual expanded white foam balls. This inexpensive foam will be messier to cut and will fall apart more quickly over time.

Another kind of foam you should avoid is *polyisocyanurate (ISO or PIR)* foam. This foam is very good for insulation, but it contains skin irritants. It's always a good idea to keep things that contain cyanide out of the water your fish and plants use. This foam is a spun-honey color and is often bonded to a silvery backing. If the foam you see has silver on one side and is labeled ISO or PIR, ask if the store has some other kind of foam sheet.

> **DEFINITION**
>
> **Extruded polystyrene (XPS)** is durable foam sheeting suitable for use in a wet environment. **Expanded polystyrene (EPS)** is foam board made of pre-expanded polystyrene beads and is also known as bead board. It is less expensive than XPS, but will break easily. **Polyisocyanurate (ISO or PIR)** is a foam insulation material that can withstand temperatures up to 400°F (200°C). It contains compounds like cyanide and can irritate skin, so it should not be placed in contact with the water that contains your fish and plant roots.

The thickness you'll use depends on the size of net pot you use. I recommend 1½-inch-thick foam sheeting if you are using 2-inch net pots and 2-inch-thick XPS if you are using net pots larger than 2 inches. You'll typically drill your holes ¼ inch larger in diameter than the supposed diameter of your net pot or cup, but always drill a test hole to make sure the hole size is correct before drilling the entire sheet.

Arranging Your Plants

Traditional gardens are planted in rows. Gardeners with small plots have started placing plants in a hexagonal pattern to cram as many plants into a given space as possible.

When you drill holes in your floating raft, though, you want to keep your plants in rows. This will allow air bubbles to travel through your bed without getting caught in the maze of root systems you get with triangular or hexagonal patterns.

The space between your rows and between the individual plants in each row will vary depending on what you are growing and how mature the plants are. In commercial practice it is common to grow the immature plants in tightly packed formation, then move the plants to another set of rafts with wider spacing a couple of weeks before harvest; that way, the mature plant can achieve its full potential.

Rob Torcellini of Bigelow Brook Farm is always coming up with great new ideas for growing with aquaponics. One idea I've seen in Rob's videos of his greenhouse is to place your plants in narrow rafts that can remain tightly clustered while your plants are small. When your plants reach maturity and need the extra space, you can insert floating strips without net pots to space out the plants and keep light from getting to the roots. This works best if you are planting a few seeds each week, so only a few strips of plants are reaching mature growth at any one time.

What Grows Beneath

With deep water culture you can use the water below your rafts for other critters. Freshwater shrimp and crawfish can do well under a floating raft. The water under a floating raft can also be an acceptable interim home for young fish too small to survive in your main tank.

If you like the idea of keeping fish or shrimp in the water beneath your plants, find out if the fish or shrimp like to eat plants. The fish will likely thrive under the plants, but you don't want your fish or shrimp to eat all your plant roots.

Other Hydroponic Growing Methods

If you look at a hydroponic catalog, you will see other ways of delivering water to plant roots, many of which involve miniature nozzles and drip systems. The tiny holes in these nozzles are easily clogged, causing a catastrophic result for your plants.

Once you have a successful system, you could experiment with these other techniques on the side. However, the small amount of water used on these drip and nozzle systems may not be adequate to filter water for your fish and maintain the biological processes necessary for robust plant growth.

Ways to Filter Your Water

As I've discussed, you need to filter particles out of the water before it enters your grow beds. The particles will be bits of leftover fish food, fish waste, dust, sand, grit, and leaves or stems bits that might fall into your tank.

There are a variety of ways to filter solids out of your water. The first is to have your deep water or nutrient flow grow beds in line after media beds. If you don't have media beds or find you still need some filtration, I suggest the following methods to filter your water.

GREEN TIP

If you combine growing in water with growing in media, the volume of your media grow beds should be roughly equal to the volume of your fish tanks. To maximize filtration of fish solids by the media, arrange your water grow beds so their water is the overflow out of the media beds.

Let Gravity Remove the Solids

A swirl filter is a circular tank where gravity pulls solids off the top layer of water and allows them to settle in the bottom of the filter, while clean water leaves the tank from the top of a standpipe in the center. In a swirl filter, the water enters the secondary tank at an angle, creating the swirling motion that gives this filter its name. This swirling motion makes the water travel around the tank so time and gravity can make the solids fall into the bottom of the tank.

A swirl filter can be made from a simple barrel with the same kind of plumbing you would use for a grow bed. A challenge with swirl filters is the need to remove the concentrated solids that collect at the bottom of the swirl filter. If you install a spigot near the bottom of your swirl filter, you can drain out the solids periodically. This sludge of organic material, also called fish emulsion, makes a great addition to compost for any traditional garden you may have.

Screen Solids Out of the Water

Another way to remove fish solids is to put the water from the fish tank through screens. The water passes through a series of mesh pads that are nearly an inch thick each. The first mesh is coarse, and subsequent screens become finer. The solids are captured in the series of screens rather than clumping on the same screen, allowing them to gradually dissolve back into the water.

After this series of screens, the water goes into a final stage where gravity pulls any remaining solids to the bottom of the pool as the clarified water spills over the wall at the far end.

Screen systems like this are usually sold as an optional piece of gear in a kit system. They can take up several feet, and may be paired with a swirl filter if the water needs additional filtration.

Use High-Tech Filters

For someone with a large garden or a commercial operation, there are commercial filter systems for removing solids. These high-tech filters were developed for aquaculture, where there are no media beds or plants to capture the fish wastes. Some examples are bio-filters used with koi ponds, rotating drum screens, bead filters, and sand filters. One source for larger filters is Aquatic Eco-Systems, which has a nice website (aquaticeco.com) where you can research the cost and capabilities of these filters.

DIY Plans for Growing in Water

Here are a couple of inexpensive projects you might want to build if you want to use nutrient film technique or filter solids out of your water. I don't give separate instructions for a deep water channel grow bed, since that is simply a regular grow bed filled with water that has a foam raft floating on the surface.

NFT Tube Made from a Fence Post

Square PVC fence posts make nice tubes for growing plants using nutrient film technique. The flat sides make it easy to drill holes for net pots and bulkhead fittings. End caps are inexpensive and can be made watertight with nontoxic silicone sealant. This basic design can be adapted to the size of the space you have. Plumbing details will vary depending on your pump and drain configuration, so have been omitted in these instructions.

Supplies:

6' of 4"×4" PVC fence post (under $20)

(2) 4"×4" PVC post caps (under $2 each)

1 tube of nontoxic silicone sealant

2 bulkhead fittings

(12) 2" net pots (can use 3" net pots if desired)

2 liters expanded clay beads or expanded shale

2 short pipe stubs to fit inside the bulkhead fittings

Tools:

Drill

Hole saw to cut net pot holes (2¼" for 2" pots or 3¼" for 3" pots)

Hole saw to cut holes for bulkhead fittings (consult bulkhead details)

Measuring tape

Permanent marker

Length of 2×3 lumber (can buy a full 8' board or just use a scrap as small as 4" in length)

1. Place the fence post on a table.

2. Mark the middle of a side 3" from either end of the post. This will be the top of your post or tube.

3. Using the measuring tape as a guide, make a mark the top of the tube every 6" between the two marks you made in Step 2. If you want your net pots to be spaced only 3" apart, make marks every 3".

4. Flip the post over and mark the middle of the bottom side of the tube 3" from either end.

5. Drill holes in this bottom side for your bulkhead fittings.

6. Flip the tube back over and drill holes in the top of the tube for your net pots. Place the 2×3 into the post to prevent the drill from accidentally making a hole in the bottom of the post.

7. Install your bulkhead fittings. If desired, add the short stubs inside the post to increase the water depth in the post when your system is operating.

8. Put a bead of silicone around the inside of one of the post caps.

9. Slide the post cap onto one end of the post. Use a finger to smooth the silicone around the inside of the post where it connects to the post cap. If you can't reach inside, put a bead of silicone around the outside where the post cap and post meet and smooth that with your finger.

10. Repeat Steps 8 and 9 with the second post cap.

11. Let the silicone cure for 24 hours.

12. Plumb your NFT tube to your pump and drain.

13. Insert your net pots full of medium.

14. Add seeds or seedlings.

Swirl Filter

A swirl filter removes fish waste and other solids from the water. Place a swirl filter in your system between your fish tank and any grow beds that use only water. These plans use a 55-gallon barrel, but if you have a small garden, you can adapt these plans to a smaller container and smaller diameter piping. For example, a great small container would be an inverted 5-gallon water bottle with a hole in the base (now on the top). You would use a flexible PVC coupler on the neck (now on the bottom) to connect it to the ball valve plumbing for draining accumulated fish waste. A 1" pipe, fittings, and uniseals for plumbing through the sides would be perfect for a small system. However, if you have room for the larger swirl filter, you won't have to drain it as often.

Supplies:

(1) 55-gallon barrel

(3) 2" bulkhead fittings

10' of 2" PVC pipe

(1) 2" ball valve

(2) 2" 90-degree elbows

Tools:

Pipe cutter for PVC (can use miter saw)

Hole saw for bulkhead fittings

PVC glue, if desired

Drill and ¼" bit

1. Cut three holes in your barrel near the top, bottom, and middle.

2. Install bulkhead fittings in the three holes.

3. Cut two 3" length of PVC pipe.

4. Use one 3" length of PVC to join the ball valve to the bottom bulkhead fitting. Glue with PVC glue following instructions on the package. You'll use this ball valve when you want to empty the swirl filter of accumulated fish emulsion.

5. Cut two 1' lengths of 2" PVC pipe.

6. Install one of the 1' lengths of 2" PVC pipe inside the bottom of the barrel, leading from the center of the barrel to the bottom bulkhead fitting.

7. Fit the second 3" length of PVC inside the barrel in the bulkhead fitting at the middle of the barrel.

8. Add a 2" elbow to the 3" pipe inside the top bulkhead fitting. Adjust the elbow so flow will jet out along the side of the barrel, creating a swirling motion in the water in the barrel.

9. Add an elbow to the end of the second 1' length of pipe.

10. Fit the second 1' length of 2" PVC pipe to the inside of the top bulkhead fitting. Twist the elbow so it is facing directly up. Optionally, you can add a short length of PVC pipe to make the water level rise above the top hole in your barrel.

11. Plumb the outside of the barrel to your pump and your floating raft grow bed using the rest of the 10' pipe.

The Least You Need to Know

- Growing in water can reduce the weight of your system, but you may have reduced success growing certain crops.
- Nutrient film technique will allow you to grow without heavy grow beds.
- Deep water culture grow beds are relatively heavy, but give you temperature and pH stability.
- If you want to grow only in water, you will need to filter your water using a swirl filter or screens.
- If you put NFT or DWC grow beds downstream of media beds, you might be able to skip separate filters.

Nutrients and Plants

In Part 3, we cover the things you need to do to grow plants in your aquaponic system, including planning your garden design, starting the plants from seeds or cuttings, finding fish-safe pest control, and maximizing your harvest. Chapter 10 covers how to develop the biological filter that will transform fish waste into plant fertilizer, as well as how to measure and adjust the chemistry of your system. Chapter 11 talks about popular garden vegetables and the conditions where they grow best. Chapter 12 discusses how to start plants, transplant them in an aquaponic system, and start seeds from cuttings. Chapter 13 tells you how to deal with pests organically; this is important because you don't want to use anything on you plants that could harm your fish. Chapter 14 finishes off the plant part by explaining how to trick your plants into producing more than they normally would.

Making Fertilizer Out of Fish Waste

Chapter 10

In This Chapter

- Forms of nitrogen and why they matter
- Jump-starting the nitrogen cycle with ammonia
- Other additives for your aquaponic garden
- Adjusting pH
- Testing your water

When we give an overview of aquaponics, we'll sometimes just say that the fish fertilize the water for the plants, and the plants purify the water for the fish. But it's not as simple as that; your brand-new grow bed isn't able to convert fish waste into plant food just yet.

In this chapter I'll talk about how to nurture your garden's ability to turn poisonous ammonia into the fertilizer called nitrate. We'll talk about the different forms of nitrogen and how they affect fish so you can avoid killing your fish while your garden is maturing.

This chapter talks about how to make the measurements to track your garden's progress and how to adjust your water chemistry to maximize the health of your plants and fish.

Beneficial Bacteria and the Nitrogen Cycle

Your plants need nitrogen to thrive. Nitrogen is a chemical necessary for life on Earth and a key component in protein. But even though air is mostly nitrogen gas, plants can't use the nitrogen in the air. Ammonia is a form of nitrogen that comes from fish waste, including leftover food, fish gills, and fish poop. But plants can't use ammonia, either.

Plants require nitrate, a form of nitrogen that is created out of ammonia by beneficial bacteria, to fuel their growth. Once you have a healthy population of these bacteria, your garden will be able to effortlessly transform ammonia from your fish into nitrate for your plants.

The beneficial bacteria are too small to see, but we can measure whether or not they are in the garden by the amount of ammonia, nitrite (an intermediate form of nitrogen between ammonia and nitrate), and nitrate we see in the water. Later in the chapter I'll talk about how to perform the simple tests to measure the presence of these chemicals.

When an aquaponic garden is new, there is nothing in the water. When we test the water, the results tell us there is no ammonia, no nitrite, and no nitrate.

We attract the bacteria by giving them food. And the first food they need is ammonia. Later in this chapter I'll talk about how to introduce ammonia to your garden.

After a week or more, the ammonia levels will begin to drop, and you will start to see nitrite in the system. This is the signal that you have a small population of the bacteria, called nitrosifying bacteria, that eat ammonia and produce nitrite.

We'll keep adding ammonia to the system to feed the nitrosifying bacteria, and our tests will show that the ammonia is all being converted to nitrite. After another week or so, the nitrite will begin to disappear and we'll see nitrate. This means we have attracted another kind of bacteria. These bacteria, called nitrifying bacteria, eat nitrite and transform it into nitrate, which is plant fertilizer. When you have both nitrosifying and nitrifying bacteria present, most people just refer to them as nitrifying bacteria. The process of developing these bacterial elements of your garden is called *cycling*.

DEFINITION

Cycling is the process of introducing ammonia to an aquaponic system to produce a robust colony of nitrosifying and nitrifying bacteria. A fully cycled system is one where all the ammonia and nitrite are continually transformed into nitrate.

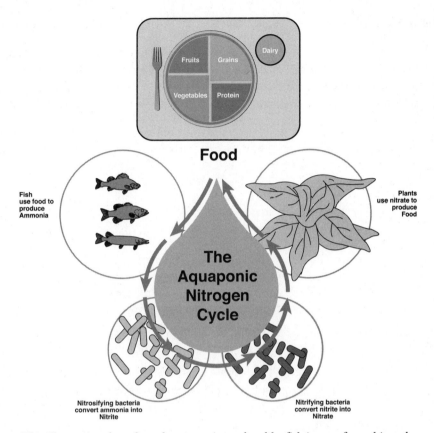

This illustration shows how the ammonia produced by fish is transformed into the nitrate plants need for robust growth.

Cycling Your Garden

You can simply add fish to the new water in your fish tank and plant seedlings in your gravel and never measure the ammonia, nitrite, and nitrate in the water. But water chemistry has a huge impact on the health of your fish and plants. It's worth your while to note how your system matures over time so you can maximize your harvest and keep your fish and plants healthy.

If you can quickly establish a robust colony of nitrifying bacteria, you can support more fish and plants in your aquaponics system. Let's talk about the different forms of nitrogen so you can understand how each affects your fish and plants.

Fish Poison: Ammonia

To start the cycle, you need to allow a large amount of ammonia to exist in your tank and grow beds. Unfortunately, this large quantity of ammonia can potentially kill your fish. You can either use cheap fish whose possible death you won't mourn, or you can add ammonia using some other method to cycle your system before adding live fish.

Following are some proven ways to put ammonia into your garden to start the cycling process.

Ammonia. The first way to add ammonia is to simply add *ammonia sulfate* crystals or pure *liquid ammonia*. If you're good with chemistry, you can calculate the amount of ammonia required to raise the ammonia levels to 0.5 parts per million (ppm) or 0.5 milligrams per liter (mg/L).

If your chemistry is rusty or if you can't figure out the strength of the products you are adding from the packaging, you'll need to test your water using the techniques discussed in the chapter. Carefully measure the ammonia and add a little at a time until your ammonia test kit gives you a reading of 0.5 parts per million (ppm) or 0.5 milligrams per liter (mg/L). Record how much ammonia that took.

Add that same amount of ammonia each day and test the concentration of ammonia and nitrite in the water. As ammonia levels increase towards 5 ppm, you should begin seeing nitrite. Once nitrites appear, halve the amount of ammonia you're adding and start testing nitrates. Once ammonia and nitrite levels have dropped to zero and nitrates are appearing, it is safe to add fish.

Ammonia seems to be the fastest way to establish a robust colony of beneficial bacteria, but it can be hard to find pure ammonia without added perfumes or detergents. If the ammonia is colored or if it foams when you shake the bottle, don't use it. If the label says it is clear ammonia, pure ammonia, 100 percent ammonia, or Pure Ammonium Hydroxide, it's fine to use. Most stores sell the foamy perfumed stuff, but you should be able to find pure ammonia at professional cleaning stores or hardware stores.

Fish. Fish add ammonia to your tank whenever they breathe, urinate, or poop. Goldfish create a lot of ammonia in their water and are able to tolerate more ammonia than other sorts of fish. For these reasons, they are a great fish to use as you build up ammonia levels in your tank.

Another option is to use a small population of juvenile fish, also known as fingerlings, of your intended fish species. The fact they are younger, smaller fish means they won't produce as much ammonia as a full population of mature fish. Less ammonia means a smaller population of beneficial bacteria, but it also means each individual fish isn't ingesting as much poison with every gill-full of water.

SOUNDS FISHY

Cheap feeder fish from pet stores or fish from local lakes and ponds can carry diseases and may contaminate your system. It's best to buy from a reputable fish dealer who can ensure that you get healthy fish.

Organic matter. Rotting organic matter gives off ammonia. Some folks will simply put a dead fish or two into their tanks to produce the initial ammonia bloom. Since the fish are already dead, there's no worrying about whether the ammonia in the water will kill them.

Another organic source of ammonia is aged urine, known during preindustrial times as lant. It was extensively used back then for cleaning, improving penetration of dyes in cloth, and flavoring ale. Lant would be fermented for a month or more in a closed container to allow the ammonia to develop properly. Storing bottles of urine, however, is probably not your cup of tea. To quote most of my friends, "Eeew!"

Oxygen-Binder: Nitrite

Nitrite is less toxic to fish than ammonia, but it can still kill your fish because nitrite prevents blood from absorbing oxygen. The types of bacteria that convert ammonia into nitrite are happiest and most productive between 70° and 80°F. As temperatures plummet below 50°F or rise above 100°F, these bacteria will stop feeding on ammonia and can die.

Because nitrite prevents fish blood from absorbing oxygen, nitrite poisoning is referred to as brown blood disease. High levels of nitrite damage your fishes' nervous systems, livers, spleens, and kidneys. Even low concentrations can cause long-term damage. When nitrite levels are high, fish can suffocate even if there is plenty of oxygen in the water.

Folks with ornamental fish aquariums add methylene blue to a tank to improve the ability of fish to carry oxygen in their blood, thus preventing fish deaths. Although it's not clear whether methylene blue is toxic to plants and food fish, to be on the safe side, don't add it to your aquaponics system. These nitrite concentrations will only last one or two weeks, and in most cases won't be high enough to kill the few small fish you would have in a new aquaponic system.

Plant Fertilizer: Nitrate

Nitrate is what you want. Nitrate is the primary source of nutrition for your plants and can be tolerated well by fish in concentrations much higher than either nitrite or ammonia.

The bacteria that eat nitrite are also happiest between 70° and 80°F, and they can die if the temperature drops below 50°F or rises above 100°F.

You'll never have to actually interact with nitrifying bacteria. They'll show up and do their job, like a silent, invisible work force. As long as ammonia and nitrite are nearly zero and nitrate is present, the bacteria are in place and doing their job. If your system is perfectly balanced, the plants will be consuming the available nitrate, so you may get readings at or near zero for ammonia, nitrite, and nitrate.

Other Suggested Additives

Aquaponics systems use the output from the fish, so any nutrients present in the fish food will eventually end up in your garden. There are two nutritional additives, though, that the average aquaponics gardener might want to have on hand.

Adding Iron for Green Plants

Most fish food doesn't contain significant amounts of iron. A lack of iron will prevent your plants from producing sufficient chlorophyll for photosynthesis, the process of converting sunlight into energy. When your plants don't have enough iron, their leaves will become pale.

The kind of iron you want to use is chelated iron, a powdered form that dissolves easily in water. Metal iron and rust will not add the kind of iron your plants can use. A teaspoon of chelated iron for a 200-gallon tank should make your plants develop lush, green growth. Don't worry if leaves that had previously been yellow remain that way—look at the new growth.

If you don't see the green growth you want, wait a week or more before adding more iron. Too much iron can harm your fish, so it's better to have slightly yellowed leaves than damaged fish.

Using Norwegian Kelp to Add Vitamins

Seaweed or kelp is a rich source of minerals, and Norwegian kelp is particularly rich in the wide range of nutrients required by plants. Maxicrop and Seasol are common commercial brands of Norwegian kelp extract available in the United States and Australia. Norwegian kelp seaweed contains over 60 nutrients, vitamins, and beneficial enzymes. These nutrients include calcium and potassium, neither of which is usually found in commercial fish food. The seaweed extract will make your water turn a rusty color at first. Don't be alarmed—it doesn't seem to bother the fish or the plants.

GREEN TIP

Some forms of seaweed extract come with chelated iron already added. This is convenient, but I recommend buying regular seaweed extract as well. Over time you can develop a concentration of iron that is too high for your fish if you only use the seaweed extract that comes with the chelated iron already added.

Altering pH

As I discussed in Chapter 3, pH is a measurement of whether water is acid, neutral, or alkaline. Your fish and plants will be healthiest when your water is either neutral (a pH of 7.0) or slightly acidic (a pH between 6.0 and 7.0). It's good to check pH at least every month, because rain, tap water, and the bacteria in your system can all change the pH of your garden. When your water is no longer neutral, there are a few simple ways to restore the balance between acidity and alkalinity in your garden.

Reducing pH

If your water is alkaline, with a pH above 7.5, you'll want to reduce pH. The best way to do that quickly is to add an acid. The best types of acid to use are hydrochloric acid, also known as muriatic acid. You can find muriatic acid in the pool supply section of your local hardware store. Use a plastic spoon to add a small amount of the acid to a section of the grow bed away from your standpipe. That way the acid gets diluted by all the water draining from the grow bed before it is reintroduced into the fish tank, preventing concentrated acid from coming in contact with your fish.

Some folks recommend lemon juice or apple cider, but it takes large quantities of either of these juices to significantly change your pH. Aquarium supply stores carry a chemical called pH Down, but the pH Down used in aquariums contains sodium, which can damage plants like strawberries.

Increasing pH

When I first started doing aquaponics, I couldn't imagine needing to increase my pH. The water I draw from the tap is very alkaline and my first grow bed used river rocks that kept my pH high. But in a mature garden, the bacteria produce small amounts of acid as they transform ammonia into nitrate, so in time you may need to add something to offset the acid. Hydroxide or carbonate/bicarbonate compounds of calcium and potassium are the recommended way to keep your garden from becoming too acidic. Not only will these keep your water neutral, the calcium and potassium are necessary nutrients for healthy plants. Stir a small amount of these powders into the media where water comes into your grow beds, or sprinkle the powder into your filter if you don't use media. Start with small amounts and measure your water the next day to see the impact on pH. Over time you'll get used to the amount you need to add to your system to obtain the desired effects.

A simple, natural way to keep your garden from becoming too acidic is to add crushed eggshells or seashell grit to a corner of your garden. The shells will stop dissolving when your pH rises above 7.5, so there is little danger of making your pH too high.

Measuring Your System

When you are growing in soil, testing your system isn't easy. You have to dig up various sections of your garden, allow the soil to dry, then either purchase a soil test kit or send it off to a lab. But because an aquaponic garden uses water, you can use the simple test kits developed for aquariums. The standard freshwater master test kit sells for around $20 and contains everything you need to measure pH, ammonia, nitrite, and nitrate hundreds of times.

In addition to the measurements you can make with a standard aquarium test kit, I recommend you measure and record temperature. You can also measure dissolved oxygen (DO) if you are concerned about whether or not your fish are getting enough oxygen to stay healthy.

It's a good idea to record these measurements in a log, including what you've done to your system and what you notice about your plants and fish. I recommend testing daily for the first few weeks, then weekly or monthly as the water chemistry stabilizes.

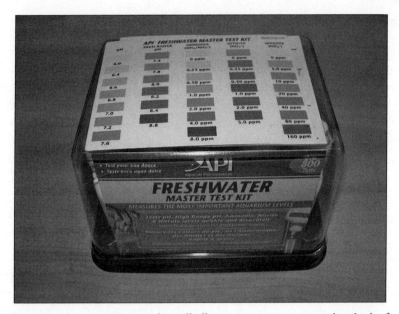

An inexpensive aquarium test kit will allow you to test your water hundreds of times. After your system has cycled, you should test your water every week or so.

Testing Your Water Chemistry

The inexpensive test kits I recommend contain glass tubes with caps and squeeze bottles of chemicals. The standard aquarium test kit doesn't contain the chemicals for testing dissolved oxygen. Salifert offers a dissolved oxygen test kit that is affordable and works much like the test kits for pH, ammonia, nitrite, and nitrate.

Before you begin, rinse out your tubes. I fill the tubes about half full, put the cap on, shake vigorously, and discard the water. If I'm not sure the tube is clean, I repeat this step.

Add water to the fill line marked in the glass tubes. When I overfill, I simply shake the tube towards my grow bed to make a few drops fly out. Over time you'll get very good at quickly getting the level exactly right. Add the recommended number of drops from the squeeze bottle and then check the color of the water against a card to determine the water chemistry.

Use the plastic caps that come with the test kit to cap the test vials instead of using your fingers. Your fingers could introduce contaminants that will affect the measurements. Also, some chemicals used in the test kit are not skin-friendly. Below are the standard instructions for measuring each major aspect of water chemistry. Testing pH is quick and simple. Testing ammonia, nitrite, and nitrate takes 5 minutes per vial. If you do them all at the same time, it takes about 5 minutes to test your water.

DID YOU KNOW ...

Hydroponic water testing equipment uses electricity to determine water chemistry. That is because the chemical fertilizers used in hydroponics contain salts, which changes the electrical properties of water. Because you are establishing a natural ecosystem, these salts won't be in your water, and these electrical measurement devices won't accurately reflect the nutrients in your water.

Follow these steps to test pH:

1. Add 5 milliliters (ml) of water from your system to a clean test vial.

2. Add 3 drops of pH test solution to the vial (5 drops if using the High pH test solution).

3. Cap the vial and invert a few times. Color develops immediately.

4. Compare the color of the water in the vial to the guide card that comes with the test kit.

5. Record the pH based on your estimate of the best color match.

Follow these steps to test ammonia (NH_3):

1. Add 5 ml of water from your system to a clean test vial.

2. Add 8 drops from the first ammonia test bottle to the vial.

3. Cap the vial and shake for 5 seconds.

4. Add 8 drops from the second ammonia test bottle to the vial.

5. Cap the vial and shake 5 seconds.

6. Wait 5 minutes for color to develop.

7. Record the ammonia concentration in mg/L or ppm based on your estimate of the best color match.

Follow these steps to test nitrite (NO_2):

1. Add 5 ml of water from your system to a clean test vial.

2. Add 5 drops from the nitrite test bottle to the vial.

3. Cap the vial and shake for 5 seconds.

4. Wait 5 minutes for color to develop.

5. Record the nitrite concentration in mg/L or ppm based on your estimate of the best color match.

Follow these steps to test nitrate (NO_3):

1. Add 5 ml of water from your system to a clean test vial.

2. Add 10 drops from the first nitrate test bottle to the vial.

3. Cap the vial and shake for 5 seconds.

4. Shake the second bottle of nitrate test solution for 30 seconds.

5. Add 10 drops from the second nitrate test bottle to the vial.

6. Cap the vial and shake for 60 seconds.

7. Wait 5 minutes for color to develop.

8. Record the nitrate concentration in mg/L or ppm based on your estimate of the best color match.

Measuring Dissolved Oxygen

If your fish are gulping at the surface as though they can't get enough oxygen, you'll want to test the dissolved oxygen in your system to make sure they have enough oxygen in their water. If they have enough oxygen, it might be some other problem with the water, such as excess nitrite, and a water change of roughly 25 percent is in order.

Dissolved oxygen is measured in the same units as your nitrogen compounds, in either mg/L or ppm. The instructions are similar to the other vial-based test kits:

1. Add 5 ml of water from your system to a clean test vial.

2. Add 5 drops from the first bottle of oxygen test solution (O2-1) and swirl gently for 20 seconds. Do not shake—this could change the oxygen content of the water.

3. Add 6 drops from the second bottle of oxygen test solution (O2-2) and swirl gently for 15 seconds. Allow solution to stand for 1 minute.

4. Add 6 drops from the third bottle of oxygen test solution (O2-3) and swirl for 20 seconds. Allow to stand 30 seconds.

5. Record the dissolved oxygen concentration in ppm based on your estimate of the best color match.

6. Record water temperature, since water temperature affects the maximum possible level of dissolved oxygen.

The amount of oxygen your water can carry will decrease as water gets hot. Compare your measurement to the 100 percent oxygen saturation in the following table. The levels in the table show the maximum amount of oxygen that freshwater can naturally hold at sea level.

Temp in °C	Dissolved Oxygen (ppm)	Temp in °F	Dissolved Oxygen (ppm)
5	12.8	35	14.0
10	11.3	45	12.1
15	10.1	55	10.6
20	9.1	65	9.4
25	8.2	75	8.4
30	7.5	85	7.6
35	6.9	95	6.9

Now you know how to create optimal conditions for your plants and fish. In the next chapter, I'll discuss the plants you can grow while you're waiting for the nitrogen cycle to get established.

The Least You Need to Know

- It will take a few weeks before a new aquaponic system can transform ammonia (poison) into nitrate (fertilizer).
- There are many ways to add ammonia to cycle your system without risking valuable fish.
- Keep your system pH between 6.0 and 7.0 to keep your fish and plants healthy.
- Water-soluble (chelated) iron and seaweed extract will add nutrients not present in fish food.
- Measure your water chemistry daily until all the nitrogen is showing up as nitrate rather than ammonia or nitrite. Continue to measure your water chemistry periodically, weekly or monthly, at least.

Which Plants Grow Best?

In This Chapter

- Planning your garden
- Plants for spring, summer, fall, and winter
- Herbs, ornamentals, and floating plants
- Extending aquaponics to soil gardening

Almost any plant you grow in a traditional garden can grow in an aquaponic garden, particularly if you are using media-filled grow beds.

There are a few minor differences between growing in an aquaponics garden and growing in a traditional soil garden. For the most part, however, you can learn from the extensive experience base of traditional gardening. In case you don't already have a shelf full of gardening books, let's cover a few basics in this chapter.

Using a Planting Guide

Planting guides help you know what vegetables grow well in your local area and when you should plant them. These guides are often available from local gardening groups, agricultural extension services, and businesses that sell plants. Information usually contained in planting guides includes the following:

- Distance between plants for each crop
- Approximate yield per average row
- How many row feet you need to feed a person
- The amount of seed (or number of plants) you need per row

- When to plant seeds or relocate transplants

- When you can expect to harvest each crop

If your area experiences winter, this guide should tell you the average date of the last killing frost in spring and the average date of the first killing frost in fall.

If you have access to the internet, there is a great website created by Kristee Rosendahl called smartgardener.com. Smartgardener lets you create a picture of your garden, decide what plants to use, and place them in your garden to avoid them casting shade on their neighbors, and then the site sends you e-mails with recommended tasks. The only bad thing about Smartgardener is I can't turn off reminders for all the dozens of chores soil-based gardeners have to do (like weeding, watering, and amending soil).

If you have a smartphone or tablet device, there are several gardening apps that will help you plan your garden, making the job of planning, planting, and harvesting your garden easy and fun.

GREEN TIP

For inspiration on what to plant next year, buy a half share in a local Community Supported Agriculture (CSA) farm. The farm will deliver locally grown, fresh produce to you each week, giving you an idea what grows well locally. CSAs will often provide recipes for the crops in each week's box, since many customers aren't used to eating the quantity and variety of vegetables the CSA produces. Ask health-conscious friends to see if there are any good CSAs in your area.

Intensive gardening was popularized in the United States by Mel Bartholomew with his Square Foot Garden method. He advocated small grow beds where a gardener could easily reach the plants without having to step into the garden.

In Square Foot Gardening, the garden is divided with a grid, clearly marking each square foot. The recommended number of desired plants is then planted in each square. There are over 100,000 gardeners using the Square Foot Garden method, which makes it easy to find accessories such as supports and trellises for climbing plants.

Aquaponic gardens are perfect for intensive gardening since you are delivering nutrient-rich water right to your plant roots and only need enough space around each plant so it can grow properly.

The following table lists some crops that you might plant in your aquaponic garden. The values in this table for rows are based on traditional soil gardens. The last column tells you how many plants you could expect to put in a square foot of your aquaponic garden.

Example Planting Guide Data Sheet

Crops	In Rows	Between Rows	Yield: 10' Row	Days to Harvest	Plants per Square Feet
Hot Weather					
Tomatoes	18-36"	36-60"	15-45 lbs	80	¼
Peppers	12-24"	30-36"	5-18 lbs	80	1
Eggplant	18-24"	30-42"	10-12 lbs	80	1
Melons	36-48"	>60"	8-40 lbs	85	½
Warm Weather					
Summer squash	18-36"	36-60"	20-80 lbs	50	½
Winter squash	24-48"	>36"	10-80 lbs	85	½
Beans, pole	4-12"	36-48"	6-10 lbs	60	8
Corn	6-12"	24-36"	7-10 lbs	70	1–4
Cool Weather					
Beets	2-3"	12-24"	8-10 lbs	55	9
Carrots	1-2"	15-30"	7-10 lbs	70	16
Lettuce	3-10"	12-24"	4-10 lbs	50-75	9
Swiss chard	6-12"	18-30"	8-12 lbs	50	1–4
Cold Weather					
Cabbage	12-18"	30-36"	10-40 lbs	60	1
Peas	1-3"	12-36"	2-6 lbs	60	8
Mâche	1-3"	3-6"	4-10 lbs	90	16
Spinach	3-6"	15-30"	4-6 lbs	35	9

We are used to eating a wide range of vegetables that have been refrigerated and shipped from around the world, so some of us never developed a sense of what plants grow in which seasons. If you are growing in a climate-controlled space, you can grow whatever plants suit your fancy. But if you are growing outside, you will get the best yield if you grow plants during the season recommended in planting guides and on seed packets.

Strictly Summer Plants

These are plants that can't tolerate cool weather and are killed by frost. They love the heat of summer and are often referred to as very tender plants. You will typically want to start these plants indoors as seeds a couple of months before the last projected frost. After about three months, they will be large enough to safely plant in your outdoor garden.

Tomatoes

Tomatoes are tasty and full of vitamin C and are the most popular of the nightshade vegetables. They were among the vegetables the Aztecs cultivated. Tomatoes grow in either bushes or vines. The bush varieties are called *determinate*, meaning that they reach a certain height and stop growing. Because the bushes are fairly compact, these kinds of tomato plants usually don't need cages or trellises. Tomatoes can take up a lot of space, but if properly trellised, a single plant should need no more than a 2-foot by 2-foot area.

Vine tomato varieties are called *indeterminate*, because they keep growing until cool weather kills the plant. As the vine grows, older leaves will wither and die. It is useful to create a cage or trellis for these vines.

Tomatoes are self-pollinating, meaning they can produce fruit from a single flower without relying on wind, insects, or human intervention to enable the pollen to reach the reproductive portion of the plant. Many indoor growers like to ensure pollination by tapping the blossoms or using a brush to make sure the pollen from the bloom reaches the reproductive portion of the flower.

> **DEFINITION**
>
> **Determinate** plants stop growing at maturity and put their energy into producing fruit. **Indeterminate** plants continue to grow, with the older branches and leaves withering to focus energy on the new growth.

Peppers

Sweet peppers and chili peppers were domesticated 6,000 years ago in Central America and were among the foods Christopher Columbus brought to Europe after his visit to North America.

Peppers are part of the nightshade family. They do best planted near other night-shade plants as well as near onions, carrots, and basil. It's best to keep peppers and other nightshade vegetables away from beans, corn, and plants in the cabbage family.

If you live in a windy area or if your pepper plants grow too large to support them-selves, you can drive a yard-long stake into the ground and tie the stem to it with something soft, like old panty hose. Peppers are self-pollinating, making these a good plant for an indoor garden.

Peppers require warm weather to grow. If you have a short summer, you can start pepper plants inside or purchase plants that are already started from a nursery.

You can harvest peppers while they are still green or wait until they turn red or yel-low, when they will have more vitamin C.

Eggplant

Eggplant is another member of the nightshade family popular among gardeners. The plant is native to India, and spread to Europe during the Middle Ages.

Each plant should produce two to three fruits, which are usually purple with white flesh. Eggplant should be harvested while they are glossy. When they become dull and lighter in color, they are overripe and are best sent straight to the compost bin.

Slender eggplants like these are perfect for making ratatouille, a classic summer dish that also includes zucchini, summer squash, peppers, and tomatoes.

Melons

Melons like cantaloupe and watermelon originated in Africa, but their sweet flesh has made them a favorite food around the world. Melons grow on vines with large leaves and can take up a lot of space if left to grow along the ground. In small gardens, melons can be trained on trellises to maximize production in the small space available. Melons are not self-pollinating, relying on insects for pollination.

Warm-Weather Plants

Warm-weather plants don't like frost but can often be seeded or transplanted into the garden as soon as danger of frost is past, even if the weather is still cool. You will also see these plants referred to as tender.

Squash

In the eternal categorization wars of fruit and vegetables, botanists will call squash fruits. But most cooks, parents, and children consider squash to be vegetables. Squash, like tomatoes and peppers, originated in the Americas.

Summer squash have soft skins and should be eaten during the warm season in which they are grown. Winter squash can last many months after the autumn harvest; they keep well for use later in the winter because of their tough skins.

Squash plants take up a huge amount of area per plant—I like to encourage my squash plants to do their growing outside of my greenhouse, even though their roots stay in my aquaponic grow beds.

The squash plant will put out both male and female flowers. You can tell the male flowers because their stems are straight and skinny. The stems of the female flowers are rounded, and these stems will develop into squash if the flower is pollinated.

The large golden squash blossoms can be prepared as food in a variety of ways, which is great when you're faced with dozens of male squash blossoms and hardly any of the female squash blossoms that have potential to become squashes. My favorite squash blossom recipe is squash flower tempura, where the flowers are dipped in a light batter and deep-fried.

Green Beans

The common green bean was another crop Columbus brought to Europe in 1493. Green beans are classified as either bush beans or pole beans. Bush beans mature quickly and will produce their beans over a short two- to three-week period. You need to start successive plantings to keep a steady supply of beans coming through the duration of the growing season.

DID YOU KNOW ...

The beans in Europe prior to Columbus's journeys were broad beans with tough, inedible pods. The American beans could be eaten while still green in the edible pod, which is why they're called green beans.

Pole beans take longer to mature but will continue to produce beans until fall frosts kill the plant. Pole beans are best grown up a vertical support, which can be a simple as a string hanging from a sturdy bar overhead.

Bean plants are considered green fertilizer, because they absorb nitrogen from the air and enrich the ground in which they grow. Green beans are considered pod beans because they can be eaten in the pod. You can also grow shell beans, any of the hundreds of bean varieties that are meant to be shelled after the beans are mature.

Sweet Corn or Maize

Corn was originally the generic name for cereal crops like wheat, barley, oats, and rye. The bright yellow grain we now think of as corn was introduced to Europe by Columbus and fellow explorers.

The corn plant produces a tall stalk that yields two to three ears apiece. Because corn requires a lot of nitrogen to thrive, it is traditionally spaced 12 inches apart. But if the corn is supplied with adequate nitrogen, possible in an aquaponics system, corn can be planted as closely as every 6 inches, or four plants per square foot.

Native Americans would plant corn, beans, and squash together and referred to these plants as the Three Sisters. The beans would pump nitrogen into the soil. The corn would provide a tall stalk for the bean plant to climb, and the squash leaves would shield the ground like mulch, with the prickly hairs on the vines deterring pests. After the plants matured, dishes combining beans and corn provided complete protein, reducing the need to raise domestic animals for food.

Cool-Weather Plants

Many popular garden crops will actually fail during the heat of summer. These cool-weather crops, or semi-hardy plants, do best in the cool of spring and fall. With an aquaponic system that bathes the roots in cooling water, these semi-hardy plants can be grown throughout the summer except in the hottest climates.

Beets

Beets were probably domesticated around the Mediterranean Sea, before they spread to ancient Babylon and China. We usually think of the sweet, red root vegetable when people talk about beets, but the leaves are also very good to eat.

Beets can be sown two to three weeks before the last spring frost and can continue to be sown up to two months before the first killing frosts of fall. The leaves are edible and make a colorful addition to raw salads or a flavorful stir-fry.

In a new media-based aquaponics system, the root of the beet might not develop. But once a system has had a year to mature, you should be able to get beetroots from your plants. The crown of the root will begin to protrude from your growing medium, giving you an idea of the size of the root. Feel free to pull the beet up to check it—you can always put it back in the grow bed if you don't want to eat it yet.

A beet straight out of an aquaponic garden. The leaves can be eaten raw or cooked.
The sweet root is boiled and peeled.

Beetroots are usually prepared by boiling whole for 45 minutes, then slipping the skin off. Pickled beet eggs is a family favorite, a recipe that makes colorful and flavorful use of the bright red liquid left over from boiling the beets.

Carrots

The carrot is native to Europe and southwestern Asia. Both the greens and the root of the carrot are edible, though the root is the portion most of us are used to eating. Carrots don't transplant well and take a long time to germinate, but they can be planted a few weeks before the last spring frost and as early as 14 weeks before the first fall frost.

GREEN TIP

Small seeds like carrot seeds can be pulled down between the rocks in your grow bed. To help these seeds stay put, I like to twist individual seeds in a scrap of single ply tissue. The moist tissue holds the seed in place during the flood and drain cycles, but doesn't impede the seed's growth once it starts to germinate.

Carrots need a foot of grow bed depth to grow a decent root. Your choice of medium will have an impact on how straight the roots grow. Or you can grow round Parisian carrots that mature quickly and don't need much grow bed depth.

Carrots are a wonderful crop to plant in the fall to harvest in winter. The cold of winter makes carrots sweet, making for a delicious homegrown treat you can't buy in stores.

Leafy Greens

Leafy greens refers to all the salad greens, including leaf lettuce, head lettuce, chard, and mustard. There are approximately a thousand species of plants with edible leaves, and within each species there can be hundreds of varieties. Beets are actually one of those many species, though most folks don't think of it as a leafy green.

Lettuce is the green most people think of in this category. It was first cultivated in Egypt and spread to Europe and North America. It is now eaten worldwide.

Some varieties of leafy greens, like iceberg lettuce, are extremely low in nutrition. But other varieties can contain significant amounts of vitamin C, particularly when they are young.

Leafy greens grow best in cool weather, where the cold keeps the plant from blooming. In warm weather, leafy greens will bolt, or quickly bloom and go to seed. Once the plant is allowed to bloom, most leafy greens become tough and bitter.

A single mustard seed produced this delightful leafy plant, which I was able to harvest one leaf at a time for months.

Cold-Weather Plants

Cold-weather or hardy plants can often be planted outside several weeks before the final frost of spring and may also be sown a second time as fall approaches. These plants may fail to thrive in the heat of summer, even in an aquaponics system.

It may be possible to grow these plants during winter under a low hoop house with row cover. Some of these plants can even survive freezing conditions. See Chapter 18 for more on greenhouses, hoop houses, and row covers.

Cabbage and Other Brassicas

Cabbage and other members of the brassica family can be grown in very cold weather. Kale is a popular brassica because it is particularly rich in vitamins and can help prevent cancer, as can many vegetables in the brassica family.

Bok choy is a member of the cabbage family used frequently in Asian cooking. The crisp stems and leaves are cut up and used in stir-fry. When grown in proper conditions (early spring or fall), bok choy can mature as soon as 35 days after seedlings emerge.

The easiest brassica to grow is the radish. Radishes can mature within three weeks after seedlings emerge. Many find raw radishes to be bitter, but they are delicious when simmered in a scant covering of water with onions, salt, and pepper, and then topped with a generous dollop of butter.

Peas

Peas are starchy round vegetables that grow in a pod. The earliest evidence of humans using peas was found around the Fertile Crescent, near the time when humans first began to grow food rather than merely gather it.

Peas are a good source of vegetable protein, and fresh peas from a home garden can be so sweet that children treat them like candy. There are a wide variety of peas, allowing you to select plants that fit your gardening style (compact plants, vining plants, climbing plants), color preference (green, purple, yellow) and taste (from stir-fried snow peas to mushy peas and sausage).

The practice of eating peas in the pod was a royal fad in the 1600s. So when you eat fresh peas from your garden, you can truly say you are eating like a king.

DID YOU KNOW …

Peas played an important role in science because their pollination can be easily controlled. In the 1800s, Austrian monk Gregor Mendel meticulously experimented with nearly 30,000 individual pea plants, leading him to develop the principles that led to modern genetic science.

Mâche

Mâche may not be familiar to most modern gardeners, because it is slow to mature and can't be easily harvested using machines. But most of us have heard of mâche by its alternate name, rapunzel. Rapunzel was the delicious plant in the witch's garden that tempted a pregnant peasant, who was forced to give up her golden-haired infant in payment. Mâche is also known as lamb's lettuce, field salad, and corn salad because it is so often found in fields.

Mâche grows wild in many parts of Europe, North Africa, western Asia, and both Atlantic and Pacific coasts of the Americas. The royal gardener of King Louis XIV introduced mâche to the world, and it was grown commercially in London in subsequent years until the industrial age made other vegetables more economical.

Mâche can endure freezing conditions, though it will do better if given some protection from the elements. Mâche is much more nutritious than many traditional greens, having more vitamin C, B vitamins, vitamin E, and omega-3 fatty acids than lettuce. Like all leafy greens, mâche tastes best if it's harvested before flowers appear.

Spinach

Spinach spread from Asia throughout Europe around the time of the Crusades, where it became popular as one of the few crops that would grow quickly in early spring during Lent, the 46 days before Easter Sunday when Christians give up meat. The first written mention of spinach is found in China, where spinach was known as the "Persian vegetable." Today China produces 85 percent of all spinach grown in the world.

Spinach is loaded with nutrients and antioxidants, and research is constantly turning up new reasons we should add spinach to our diets. Boiling spinach can remove many of the nutrients, but microwaving spinach does not affect nutrient levels as much.

There have been a couple of contamination scares involving spinach, but these scares were caused by contamination due to wild pigs and mass production, neither of which should occur with plants grown in your aquaponic system.

Beyond Garden Vegetables

You can grow more than vegetables in your garden. In fact, it would be easier to simply list the few plants that don't thrive in aquaponic systems. Following are a few categories of plants you might be interested in adding to your system.

Herbs

Herbs are the spice of life. It is wonderful to be able to nip down to the garden and gather fresh herbs to season a meal or garnish your plate. You pay a pretty penny for these in the store, but they continue to grow in your garden, easily replacing the bits you snip off in a matter of a few days.

Basil is probably the herb that provides the most value if you are considering specializing in herb production to earn a bit of money on the side. Basil grows quickly and can be propagated through cuttings very easily. Simply snip off excess branches and stick them straight into the grow bed to root and form a new plant. I'll often cut a slit up the middle of the woody stem just to increase the amount of water and nutrition the cutting can get before roots form.

Mint is one herb to grow with caution. Mint grows aggressively, and its root systems can quickly overwhelm other plants in the same grow bed. I enjoy taking a few branches from the mint, stripping off the leaves, and steeping them in boiling water to yield fresh mint tea.

Trees

I was fascinated when I first saw people growing banana trees, papaw trees, and citrus trees in their aquaponic gardens. I'd always thought that a tree's root system was like an underground mirror of its aboveground branch system.

Contrary to my naive understanding, the majority of a tree's roots will remain in the top 2 to 3 feet of the ground, so it isn't a terrible hardship for a young tree to adapt to the confines of a grow bed. However, if you wish to grow trees, you may want to use a grow bed that is more than a mere 12 inches (300 millimeters) deep.

Flowers

It is common to plant marigolds in an aquaponic garden because marigolds repel many common garden pests (see Chapter 13). But you can plant other flowers as well, such as the vinca I transplanted into my Windowfarm.

Because aquaponics has primarily been focused on food production, there is relatively little information about growing flowers. Almost all species of flowers can thrive in a pH range of 6.0 to 7.0. If you love flowers, I encourage you to experiment to see how your favorite flowers do in an aquaponic garden compared to how they grow in soil.

Duckweed

You and I will probably not grow duckweed for our dinner plates. But this high-protein, high-fat plant makes a great food for fish that eat plants. Many aquaponic gardeners add a shallow tank specifically for growing duckweed to feed to their fish.

> **GREEN TIP**
>
> Duckweed is high in protein and is a favorite food for fish that eat plants, like tilapia. Make sure the water in your duckweed tank doesn't swirl, however. Even a slow swirl can seriously reduce the rate at which your duckweed grows.

Duckweed is a small floating plant, with a small root that extends down into the water. Duckweed floating on nitrate-rich water will usually double every couple of days in summer. The rich food can either be fed directly to the fish or frozen for days when the cold and short days make it hard to grow much of anything.

Extending Aquaponics to Plants in Soil

I love the idea that my fish and plants create a complete mini-ecosystem. But despite my enthusiasm for aquaponics, there are some garden plants that simply don't work well in aquaponics.

Two plants that come to mind are potatoes and blueberries. Potatoes can actually grow in aquaponic systems, but they unquestionably do better in soil. Blueberries, on the other hand, require soil with a pH of 4.5 to 5.0, which is too acid for fish and most other plants.

You don't need to abandon favorite garden plants or resign yourself to simply growing such plants in a regular soil garden. You can use water from your aquaponics system to fertilize and water soil gardens.

Wicking Beds

Wicking beds are soil plots that rest on top of a reservoir of water. The reservoir is created using some sort of waterproof material, such as polyethylene sheeting, plastic bins, or ceramic tubs.

In a low-tech wicking bed, the reservoir is filled with a large rock material, like gravel. The desired depth of soil is shoveled in on top of the gravel. Some folks bury a pipe so they can test the depth of water in the reservoir with a stick. Others will separate the soil from the rocks with a layer of geotextile, any of a number of synthetic fabrics specifically designed for retaining soil silt. Geotextiles can be woven or nonwoven, and you may have seen them near construction sites, where they are used to reduce the amount of mud and dirt on nearby roads.

The reservoir is filled with overflow water from the aquaponic system, and the nutrients and moisture naturally travel up into the soil overhead, particularly as roots grow down into the rocky reservoir.

A patented version of the wicking concept is marketed as the EarthBox container system. This is a well-designed commercial product with aesthetic flair.

Teenagers Grant and Max Buster thought the EarthBox was pretty cool when their dad bought one. But when they read that the United Nations was using EarthBox planters to teach people in developing nations a better way to grow food, the Colorado kids designed an EarthBox-like wicking garden out of plastic buckets. Their target market is the 800 million people facing starvation in parts of the world where the food budget is around $1 per day per person.

Teenagers Grant and Max Buster with their Global Buckets, developed to improve gardening for people around the world with limited water and cash resources.
(Photo courtesy of Grant and Max Buster)

The Buster brothers call their idea Global Buckets, which they promote via YouTube and their website, globalbuckets.org. When they found out that plastic buckets are considered so valuable in some nations that locals don't want to cut holes in the inner bucket, Grant and Max embarked on a Garbage Gardening project to create gardens from items considered trash even in the developing world. As they explain, "Roots only require three essential items: water, air, and nutrients."

Sounds awfully familiar to an aquaponic gardener!

> **DID YOU KNOW …**
>
> Aztec Indians living near modern-day Mexico City created narrow gardens separated by canals to grow much of their food. The nutrient-rich lake water wicked up into the soil, providing water and nourishment to the plants. These floating gardens, or chinampas, could produce up to seven crops per year. Many consider the Aztec gardens to be the first aquaponic gardens.

Smartscaping with Aquaponics Water

Irrigation is a simple way to extend the benefit of your aquaponic garden to soil plants, but you don't want to use sprinkler and hose irrigation techniques with your fish water. These traditional techniques allow most of the water to evaporate or seep away before the plant benefits from the moisture.

Smartscaping or Xeriscaping usually refers to dry landscaping, where the little water required for desert plants is delivered directly to the plant root through small irrigation tubes. But smartscaping techniques can also be used in a humid climate to deliver nutrient-rich water directly to the roots of your plants.

The three important components of a smartscape garden are as follows:

- Using irrigation tubing to deliver water directly to plant roots

- Covering the roots with mulch to reduce evaporation

- Amending soil with compost and other materials to improve moisture retention in the root zone

My favorite example of smartscaping combined with aquaponics is found at Sahib Aquaponics in an alley behind a shopping complex in Winter Park, Florida. Sahib Punjabi uses the excess aquaponics water in his urban garden to irrigate a variety of plants and fruiting trees growing along the edge of the parking lot for the shopping complex. Though his aquaponics garden is behind a fence, the parking lot trees are available for anyone to enjoy.

Both smartscaping and wicking beds drastically reduce water evaporation and seepage. When you also use aquaponic overflow water to irrigate these engineered soil gardens, you can grow any plant that thrives in your climate.

The Least You Need to Know

- Build on local gardening guidance for planning your aquaponic garden. There's no need to reinvent most gardening wisdom.
- Work with nature to grow plants that will thrive in your weather conditions.
- In addition to fruits and vegetables, you can grow herbs, flowers, trees, and floating plants in an aquaponic garden.
- For those plants that require soil to thrive, you can water and fertilize wicking beds using water from your fish tank.

Starting, Planting, and Propagating Plants

In This Chapter

- Starting plants from seed
- Transplanting seedlings into your garden
- Propagating plants from cuttings
- Saving seeds for next season

There are three ways to get plants into your garden. You can start plants from seed, you can buy seedlings from a local nursery and transplant them into your garden, or you can take cuttings from plants that will grow new roots in your garden. In this chapter I review how each of these three methods works when you are growing in an aquaponic garden.

It's much simpler to plant an aquaponic garden than a soil garden. It's even possible to pull up a plant periodically to check on its root system, which I'd never do to a plant in a soil garden. The one drawback is small seeds getting washed away by the constant water flow, but there's a trick to address that later in this chapter.

Starting from Seed

Almost all plants started from seed at some point. Growing your plants from seed is an inexpensive option. Seeds are light and therefore inexpensive to ship. On the other hand, seeds must often be planted several weeks before the plant produced by the seed can be transplanted. So growing from seed takes more planning than it takes to simply drive to the nursery and purchase a pallet of seedlings.

Seed packets start showing up in stores about three months before the last frost date in your area. Once you have purchased your seed packets, take out a calendar and mark the average day of the last frost in your area. Then make a schedule to tell you when to start the seeds and whether they need to be started inside (or in your garden, if you are growing outdoors).

Planting Seeds to Transplant

Unless your garden is warm year round, you may want to start seeds inside in pots during your cool season. This lets you get a head start so your warm-weather plants are already partially grown when the outside weather gets warm. If you decide to plant seeds for transplant, the standard method of starting seeds works fine. You'll just need potting soil and seedling pots. You'll wash the dirt off the seedling before putting it into your aquaponic garden.

GREEN TIP

Your seeds will sprout faster if you soak them in water for several hours first, usually overnight. This is called priming your seeds. An overnight soak will be more than enough for small seeds, peas, and beans. Seeds with hard skin, like corn, may need to soak as long as 18 hours.

Prepare your seedling pots according to directions. Some gardeners like to purchase compressed pellets of potting soil that are transformed into seedling pots by adding hot water. Others like to use eggshells, yogurt cups, or cups formed from newspaper, to name only a few of the many options.

If your seedling pot isn't already prefilled with potting soil, add potting soil. When you are done, the soil should have a spongy texture and spring back when you press on it. That means there are air pockets, which will allow the sprouting plant to get adequate oxygen in the root zone. Make sure you arrange your pots on a waterproof plate or tray to keep water from seeping out the bottom of the pots and damaging or staining your counter or table.

Add your seed according to the packet directions regarding seed depth. Some people like to place a single seed in each pot, others like to add three or more. I find it useful to use a pencil to create the required depression in the soil to accept the seed. After the seed is planted, pull the surrounding soil over the seed in the depression.

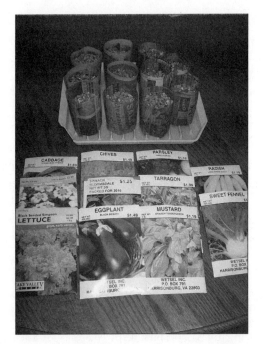

You can make your own seedling pots out of newspaper. These are filled with vermiculite, but you can also use regular potting mix.

Water the seedling pots thoroughly, cover loosely with plastic wrap to keep the pots moist, and put the pots in a warm place where there are few drafts. The top of a refrigerator is a good place, if you know you won't forget your plants. Once the plants begin to sprout, you can pull back a corner of the plastic covering and put the plant in an area with sunlight.

If you provide enough light, the plant will remain compact. Lack of light will cause the plant to stretch, hunting for good light. If you notice the top of the potting soil drying out, water the plants by adding a small amount of water to the tray and allowing the water to wick up into the seedling pots.

Some people like to use an inorganic material like vermiculite instead of potting soil and use water from their aquaponic system to provide nutrients. That is perfectly acceptable, but I find the traditional soil method to be easier for beginning gardeners.

Planting Seeds Directly in Your Garden

If you are planting hardy plants or if the packet recommends direct seeding, you can skip the step of fussing with seedling pots. Simply drop individual seeds onto the media in your grow beds. Water with care, since a vigorous watering could wash the seeds deep into the grow bed.

If you are dealing with tiny seeds, I suggest you wad the seed in a $\frac{1}{2}$-inch square of single-ply facial tissue to make a tissue ball with the seed in the center. The tissue will increase the bulk of the seed and adhere to the rocks in your grow bed. As the seed germinates, the root and stem will be able to easily push through the moist tissue fibers.

Another alternative is to buy pelleted seeds, which are coated with fine clay. The clay in the pellet holds the seed in place and absorbs water, keeping the seed moist so they sprout consistently.

Seeding a Floating Raft

If you are using floating rafts, you will want to start your seedlings in an inorganic medium, like gravel or expanded clay contained in something like a net pot. You can start the seeds outside of the floating raft, or start the seed directly in the raft.

If using a floating raft, remember to add air to the water using an air pump, air lines, and air stones. Pumping air into the water under your raft will make sure the sprouting plant gets the oxygen it needs. For more information, see Chapter 9.

Transplanting Seedlings

Whether you've grown your own plants from seed or are bringing in plants from some other place, the process of transplanting your seedlings is the same.

First, make sure the plant is sturdy enough to be successfully transplanted. You'll want your seedling to have several true leaves and a sturdy stem. It also helps if your seedling has a robust set of roots, since the roots will get damaged during the process of moving the plant to your grow bed.

A seedling tray with plants almost ready for transplant. Notice the difference between the true leaves and the round seed leaves.

DID YOU KNOW ...

The first leaves on your plant come from the seed itself and are called seed leaves, or cotyledon. They are usually smooth and round and are not considered true leaves. The first true leaves will look like tiny versions of the leaves of the plant you are growing, and they usually look very different from the seed leaves.

Rinsing Roots of Transplants

Whether you've grown your own plants or gotten them from somewhere else, it's a good idea to rinse the roots clean before plopping the plant into your garden. There are two primary reasons to rinse your seedlings:

- The soil in which your seedling was grown could carry fungus or disease.

- Small particles clinging to the plant roots will wash into your system, clouding your water and adding silt that could clog your system.

To rinse your plants, turn the pot of seedlings upside down, supporting the contents with one hand while you slide the pot off with the other. Holding the plants by the stem, dip the root ball into a small container of water and shake the plant. This allows gravity and water to loosen the dirt from the roots. You may need to use your fingers to dislodge or brush off persistent clumps. Swish the roots until they are clean.

Transplanting Your Seedlings

If you are using expanded clay or expanded shale, transplanting will be a breeze. Simply use your finger to push the roots down into the media. Water the plant and you're done. Some of the roots may be a bit bruised, but the plant should survive just fine.

If you are using gravel or river stones, you'll need to be more careful to avoid crushing the roots. I scoop a shallow hole and push the extra rocks to the edge of the hole. I place the plant roots into the hole, attempting to work it even further into the grow bed. Then I carefully push the rocks around the edge of the hole back in to surround the plant.

If you pour fish water over your transplants, the water bath will drag the root deeper into the grow bed and pull them into crevices between the rocks. The added water will also help reduce the transplant stress the plant will experience.

If you are growing in a floating raft, you may have a portion of the raft with holes spaced closely for the initial phase of plant growth when the plant is still compact and another section of the raft with holes spaced further apart for the final stage of growth. Transplanting is as simple as moving the net pot holding your plant to a different hole in the floating raft. The main difficulty will be threading the plant roots into the new hole.

An alternative to transplanting in your floating raft is to have floating strips of plants, adding empty strips to space the planted strips when they need extra room to reach their full growth.

Propagating Plants from Cuttings

Growing plants from cuttings is very easy in an aquaponic garden. This works best for plants with woody stems like basil, sage, and rosemary. You don't need to use rooting powders or special tools used by traditional gardeners to propagate cuttings.

You simply cut the stem you want to transplant, cut a $\frac{1}{2}$-inch slice up into the end of the woody stem, remove any leaves that are closer than 2 inches from the cut, and poke the cutting into your rocks. The slice in the end of the stem will both increase the water the plant can absorb and improve the likelihood that rooting will take place.

Leave the plant alone, and in most cases you will see new growth within a few days if you pull the plant out to look. After a couple of weeks new roots should be established.

Cutting Correctly

If you decide to cut your plants, make sure you cut $\frac{1}{2}$ inch or so above a set of leaves. The cut plant will put forth new branches from the base of those leaves as long as the cut section of stem isn't so close that the base of the leaves dries out. Keeping the cut somewhat close maximizes the plant's natural healing response.

Sometimes you want to reduce excess leaves or branches from your plant to focus the plant's energy on producing fruit. When this is the case, snip excess branches or suckers far enough from the main trunk of the plant so the trunk itself remains undamaged.

Sharing Plants

As you start to garden, you will realize that there are a lot of friends willing to share their extra seedlings and cuttings. You may find yourself with an abundance of some plants.

SOUNDS FISHY

People are almost always willing to share mint. That's because this delicious and fragrant plant grows like a weed—out of control. Mint is also pretty hard to kill. Make sure you've got a separate area of your garden where you can quarantine mint if you accept one from a friend.

If you are receiving plants from someone else, they will usually be providing them in a pot with soil. In that case, you can simply treat it like any seedling and rinse off the dirt when you are ready to plant it in your aquaponic garden. If you have to travel any distance with an unrooted plant, you can simply wrap the roots in a bit of wet paper towel covered with a plastic bag to keep them moist until you can get them home.

If you are sharing your plants with someone else who gardens in dirt, you may want to prepare the plant for its new life in soil. Have a container of potting soil handy. Pull the plant out of your grow bed and let it drip dry briefly. Dust the roots with the potting soil, carefully separating them so the roots aren't clumped together. This will allow the individual roots to absorb oxygen in their new soil home. Put the plant into a container and gently add potting soil until the container is full. Water thoroughly, then add any additional potting soil needed to fill the container and support the plant.

Plants used to the easy environment of an aquaponic garden might struggle to adapt to the harsher climate in a traditional garden. You will want to make sure the soil is kept moist and you've added sufficient compost or fertilizer to nourish the plant.

Saving Seeds

Before the days when you could buy pretty packets of seeds, most farmers and gardeners used seeds they saved from their own plants the year before. Those seeds were necessary to ensure next year's success. It was considered very unwise to consume or discard these seeds. The phrase "eating your seed corn" refers to the practice of consuming everything you grew without saving seeds for the next year.

The founding U.S. president, George Washington, was first and foremost a careful farmer. He took great pride in the farm surrounding his Mount Vernon estate, including the fields where he grew seeds for the next year's crops.

There are two ways to save seed for next year's garden. First, you can simply save the seeds that you didn't use. You will likely have a smaller percentage of viable plants after storage, but you can still have viable seeds for years after initial purchase. Second, you can save seed from your own garden. Seeds aren't terribly expensive so this won't save much money, but saving your own seed gives you an opportunity to maintain strains of prized plants.

If you are going to save seeds, there are a few rules of thumb to determine seeds are worth saving in the first place:

- Don't bother saving seeds from hybrid varieties. The hybrid you grew was optimized in the lab. The next generation of this hybrid will not be the same as the parent hybrid and will almost always be inferior.

- Don't save seed from patented varieties. The seeds of patented plants belong to the companies holding those patents, not to you. It is unlikely that such a company would come after a home gardener, but they have come after farmers for saving seed.

- Self-pollinated plants such as lettuce, beans, peas, and tomatoes will produce true to form as long as you didn't start with a hybrid.

- Don't bother saving seed from cross-pollinated plants like squash, pumpkins, and cucumbers unless you can keep them separated from other varieties by at least 200 yards. In the case of wind-pollinated plants like corn, you'd need to separate them by a full mile from other varieties to avoid mixed cross-breeds in the next generation. The cross-bred seeds could be okay, or they might have all the worst characteristics of each parent plant.

What You Need to Save Seed

You will want to use paper envelopes to store your harvested seeds. Paper breathes, allowing residual moisture to evaporate. It is also easy to write on paper, reducing the probability of losing track of which envelope contained which seed.

GREEN TIP

If you have time and a dry climate, you can dry your seeds by hanging the part of the plant containing seed inside a paper bag in a protected portion of your garden. The paper bag will keep out bugs and catch seeds that might otherwise fall to the ground.

The method you use to get your seeds will depend on the form of seed. You can have seeds in pods, seeds in fruits, and seeds in flower heads. Always pick seeds from the strongest plants that grew desirable fruit.

When harvesting seeds in pods (like beans and peas), allow the pod to dry thoroughly. When the pod is dry, open the pod and pop out the seeds.

When harvesting the tiny seeds in flower heads (like lettuce and dill), cut off the head before the seeds dry completely. Use an electric dehydrator to dry the seed heads.

When harvesting seeds from fruits (like tomatoes and cucumbers), press the mature seeds and pulp out of the fruit into a glass container. Add water and let sit for a few days, stirring occasionally. The good seeds will sink, and the bad seeds will float. Pour off the liquid and bad seeds, and spread the good seeds on a paper towel to dry.

Storage and Viability

Seeds are best stored in a cool, dark, dry place. The seeds should be dry enough that you can snap them apart or reduce them to powder with a hammer blow. If the seeds don't dry out enough when allowed to air-dry, you can use a dehydrator or warm open stove to help remove the excess moisture.

Typical containers used for seed storage are glass jars, metal cans, and Mylar bags. Seeds stored using professional measures could remain viable for as long as 20 years. However, most seeds merely kept dry in a cool, dark place can remain viable for three to five years.

The Least You Need to Know

- Growing your plants from seed saves money and allows you to grow unusual plants not sold in local nurseries.
- If you have a seedling that was growing in soil, you can simply rinse the soil off the roots and transplant it into your aquaponic system.
- Propagating plants from cuttings is as easy as pushing the cut stem into your grow bed medium without the fuss of rooting powders or other procedures used in traditional gardens.
- You can harvest the seeds from your crops as well.

Fish-Safe Pest Control

In This Chapter

- The biggest pests in your aquaponic garden
- Beneficial bugs
- Plants that deter pests
- Using sprays, powders, teas, and beer to reduce pest problems
- Getting rid of mosquitoes

The great thing about an aquaponic garden is that it is necessarily free of pesticides. You won't be using toxic chemicals to kill pests because they can poison your fish and pollute your plants.

However, you will have to figure out how to get rid of garden pests without poison. Natural methods may not be as convenient as pulling out a spray bottle of dangerous chemicals, but your fish will be happier and you'll know your food is safe to eat.

What Is a Pest?

A pest is anything that destroys your vegetables or fish before harvest or that tries to eat you when you visit your garden. In this chapter I concentrate on fungus and insects.

Birds, dogs, deer, and even humans can be pests, but they can be kept out using netting and fences. Insects and fungus are harder to keep out, however—and an indoor garden may be particularly hard to rid of pests, since an indoor space lacks many natural predators found outdoors.

Pest insects in your garden are herbivores that are trying to eat your plants. I group these by the kind of damage they do. The rest of the chapter deals with various remedies for these pests.

Root Borers

Various insects and larvae like beetles and grubs live in the top 8 inches of the ground. They serve a useful function in helping decompose organic matter in the top layer of the soil. Unfortunately, these insects and their larvae will also bore holes in your plant roots and can make root crops inedible.

Flies will lay their larvae or maggots near roots so the maggots can feed. Row covers made from filmy nonwoven synthetic fabric can keep the flies away from your roots. A number of beetles also lay their eggs near the roots of plants. Some common offenders are wireworms, larvae of the click beetle, and white grubs, larvae of Japanese beetles.

Sap Suckers

Several types of flying insects get their nourishment by sucking sap from the leaves of plants. These insects may be small, but the damage they can do is significant.

Aphids are notorious for collecting on the tender stems and leaves of plants. Aphids come in a variety of shapes and sizes, seemingly a different form uniquely adapted to each crop. White flies are another sap sucker that can cause significant damage to your plants. White flies tend to feed on the underside of leaves, so they may remain undetected by the inattentive gardener.

Leaf Munchers

Chewing insects are often the caterpillar form of moths, but slugs are also famous for chewing on leaves. One nice thing about these bugs is their large size, making them easy to spot and relatively easy to flick off your plants. Another way to dispose of munchers is to feed them to your fish.

Other Bothersome Pests

Plants eaten by insects are likely to be attacked by fungus or mold. A fungus can attack even when there are no insects, sending its parasitic filaments into your plants to extract energy for its own growth. Though there are some good fungi, like penicillin and mushrooms, most fungi you find in your garden should be destroyed before they can destroy your crops.

Finally, mosquitoes may not bother your garden plants, but they definitely bother the gardener and the gardener's family and friends. An aquaponic garden provides mosquitoes lots of moisture to lay eggs, but you can beat this pest and still enjoy your aquaponic garden. I discuss various methods for controlling mosquitoes later in the chapter.

Good Bugs

If the pest insects are mostly bugs that eat plants, the good kind of bugs to have in your garden are bugs that eat other bugs. These are the carnivores of the insect world, and you want them around your garden.

There are other insects that are beneficial to have around your garden; bees, for example, play a vital role in pollinating plants. But since this chapter is focused on pest control, we'll focus on the bugs that eat pests.

Ladybugs

Ladybugs love to eat bugs that drink sap, including aphids, white flies, corn borers, cabbage worms, spider mites, scale insects, and thrips or corn lice. Ladybugs are so useful for controlling common garden pests that they are sold for that purpose in major garden centers.

You can purchase packages containing hundreds or even thousands of ladybugs. Though some will undoubtedly fly away to eat your neighbors' aphids, the sap in your well-watered plants will keep attracting the aphids ladybugs love to eat; thus you should be able to retain a significant colony of these cheerful-looking red insects.

Lacewings

The adult lacewing is a beautiful creature. In addition, lacewings voraciously eat the same sort of insects that ladybugs do. Lacewings have a long thin body and four transparent wings with a silvery network of veins that give them their name.

If you are not familiar with lacewings, I recommend you find out which of the 6,000 species are native to your area and what they look like in their larval and cocoon stages. Go online to view pictures, or ask at your local garden store. It would be a pity to inadvertently exterminate an insect that is one of your best allies in destroying pest insects.

Praying Mantises

The praying mantis, with its strong jaws and powerful forelegs, is perfect for hunting insects. Mantises are the only insects that can turn their heads around to look behind them, making them uniquely intriguing as pets.

DID YOU KNOW ...

Praying mantises can make delightful pets. Unfortunately they have incredible appetites, which means the owner of a pet praying mantis has to spend a lot of time raising or buying bugs. This voracious appetite, however, is a wonderful thing if you have praying mantises around your garden.

Praying mantises are insectivorous and carnivorous, usually eating fresh insects and live meat. In the spring when they are young, mantises eat aphids, leafhoppers, mosquitoes, caterpillars, and other soft-bodied insects. As they mature over the summer, they eat larger insects like beetles, grasshoppers, and crickets.

When in Doubt

Not all insects in your garden are pests. There are some you might find flying around that are just innocent bystanders. If you are new to natural gardening and haven't learned which insects are good and which are bad, you can put up sticky paper to collect samples of your local insects. Yellow sticky paper such as fly paper is particularly good for attracting bugs. Some people will coat a sheet of seaweed with molasses and then feed the whole thing to their fish. Most communities have gardening experts who can tell you what your insects are and whether or not you should take action to deter them.

Pest-Deterring Plants

Some plants naturally repel pest insects. Adding these plants to your garden among your crop plants is one way to deter pests. Following are several common plants you can use.

Marigolds

Marigolds grow well in a media-based aquaponic garden and can be a useful plant in its own right. Luckily, many common insects hate the taste and smell of marigolds. Mosquitoes and aphids are two of the many pests a colorful border of marigolds can keep away.

Mosquitoes and aphids don't like to be near the cheerful marigold. A border will brighten your garden and help keep common insect pests away.

Garlic

Garlic and chives will repel slugs. I plant them in the edge of my grow beds, along with onions.

Peppermint

Humans generally enjoy the smell of mint plants, but ants can't abide the stuff. The only problem with mint is that it can be a pest plant in its own right because it grows so quickly and can overwhelm other plants. But if you've got an ant problem, it might be worth planting some mint in containers to protect your garden.

Lavender

Lavender is useful for deterring flying and crawling insects. As with the other plants mentioned, it is the aromatic oil that the insects detest. The oil is concentrated in the lavender flower, which is why lavender sachets are sometimes used in dresser drawers to repel moths.

The insects that are repelled by lavender include mosquitoes, ticks, and fleas. In addition to simply growing lavender in your garden, you can infuse olive oil with lavender oil and apply the oil infusion to your skin. Lavender oil might not be the most effective bug repellent, but it probably smells the nicest.

> **GREEN TIP**
>
> You can use plants to protect your fruit and vegetables from insect pests, but you can also group plants to support the health and growth of their neighboring plants. This is often called companion planting, and there are numerous guides to companion planting in print and online. Companion planting even has its own Wikipedia article.

Sprays and Powders

Plants and good bugs are great, but there are times when you want to be able to do something yourself to keep pests away. These sprays and powders are for those moments when you just want to act.

A Squirt of Water

One of the best pest control measures is to get rid of the bugs with water from a hose or spray bottle. You can use water to dislodge many caterpillars, aphids, and other nasties. At the very least, this will stop the bugs from munching on your plants while you grab something more powerful to keep them away. You can grab the grubs after you spray them off your plants and feed them to your fish.

Garlic Fire Spray

You can make garlic fire spray by blending 20 to 30 cloves of garlic and 5 to 6 hot chili peppers together in a couple of quarts (or liters) of water with a large spoonful each of salad oil and dish detergent. Filter out the remaining chunks and pour the liquid into a spray bottle. The small amount of detergent you use in this solution will not harm your fish.

Bugs hate the taste of garlic, and the oils in the chili peppers burn both insects and four-legged pests. The vegetable oil slows evaporation of the garlic and chili essences, and the dish detergent helps the spray stick to leaves. You can spray the garden every few days until the pests are gone and then again after rains or every couple of weeks to keep them away.

Molasses Spray

Animals and insects will attack a weakened animal or plant. A weakened plant does not taste as sweet to the bugs, and this lack of sweetness indicates that the plant will be easier to eat.

Molasses spray works by tricking the insects into thinking a plant is healthier than it actually is. If your cabbage, broccoli, or chard leaves are becoming holey, pull out the molasses spray. Stir a large spoonful of molasses to a quart (or liter) of water, then add a large spoonful of dish detergent. You can add a spoonful of vinegar to make this even more effective.

Spray the molasses mixture on the leaves, particularly on the underside of leaves. Avoid getting this spray on lettuce plants, however, since the sweet sticky liquid will cause brown spotting on lettuce leaves.

Diatomaceous Earth

Diatomaceous earth (DE) is a white powder made from the silica skeletons of single-celled algae. The silica skeletons have incredibly sharp edges on a scale that damages worms and insects.

The sharp edges can cut slugs and worms, irritating them and potentially cutting them. Additionally, the dry crevices in the powder absorb the waxy coating on bugs, causing them to crack and dry out. Even if the damage isn't fatal, DE can discourage bugs from bothering your plants. Products that contain DE are regulated by the Environmental Protection Agency, so make sure you read any cautions that come with purchased DE to ensure you use it properly.

Teas

I've talked a lot about how to deter insect pests, but a fungus can do great damage to your garden as well. One way to control the fungus is to uproot the affected plant and throw it away (preferably not in the compost bin). But you may be able to rescue your plants by spraying or dowsing them with a tea.

Chamomile Tea

Chamomile tea is a mild fungicide that can be used to prevent and treat a fungus. You can make the tea from dried chamomile flowers or from standard chamomile tea bags.

You can proactively help prevent fungus by soaking your seeds in chamomile for a few hours before planting them. Additionally, you may be able to save plants that are just developing a fungus; keep a spray bottle of chamomile tea brewed to normal strength handy to spritz new seedlings at the first sign of fuzz or mold. It's useful to add a bit of dish detergent to get the chamomile tea to stick to the leaves.

Compost Tea

Compost tea is made from worm castings, which is the stuff that has passed through a worm's guts. Worm castings are unusually rich in beneficial bacteria. Compost tea is made by filling a pillowcase or tea towel with worm castings and adding an ounce of molasses to a 5-gallon bucket of warm, nonchlorinated water. Include several air stones to add oxygen. The molasses sugar, warmth, and oxygen cause the beneficial bacteria to multiply at an accelerated rate.

Let the bubbler run in the mix for two or three days until you have a nice head of foamy gunk on the surface, then strain the tea through an old pillowcase to fill a spray bottle. Immediately spray the compost tea on the leaves of your plant and pour it into your grow beds. The beneficial bacteria will suppress fungus, detoxify your plants, and make it easier for the plants to absorb nutrition. The bacteria in compost tea will benefit your fish as well.

DID YOU KNOW ...

New gardeners may think compost tea is the brown liquid that leaks out of the bottom of a worm bin. The brown stuff looks like tea, after all. This brown liquid won't harm your plants, but it won't provide the benefits of a true compost tea. True compost tea is a brew of worm castings and molasses where the beneficial bacteria are encouraged to grow by adding lots of air with an air stone. At the end of the brewing process, compost tea will probably have a layer of frothy foam on the top, making it look more like compost beer.

Beer

Beer is as old as farming and is the most popular alcoholic drink, bar none. Luckily, pests like slugs and snails love it too.

Slugs love a moist environment, and an aquaponic garden must seem like slug heaven. You can lure them to their deaths by putting a shallow container of beer out in the garden for them. The slugs will flock to the beer and drown.

What to do with the dead slugs? You can always see if your fish like them. Drop one of the slugs into your tank and see what happens. The worst that could happen is your fish ignore the slug, in which case you can dump the dead mollusks in the compost bin.

Controlling Mosquitoes

If you're like me, the most irritating pests in your garden will be mosquitoes. I was thrilled when I found out how many options I had for controlling the mosquitoes that plagued me. I've already mentioned a few plants that are supposed to deter mosquitoes, like marigolds and lavender. But in the rest of the chapter I'll talk about things that profoundly reduce mosquitoes around your garden.

Bacillus Thuringiensis

Bacillus thuringiensis (Bt) is soil bacteria that kills insects and doesn't hurt anything else. You can find Bt in most hardware stores. One specific strain of Bt is extremely effective at killing mosquito larvae and is sold as dry granules or donut-shaped floating chunks of Bt, commonly called dunks. Bt mosquito dunks and granules are considered extremely safe because they only hurt mosquito larvae.

A single donut-shaped dunk will kill mosquito larvae in 100 square feet of surface water for 30 days.

Neem Oil

Neem oil comes from an evergreen tree that grows in India. Diluted neem oil can be effective as a pesticide and can control various fungal diseases, such as powdery mildew, on animals and plants.

When neem oil is added to kerosene to create a 1 percent solution and burned in a lamp, the small amount of neem in the lamp smoke is more than 80 percent effective at repelling the mosquitoes that cause malaria, dengue fever, and West Nile virus. A tablespoon of neem oil in 6 cups of water will produce a 1 percent solution.

SOUNDS FISHY

Be careful and wear gloves when handling pure neem oil—it is very strong. It has been shown to cause infertility in rats and can irritate your skin and eyes.

Bug Zappers

If a bug is attracted to light, a bug zapper will kill it. These electronic devices emit a blue glow that attracts bugs. When a bug gets close, an electrical field kills it.

A great thing about a bug zapper is that dead bugs generally fall below the bug zapper. You can therefore use a bug zapper to both kill bugs and supplement the feed your fish get.

The Least You Need to Know

- Aquaponics forces you to give up pesticides, but there are lots of options for getting rid of pests that are completely safe for your plants and fish.
- Beneficial bugs will feast on any pest insects attracted to the lush plants in your garden.
- Careful use of plants can make your garden unattractive to pest insects.
- There are a variety of liquids that will deter or kill pests, including water, beer, sprays, and teas.
- Mosquitoes are irritating, but you have many options for repelling and killing them in an aquaponic garden.

Growing Abundant Amounts of Healthy Produce

In This Chapter

- Pruning your plants to encourage growth
- Increasing your crops and duration of harvests
- Maximizing nutrient availability
- Treating nutrient deficiencies in your plants

The plants in an aquaponic system almost grow themselves. But if you haven't gardened much before, there are a few time-honored tips and tricks that can improve the quantity and quality of the harvest you get from your system. Pruning your plants appropriately will produce more fruit, and staggering planting will extend the length of time you will be able to harvest your produce. Both of these techniques are used in well-managed traditional gardens.

The water in an aquaponic garden provides a unique ability to control water chemistry and nutrients. With proper management, research shows that most plants grow faster and larger in an aquaponic garden than they do in either soil gardens or hydroponic gardens.

Pruning

Pruning refers to the selective removal of parts of a plant to improve plant health, yield, and quality of flowers or fruits. There are also times when you will prune an aggressive plant to prevent it from overwhelming its neighbors.

Pruning is a term used for fruiting or woody plants; if you have leafy greens, the proper term is *thinning*. However, many of the same principles apply.

DEFINITION

Pruning means to cut off parts of a fruiting or woody plant to improve the plant's health or shape. **Thinning** is when leafy plants are cut or pinched back.

Rules of Thumb

The purpose of pruning is to minimize disease and maximize the production of fruit. Here are some tips for proper pruning:

- Pinch with your fingers rather than cut where possible. Cutting slices through cell walls, increasing opportunities for fungus and bacteria to damage the plant.

- Never prune, handle, or fasten branches that are wet. Moisture will increase the probability of infection where the plant is pruned or tied.

- Cut off branches that grow to the ground. Leaves and fruit on the ground are more likely to rot and get infected.

- Prune to give plants and fruit enough room to thrive. Better a few well-formed fruit than many small fruit.

- For fruiting plants like tomatoes, cut off sides shoots or suckers that form in the intersections between the leaves and the main stem. These shoots are called suckers because they suck away energy that could go toward fruit production.

Pinching Off New Growth and Flowers

Pinching or deadheading refers to cutting dead flower heads off your flowering plants, but it can also refer to any time you cut the tip off a plant.

Normally, fruiting plants try to put out a central shoot bearing flowers, produce fruit, and then die. When you pinch off this first flower, however, the plant redoubles its efforts to reproduce. The plant will produce more flowers and rush fruit to ripeness when you pinching off excess flowers and new growth. Here are some particular examples of how you can pinch off growth to encourage your plants to grow more edible food:

- Pinching off the central stem will encourage new shoots to grow from the base of each leaf just below the cut. This encourages a leafy plant, like basil, to become bushier.

- Leafy greens live to set seed and die. Once the seed head has fully emerged, the leaves become bitter. If you see the seed head start to emerge, pinch it off to keep the leaves edible.

- Flowers exist to pollinate and be pollinated to produce fruit and seeds. If you pinch off the first flowers in a prolific plant like tomato, the plant will redouble its effort to set flowers, resulting in more fruit.

- Toward the end of the season, pinch off the growing tip of the plant and any suckers that develop. The plant will divert its energy toward ripening the fruit it has already set.

Pruning will not merely convince the pruned plant to produce a larger crop; you can often use the prunings to start new plants.

This patch of basil has gone to seed, meaning that the plant has produced flowers. When a plant flowers, the taste of the leaves can become bitter.

Extending Your Harvest

If you are planning to can most of your vegetables, it is beneficial to have your crops mature at the same time. But most home gardeners will also want to eat fresh vegetables from their gardens over the course of the summer.

There are a few tricks for increasing the amount time you can produce a variety of fresh food in your garden during late spring through fall and even winter.

Staggered Planting

If you want to spread your harvest over several weeks, you can use ever-bearing varieties of your favorite crops. Ever-bearing plants produce fruit over an extended period of time instead of all at once. Unfortunately, ever-bearing crops usually achieve an extended harvest by sacrificing either flavor or volume.

If you don't want to use ever-bearing plants, you can still extend your harvest. You just need to spread out the time over which you plant seedlings.

As I mentioned in Chapter 11, it's helpful during winter to plan out when you'll be starting various seeds. You'll need to start a few seeds for several crops every week over an extended period of time. For a huge community garden or commercial greenhouse, this shouldn't be a problem. You'll already have lots of pallets of seedlings to start every month. But if you are growing food for just your own family, you'll want to start only as many plants as you plan to eat or store. Plant the seedlings in your garden when several true leaves have emerged.

GREEN TIP

You can create your own seedling pots from newspaper. Find a bottle or similar tube shape about the size you want your pot to be. Cut or tear two to three pages of newspaper so the pages wrap around the bottle a couple of times with edges that can fold together at the bottom. Slide the newspaper off the bottle or tube. Fill the newspaper pot with soil and place in a water-tight dish. Plant your seed, label the pot, water, and wait for seedlings to emerge.

Multi-Layer Gardening

As you become familiar with the amount of time your plants require to mature, you can start doubling up your plants. Place the new seedlings in the garden at the base of crops you expect to harvest in a few weeks. When the young plant is ready to put on mature growth, you'll be clearing out the older plant.

Alternately, you can grow compact plants in pots hung above your grow beds. As long as the plants in the pots keep to themselves, enough light should get through to plants in the grow beds below.

Harvesting in Season

You can trick your plants into growing any time of year, but your plants evolved over thousands of years to thrive during particular seasons. One easy way to maximize the yield of your plants is to grow them during a time of year that enhances their productivity. This may be different from the ideal conditions for the plant to set seed.

For example, lettuce loves warm weather—but in warm weather, it can immediately go to seed and die. Since you want to eat lettuce leaves, plant it in cool weather conditions that discourage the lettuce from going to seed. This stretches out the time it takes the lettuce to mature and go to seed, which maximizes the production of edible leaves.

The Importance of pH

You learned in Chapters 3 and 10 that pH is a measure of the acidity or alkalinity of the water in your aquaponic garden. We've talked about how your fish and plants want the water to be at a pH between 6.0 and 7.0. But the importance of pH bears repeating in this chapter since it can have such a significant impact on the health of your plants. Plants will grow healthier and be more nutritious when the pH of the water matches the pH the plant needs.

Effect on Nutrient Availability

If your plants are looking sickly or tasting bitter, the first thing to check is pH. You can add nutrients to your water all day long, but they won't be accessible to your plants unless the water is at the proper pH.

Even if your pH was in a good range when you tested it a week or a month ago, check your pH periodically.

Your nitrifying bacteria will add acid to the water as they convert ammonia waste into nitrate, reducing the pH of the water. They also consume carbonates, making the water softer. The acid and soft water won't be good for your fish, increasing the probability of open sores and infection. Luckily, the substances you add to correct pH will also help protect the fish.

Most nutrients are available at pH between 6.0 and 7.0. As pH moves outside that range, your plants will be unable to access the nutrients in the water.

Altering pH

If your pH is too high or too low, you want to bring it into the range that is most productive for your plants. Veteran aquaponic gardeners suggest adding hydrochloric acid or muriatic acid when your pH is too high. Muriatic acid is inexpensive and widely available in stores that sell pool supplies.

In a mature garden, however, it is most likely your pH will be too low. Crushed eggshells can gently buffer pH. Acids in the water will dissolve the shells, which adds calcium carbonate that in turn increases pH and supports healthy growth. You can also buy calcium carbonate powder or calcium hydroxide if you prefer adding powder to messing with eggshells. Potassium carbonate will also increase pH and is a natural fungicide.

DID YOU KNOW ...

Your plants need calcium for proper growth and potassium to support healthy flowers. It is common for aquaponic gardeners to keep both calcium carbonate and potassium carbonate on hand and alternate between the two to increase pH when the water gets too acidic.

Treating Nutrient Deficiencies

There will be times when your plants are looking sick. Once you've confirmed your pH is in the right range (6.0 to 7.0), you'll want to determine what nutrients are missing from your system.

With a soil garden, you would need to do a lot of work with your soil to get the right drainage and nutrient balance. With aquaponics, however, the coarse rocks in your beds provide plenty of drainage. You only need to add a couple of things to your water to provide the proper nutrients for your plants.

The following table lists common symptoms your plants may exhibit. For each symptom there is both a specific nutrient lacking and a recommended additive to correct the deficiency.

Symptoms of Nutrient Deficiency and Remedies

Symptom	Problem	Remedy
Fruiting vegetable rots near the blossom-end	Calcium deficiency	Calcium carbonate (builder's lime) or calcium hydroxide (hydrated lime)
New leaves deformed and pale		[Will increase pH]
Pale yellow or white leaves with green veins	Iron deficiency	Chelated iron
New leaves small and yellow, old leaves yellow and die off	Nitrogen deficiency	Add fish, add nitrifying bacteria, or feed your fish
Leaves yellow at tips and edges, develop pinholes with yellowing edges	Potassium deficiency	Potassium carbonate (potash) or potassium hydroxide (pearl ash) [Will increase pH]
Old leaves fall off	Phosphate deficiency	Seaweed extract
Leaves turn yellow from center, veins green	Magnesium deficiency	
Yellow spots and/or elongated holes between veins	Manganese deficiency	

Seaweed extract and chelated iron will not impact the pH of your system. Calcium carbonate and potassium carbonate in small doses will slowly raise your pH. Calcium hydroxide and potassium hydroxide will produce larger shifts in pH and should be used with care.

The Least You Need to Know

- Pruning your plants properly will encourage growth and healthy fruit.
- You can plant multiple crops in the same area if they grow at different rates or occupy different vertical space. You can also extend your harvest of favorite vegetables by staggering when you plant seedlings.

- When growing outdoors, your plants will thrive if you grow them during the proper time of year to ensure to proper length of day and temperature to yield the largest crop.
- Your plants may suffer from lack of nutrients either because the pH is outside the optimal range of 6.0 to 7.0 or because they lack key nutrients. Keep a few key additives on hand to remedy any nutrient deficiencies.

Fish and Other Animals

Once the biological filter in your garden is firmly established, it's time to add your fish. First you need to decide which fish you will raise and their individual needs, which we cover in Chapter 15. Chapter 16 talks about other members of the animal kingdom that might be useful in your aquaponic garden, from worms to bees to crayfish. Chapter 17 shares advice on how your fish breed and what you can do to prevent it, since having too many fish in your tank means they will all stay small and runty. Chapter 17 also talks about how to diagnose problems with your fish and the proper techniques for helping heal them without poisoning your plants. For those of you raising edible fish, this chapter also covers how to catch, kill, clean, and cook them.

Adding Fish to Your Aquaponic Garden

Chapter 15

In This Chapter

- Why you should use freshwater fish
- All-purpose ornamental fish: goldfish and koi
- Pond and lake fish
- Fish that need cold water
- Fish that need warm water
- Popular Australian varieties of fish

At this point you've at least got a mental picture of your system, the tanks and plumbing, and whether you plan to grow in gravel or grow in water. You may even have your system set up with plants already growing strong. Now, it's time to talk fish.

In this chapter I'll tell you all about the major types of fish used in aquaponics systems, along with the benefits and challenges associated with each.

Why Freshwater Fish?

Most of us are interested in growing strawberries, lettuce, beets, spinach, tomatoes, marigolds, and other traditional garden crops and flowers. All of these plants require freshwater—water that doesn't contain salt. Strawberries in particular will refuse to thrive if there is any salt in the system.

Luckily, there are lots of options when it comes to freshwater fish:

- Ornamental fish
- Pond fish
- Cool-water fish
- Warm-water fish

SOUNDS FISHY

Not all freshwater fish will be legal in your area. Check with your local Department of Natural Resources to find out what restrictions exist in your local area. Even when a fish is legal, there may be expensive or time-consuming inspection requirements. Also, avoid fish you can't feed. Preferred fish are those that can eat the bulk fish food or pellets available online or from agricultural supply stores.

All-Purpose Ornamental Fish

Goldfish and koi are beautiful fish that have been bred to show off their bold colors. Both are considered ornamental fish because they are usually raised for show rather than for food. Ornamental fish are rarely regulated because they are usually kept in aquariums and backyard tanks rather than in large ponds and rivers that might flood into local waterways. This lack of regulation means there's no need to apply for and pay for a license or wait for a government official to come by and inspect your system.

Goldfish (*Carassius auratus auratus*)

Goldfish are inexpensive and readily available, and they prefer water temperatures of 50° to 77°F. Goldfish are a type of carp developed in China thousands of years ago from edible carp. Today goldfish are among the most commonly kept aquarium fish and have a wide variety of colors and body types.

For aquaponics, I recommend goldfish with simple bodies and tails. These can grow to be as long as 8 to 12 inches. These include the common goldfish (streamlined body, short tail) and comets (streamlined body, elongated tail). These simple goldfish are sturdy and produce lots of ammonia—a good thing in an aquaponics system. It is also usually possible to obtain common goldfish and comets quite inexpensively at local pet stores. You don't need many goldfish to supply the nitrogen needs for an aquaponics system. In fact, aquarium enthusiasts recommend common goldfish be allowed 55 gallons of water per fish, which can grow to be a foot long if they live to maturity.

Goldfish are omnivores, meaning they will eat both plant food and meat (or other fish). But although goldfish will nip at plants and other fish, they aren't known for eating their tank mates. It's best to feed them a sinking food so they don't gulp down air with their meal. They are also excellent learners. They will soon come to recognize the hand that feeds them and gather eagerly near the normal feed spot when you appear. When they don't gather around, it's a sign something is off. They will usually eat as much as you will give them, which may be well more than is healthy. Over time, overfeeding can damage the goldfish swim bladder, making it hard for them to stay upright and even making it impossible for them to swim.

Though carp is considered good eating in many cultures, goldfish sold in the pet industry may have been treated for diseases using various chemicals that can cause cancer and illness in humans or other fish. The chemicals won't contaminate other fish in your tank, but they could remain in the flesh of the goldfish.

Koi (*Cyprinus carpio carpio*)

Koi can be expensive, but they are readily available and do well in water temperatures of 32° to 77°F. Koi are another form of carp that were developed in Japan. The colorful variations we are familiar with today were developed by winter-bound farmers in northern Japan to pass the time. These colorful carp (nishikigoi or brocaded carp) were first introduced beyond northern Japan at the 1914 Tokyo Exhibition. Individual fish can be worth hundreds of dollars and can live for several decades.

Koi are ornamental fish that symbolize love and friendship in Japan. High-quality koi can cost hundreds and even thousands of dollars.
(Photo courtesy of Grow It Right Aquaponics)

Koi develop whiskers around their mouths and over time will grow to be 3 to 4 feet long, much larger than goldfish. Koi produce thousands of offspring from a single *spawning*. The large majority of these koi offspring are considered inferior. However, your garden doesn't care what color your fish are. As long as the fish are healthy, you can use inferior (and less expensive) koi in your garden.

DEFINITION

The term **spawn** refers both to the act of producing fish eggs and to the fish eggs themselves.

Koi are omnivorous fish, eating plants as well as koi food. Koi food is designed to float to encourage koi to come to the surface, and the koi can be trained to take food from your hand. Koi will stop eating if the temperature drops below 50°F. Any food you give them in cold weather will either spoil in their stomachs or in the tank, causing sickness and possibly death.

All-Purpose Pond Fish

If your garden is outside, the best fish for your locality are native fish. The fish in local ponds, lakes, and rivers are already adapted to local conditions. If you were to have an accident where your fish got into local waters, native fish would be far preferable to nonnative species. Fish from the other side of the world can become invasive species if accidentally introduced into local waterways.

I recommend you start with fish that can thrive on pellets. These include catfish, yellow perch, and bluegill. Minnows are another option that are low maintenance and locally available. Ask your local agricultural store if they know of a vendor who sells pond fish. These vendors usually travel to agricultural stores every few weeks so people can buy fish for their outdoor fishing ponds. You may also be able to find someone who will ship fish to you directly.

Channel Catfish (*Ictalurus punctatus*)

Catfish are moderately expensive and prefer water temperatures of 50° to 75°F. Catfish are a smooth-skinned fish native to northeastern portion of the Americas from Mexico to Canada. They are omnivores and will eat pelleted fish food. Like most fish, catfish are particularly fond of worms. Catfish can be obtained from companies supplying fish for ponds and are usually sold when they are 2 to 4 inches in length.

Catfish in captivity will reach a mature weight of 2 to 4 pounds and a length of about 18 inches. When stocking catfish in an aquaponics system, the recommended ratio is one catfish per 20 gallons of grow bed volume, since catfish need well-filtered water. Because catfish are relatively long, they are best kept in a tank that has a diameter of at least 4 feet (for example, a 300-gallon stock tank). Unlike the social goldfish and koi, catfish like to avoid interaction with humans and will usually stay near the bottom of the tank except during feeding time.

Channel catfish have sharp spines on the fins behind their gills and along their back. These spines can puncture rubber and plastic tank liners as the fish search the edges of their habitat for food. The spines can also puncture your skin if you aren't careful when harvesting the fish.

Catfish is a popular food fish in the United States, so you will not lack for catfish recipes if you decide to eat yours. A mature catfish is large enough to feed an entire family and lacks scales, making it easier to prepare. Some folks dislike catfish because they are bottom feeders in the wild with a muddy flavor. But catfish raised in aquaponics systems and fed on pellets tend to not to have that muddy flavor.

Fathead Minnows (*Pimephales promelas*)

Minnows are inexpensive and prefer water temperatures of 50° to 70°F. Minnows are small and hardy fish that breed prolifically. They like to sift around in the muck at the bottom of a tank to find their food.

Minnows are usually sold as bait fish, and you'll notice many fishing lures look an awful lot like minnows. Minnows can coexist with other pond fish if those fish are well fed or if there is plenty of shelter in the tank. But if the larger fish get hungry, the minnows in the pond will become a snack. Minnows are put in large ponds to feed larger fish, where they can usually find cover and reproduce fast enough to maintain a good population despite getting eaten by the larger fish.

Minnows in a tank won't have as many places to hide, so your population of minnows might disappear if you keep them in the same tank with larger fish.

DID YOU KNOW ...

If you put minnows in a sump or deep water grow bed, they will eat the gunk that collects at the bottom of these tanks. They will also eat small insects and larvae on the surface of the water, like mosquito larvae.

Bluegill (*Lepomis macrochirus*)

Bluegill are inexpensive and do well in water temperatures of 34° to 75°F. The large temperature range over which this fish thrives, combined with the great taste of this smaller fish, make it a great option for home aquaponic gardeners who want to raise food fish outdoors. Bluegill are also a favorite fish for young anglers because they are easy to catch. They are increasingly a favorite fish for North American aquaponic gardeners because they will eat pellets, can be kept in a smaller tank than catfish, and are good eating. Bluegill can grow to be several pounds in the wild, but will usually remain smaller than a pound when raised in tanks.

Bluegill breed early and often once water temperatures warm to 70°F. The males will create dish-like depressions where they attract a female to lay eggs. The males aggressively guard the eggs and *fry* from being eaten by other bluegill. If the baby fish survive and overpopulate the tank, the other fish in the tank can become stunted. You can tell stunted fish from baby fish because a stunted fish will have large eyes.

DEFINITION

Fry are tiny baby fish, right after they have emerged from the egg.

Bluegill are fast swimmers that race towards you at feeding time, only to turn on a dime and disappear from view once they've nabbed their morsel of food. If you leave the tank uncovered, the bluegill might jump out of the tank.

Bluegill can be purchased from companies that supply fish for ponds. In ponds, bluegill and their young become food for large-mouth bass, so bluegill stunting won't usually become an issue in well-stocked ponds. If you end up with a lot of small bluegill in your tank, you can still eat them. One popular recipe is to can the fish, which makes the bones edible and can taste a bit like canned salmon.

Ice fishing for bluegill is a popular sport. Bluegill also thrive in warm waters during summer, which is when they usually breed.
(Photo courtesy of Nate Herman of Herman Brothers Pond Management)

Hybrid Bluegill (*Lepomis macrochirus*)

Hybrid bluegill are produced when a male bluegill is crossed with a female green sunfish. The offspring of this mating are fish with the large mouth of the green sunfish and the aggressiveness of the bluegill. The offspring are usually male (90 to 95 percent is typical), reducing the time and energy a group of hybrid bluegill spends mating. The large mouth, aggressive nature, and reduced energy spent producing young enable hybrid bluegill to grow faster and larger than regular bluegill.

Hybrid bluegill will feed on commercial pellets and will grow as much as $\frac{1}{2}$ to $\frac{3}{4}$ pound per year. Growth of fish in the tank will be uneven, with some individuals remaining quite small for a year or two. Over time hybrid blues can reach weights of 2 to $2\frac{1}{2}$ pounds and will live as long as 11 years.

Hybrid bluegill like shade. They are able to change color to a certain degree, so you will find them particularly hard to see in a black tank.

Hybrid bluegill can reproduce and will do so with sunfish species that are available and compatible. An experiment conducted at Meadowlark Farms in Texas indicates there is no stunting in subsequent generations, though the subsequent generations may favor the green sunfish parent of the original stock.

If you start with all hybrid bluegill stock, you shouldn't have a problem with over-crowding, but you might want to plan to harvest all your fish and start fresh every year or so.

GREEN TIP

Canned bluegill is crunchy, like canned salmon, and tastes great on crackers, in sandwiches or fresh salads, or cooked in a fish loaf or fish a la king.

This recipe for canned bluegill comes courtesy of Bayou Bill Scifre:

1. Remove the fish's head, fins, entrails, and scales. Wash the body cavity with cold, running water; drain.
2. Stuff well-drained bluegill (whole or cut in chunks) in pint canning jars as full as you can. Add salt and pepper or powdered mustard to taste (don't add water). Loosely screw on canning jar lids. Cook in pressure cooker for 110 minutes at 10 pounds of pressure.
3. When the cooking process is done and the jars are cool enough to handle, hand-tighten the jar lids.
4. Store the jars in a cool, dark place. Canned fish will last for years.

Yellow Perch (*Perca flavescens*)

Perch prefer water temperatures of 63° to 77°F, but they can also survive freezing temperatures. Yellow perch is a favorite food fish in the vicinity of the Great Lakes on the border between Canada and the United States. It is considered by many to be the finest of all panfish. Yellow perch occupy a similar ecological niche to bluegill.

In nature, yellow perch inhabit the shallow shores of lakes and ponds and slow-moving water of rivers and streams. Though they prefer warmer temperatures, they can clearly survive the cold temperatures of North American winters. In fact, yellow perch is a favorite catch among ice fishers.

Yellow perch are yellow gold and marked with six to eight dark vertical stripes. Adults typically range from 4 to 11 inches and live up to 10 years. They are carnivorous, meaning they eat meat in the wild, and require pellets containing about 50 percent protein.

Those familiar with yellow perch love the taste and texture of the larger fish. Small fish can be canned, eliminating the need to bone the fish and resulting in a delicious treat that tastes less fishy than sardines.

Cool-Water Fish

Pond fish can survive cold temperatures, but they do well in warm water as well. Following are descriptions of trout and salmon, two popular cool-water fish. Of these, trout are the only real option for a home garden, assuming you can keep the water cool enough for the trout to stay healthy.

Because you have to keep the water cool to keep the trout healthy, grow plants that will thrive in cool temperatures. See Chapter 11 for several popular vegetables that grow well in cool and cold growing conditions.

Rainbow Trout (*Oncorhynchus mykiss* and *Salmo gairdneri*)

Trout are moderately expensive and prefer water temperatures of 55° to 65°F. In the wild, trout can grow to be as large as 50 pounds, but farmed trout are usually only a couple of pounds when they are harvested. Trout is a favorite fish for many anglers—and many eaters. Rainbow trout is preferred for farming because of its rapid growth, delicious flesh, high survival, willingness to eat pellets, and ability to survive temperatures as high as 70°F. Other trout tend to be more cannibalistic and delicate. Since trout are carnivorous, their feed must contain high levels of protein and is more expensive than the pellets appropriate for omnivorous fish.

Rainbow trout are native to the western United States and are closely related to Pacific salmon. Some rainbow trout spend the mature phase of their life in the ocean like salmon.

Trout require lots of oxygen and high-quality water, like the cold, pure water in the streams where trout evolved. Farmed trout are traditionally raised in flow-through raceways fed by mountain streams.

For the home grower, a circular tank containing at least 300 gallons of water is recommended. Trout want to swim, so continuous feed from the water pump will help rotate the volume of water within the tank. Because trout need extremely pure water, make sure to fully cycle your system before introducing fish. Invest in an oxygen test kit, and make sure the water is consistently oxygenated to near-saturation.

A basket of rainbow trout harvested from a commercial-style flow-through raceway.
(Photo courtesy of Ken Semmens, West Virginia University Extension)

Salmon

Salmon typically require cooler temperatures than trout (52° to 58°F) and aren't as hardy as trout. Their distinctive pink color for which salmon are famous comes from the plankton they eat in open waters. If you raised salmon in your aquaponic garden, the flesh would be white and taste like trout.

Young Chinook salmon can be raised in land-based tanks and then transferred to net cages in the ocean to mature. Over the past 20 years salmon farming has matured to the point that over half of all Chinook salmon on the market come from fish farms. Chinook salmon have been used in combined aquaculture/hydroponic systems in New Zealand but little information is available about salmon aquaculture in the United States. Since few home gardeners have access to the ocean net tanks required for the mature stage of a Chinook salmon's life, these salmon aren't an option for a home aquaponic garden.

Kokanee are landlocked freshwater salmon found throughout western North America, as well as in Nantahala Lake in North Carolina and Saiko Lake in Japan. Kokanee are genetically identical to sockeye salmon but usually grow to no more than 14 inches long and 3 to 4 pounds. In nature, kokanee eat plankton, insects, small crustaceans, and small fish. Kokanee in captivity are prone to bacterial kidney disease. Additionally, sockeye salmon, including kokanee, die after spawning. It is therefore impossible to maintain brood stock.

> **SOUNDS FISHY**
>
> Because salmon is a popular eating fish, unscrupulous people will promise you that salmon can be raised in an aquaponic system. This isn't a complete lie, but salmon are not an option for most aquaponic gardeners.

Warm-Water Fish

From fish that thrive only in pristine, frigid mountain lakes and streams, we'll now move on to fish that need warm water. These warm-water fish evolved near the equator and need their water kept warm, whatever the cost.

Because you have to keep the water warm to keep these fish healthy, grow plants that will thrive in warm weather. See Chapter 11 for several popular vegetables that grow well in the warmth and heat of summer.

Tropical Aquarium Fish

Aquarium fish are readily available and prefer water temperatures of 64° to 82°F. A wide variety of freshwater tropical fish are available to the home hobbyist, such as tetras and angelfish. Any selection of fish that would work well in a hobby aquarium tank can potentially work well in a small aquaponic system.

If you already have an aquarium and are thinking of converting it to the fish-tank portion of an aquaponics system, I recommend you get the grow bed cycled using a bucket of water as a surrogate fish tank. As discussed in Chapter 10, add ammonia and cycle the system until you no longer see ammonia or nitrite showing up on the water tests. When the grow bed is fully cycled after a few weeks, adjust the pH and temperature of the water bucket and your fish tank until the two match. Then remove the bucket and connect the cycled grow bed to your fish tank.

Tilapia

Tilapia are inexpensive if you buy them in bulk. They prefer water temperatures of 70° to 86°F, and most species of tilapia will die if water temperatures fall below 60° F. Tilapia are omnivorous and were domesticated during ancient times in lands bordering the eastern Mediterranean Sea. There are now over 80 varieties of tilapia around the world.

Tilapia are very prolific—when females are as young as 11 weeks old they start to lay eggs, which they will continue to do every two months as long as the water is warm enough. If the 200 to 1,000 eggs are fertilized, the female gathers the eggs in her mouth and broods them there until they hatch. Once the fry are able to swim about, the female resumes eating until she has another fertilized set of eggs to protect. Because the females are constantly brooding, they tend not to gain as much weight as males. Females and their young are associated with overcrowding and stunting in the rest of the population, making male fish highly desired.

Tilapia can grow from fingerling to plate size in nine months, making tilapia a favorite fish for aquaponics—but only where it is legal.
(Photo courtesy of Pat Chiu)

Males can be created using a variety of methods. The most natural is to cross female Mozambique tilapia with male Zanzibar tilapia. Another method is to bathe the newly spawned fish in hormones like testosterone, reversing the sex of the female fish. An alternate method of controlling population is to crowd the fish so they are less likely to breed. Tilapia may also kept in nets suspended over the bottom of the fish tank, so that any eggs released by females are unlikely to be fertilized and, in any case, will not be able to be collected by the female for brooding.

Tilapia kept in warm water gain weight rapidly, growing to plate size in as little as nine months. Tilapia flesh is white and relatively flavorless, allowing tilapia to be successfully used as a protein base in a wide range of dishes.

Because tilapia are so prolific yet temperature sensitive, they can significantly disrupt local ecosystems if they're released into the wild. Tilapia are illegal in much of Australia and are illegal or highly regulated in many portions of the United States. On the good side, there is a wealth of information available on tilapia and aquaponics. Tilapia will eat commercial fish food and just about anything else you might choose to put in the tank. If you have warm conditions and the laws allow it, tilapia is one of the best fish to use for aquaponics.

Pacu (*Colossoma macropomum*)

Pacu prefer water temperatures of 73° to 82°F and grow to be extremely large—up to 3 feet long and 55 pounds in the wild. Pacu are a gentle Brazilian fish with straight, human-like teeth. They are primarily vegetarian.

Theodore Roosevelt wrote that pacu were "good-sized, deep-bodied fish" and "delicious eating." Wild stocks of pacus are overfished; they are preyed upon by subsistence fishers, commercial fishers, and sportsmen. Pacu make an excellent fish for warm-water tanks due to their ability to tolerate poor water conditions and their primarily vegetarian diet. The flavor of farmed pacu is comparable to hybrid striped bass, tilapia, and rainbow trout.

Pacu require very large tanks due to their colossal size. Though they are peaceful, it is better to keep them in a separate tank from much smaller fish.

DID YOU KNOW ...

Many hobbyists decide to discard their pacu when the fish grow too large. If your local fish store sells pacu, ask if they know of any owners looking to give their pet another home. For more information on encouraging responsible consumer behavior toward fish, visit habitattitude.net, a website for aquarium hobbyists and pond owners sponsored by U.S. Fish and Wildlife Service.

Australian Fish

Aquaponics became particularly popular in Australia in 2006, after the popular TV show *Gardening Australia* aired a tour of hobbyist Joel Malcolm's backyard paradise. Australia is relatively close to the equator, and most towns enjoy warm weather year round. Joel has since founded the website/magazine/store front/forum known as Backyard Aquaponics. Backyard Aquaponics is a leading reason for the popularity of aquaponics. The following types of fish are available in Australia and are featured in various articles and videos you will come across, even if you don't happen to live in Australia.

The popularity of aquaponics in Australia means Australian fish are often discussed in online aquaponics forums. Popular species include jade perch (top, held by Murray Hallam), silver perch (middle), and barramundi (bottom).
(Photo courtesy of Murray Hallam, Colin Wilson, and Ecofilms)

All these fish are weaned at the hatchery to commercial feed, usually high-protein pellets. If you wanted to raise any of these Australian fish species, check to see if they can be legally kept in your area. If they're not prohibited and if you live near a major airport, hatcheries like Ausyfish (www.ausyfish.com) are happy to ship them to you.

Barramundi (*Lates calcarife*)

Barramundi are native to Southeast Asia and northern Australia. They prefer water temperatures of 78° to 86°F. Barramundi are large, tasty fish also known as Asian sea bass. Barramundi usually only grow to be a couple of feet long and about 6 pounds.

Barramundi produce a lot of waste, and they like clean, moving water. Even in media-based systems, it is usually necessary to add a swirl filter to make sure the water stays adequately clear. It is also necessary to divert part of the pump outflow to the fish tank to keep the water moving enough to keep the barramundi happy. Barramundi will eat their tank mates, so for every 100 fish you might start with, you can expect to lose 20 to 30 as food to their mates.

Silver Perch (*Bidyanus bidyanus*)

Silver perch are native to southeastern Australia and prefer water temperatures around 75°F. Nearly extinct in the wild, in captivity they usually reach mature size at 3 pounds and 12 inches long.

Silver perch are bred extensively in aquaculture. Farmed fingerlings are weaned to commercial feed and can be purchased relatively inexpensively in Australia.

Jade Perch (*Scortum barcoo*)

Another native to Australia, the jade perch has an iridescent skin marked with characteristic dark splotches. They prefer water temperatures around 77°F but will tolerate temperatures up to 104°F. Jade perch is a freshwater finfish frequently found in aquaponic gardens in its native northern Australia. Like silver perch, jade perch in captivity usually reach mature size at 3 pounds and 12 inches long. Farmed jade perch fingerlings are weaned to pellets early in life and can be purchased from Australian hatcheries like Ausyfish.

SOUNDS FISHY

Studies show silver perch and jade perch are unusually high in omega-3 fatty acids. The health benefits of fish oil were first hypothesized during the 1970s when scientists tried to determine why Greenland Inuit people didn't suffer from heart disease. The omega-3 fatty acids that suppress heart disease come from the algae and plankton fish eat in the wild. So you need to feed your fish a diet high in omega-3 fatty acids (flax, algae, plankton) for your fish to be high in omega-3 fatty acids.

Murray Cod (*Maccullochella peelii*)

Murray cod are native to southeastern Australia and prefer water temperatures around 75°F. They are touted as excellent eating fish. The number of Murray cod in the wild has declined sharply in recent years. Fish raised in tanks are usually harvested when are plate sized, just over a pound. Murray cod are a fast-growing fish and are best grown in densely stocked tanks to prevent territorial aggressive behavior.

Sleepy Cod (*Oxyeleotris lineolatus*)

Sleepy cod are native to tropical regions of northern Australia. They prefer water temperatures around 77°F but will tolerate higher temperatures. Sleepy cod generally weigh no more than 6 pounds and live in oxbow lakes and slow-moving water in rivers and creeks.

Sleepy cod are highly prized as eating fish, with white flaky flesh that is mild and low in fat. They do better in tanks, and should be kept crowded and well fed for best growth rates.

The Least You Need to Know

- Use freshwater fish since most vegetables and fruits can't grow in saltwater.
- Know what fish are legal in your community and available in your country. There are substantial fines in some places for keeping fish without a proper license.
- Goldfish and koi can be excellent fish for aquaponics, but they shouldn't be eaten since they may have been treated with chemicals that cause cancer in humans.
- Pond fish like catfish and bluegill will thrive in a wide range of temperatures and make an excellent choice for an outdoor garden in North America.
- Cool-water fish can't survive in warm water (above 65°F). As long as you must keep the water cool for your fish, plan to grow cool-weather crops like spinach.
- Warm-water fish can't survive in cool water (below 70°F). As long as you must heat your fish tank, plan to grow warm-weather plants.

Other Useful Animals

In This Chapter

- All about beneficial worms
- The good guys: black soldier flies
- Helpful honeybees
- What chickens, ducks, and quail can do for your aquaponic garden
- Freshwater shellfish to add to your garden

Aquaponics mainly involves fish, but there are other animals that you might find useful to include in your garden system. Adding other animals to the mix will make your garden more complex. But if you are creating an aquaponic garden as part of an overall focus on sustainability, the addition of other animals can help you get rid of waste, supply you and your fish with other sources of protein, and help control pests.

Composting Worms

Composting worms are the fabulous creatures that transform your kitchen scraps into worm castings—the bacteria-rich black gold worshipped by so many gardeners. They can eat their weight in decomposing food in as little as two days. As the rotten waste travels through a worm's gut, it is cleansed of fungus and dangerous bacteria.

Red Worms vs. Burrowing Worms

Most species of earthworms can't tolerate warmth or crowding, so it takes special worms to handle the high worm densities and warm conditions you'll have when worms are composting rotting food.

Red wigglers and European nightcrawlers are two of the worm species that are adapted to composting scraps. They both tolerate temperatures from freezing all the way up to 95°F, but they prefer temperatures between 55° and 77°F. The popularity of composting has created a market for these worms, and they can be purchased from online vendors who will ship bags of several hundred or even several thousand worms. There are numerous websites and books discussing worm composting. Three popular websites for composting worms are www.redwormcomposting.com, garden-worms.com, and unclejimswormfarm.com (see Appendix B for details).

Worms adapted to breaking down compost are different from the earthworms you find in most gardens. Composting worms like these red wigglers can be purchased from online sources.

What Worms Eat

Worms eat the microbes that decompose organic matter. But worms definitely have preferences when it comes to what decomposing trash they will eat.

Worms prefer the kinds of food they would encounter on a forest floor. Rotting vegetables and fruit are prime eating. Leaves and seeds also fall into this category, though the leaves and seeds a composting worm might get from your kitchen would likely be from tea bags or coffee grounds. Worms deal well with crushed eggshells and particularly enjoy aged manure. In fact, red wigglers are also known as manure worms.

Worms don't like processed foods that are starchy, sweet, or oily. Too much pasta, bread, and rice may cause a worm bin to stink, as will oily, spicy, or sugary foods. Worms are also indifferent about citrus and grass clippings. Citrus oil kills bacteria, and both citrus fruit and grass clippings are more acidic than worms prefer.

SOUNDS FISHY

Composting toilets are all the rage and are even endorsed by high-profile celebrities—but don't feed composting worms human or pet waste. Composting worms do well in the manure of plant-eating animals like rabbits and chickens, where the waste is mostly high-fiber decomposing vegetation. The waste of omnivores like humans, cats, and dogs attracts flies and maggots, not composting worms.

Worm Reproduction and Harvesting

A population of composting worms can double in size every month under the right conditions. If the worms feel too crowded, they simply won't reproduce, so you don't have to worry about having population overload with your worms.

To harvest worms, tumble compost from the top 6 inches of your worm bin in a basket of $1/2$-inch wire mesh. The compost will fall out, leaving the worms behind. Alternately, you can shine a light on the compost and gradually pull off the outer layers of compost as the worms burrow deeper and deeper, away from the light. Eventually you'll get a pile that is made up of more worms that it is compost.

How Worms Help Your Aquaponic Garden

My favorite way to use composting worms is to simply let them loose in my grow beds. They will go about their business eating decay within the bed and breeding to capacity. In the process they will produce worm castings, which will naturally dissolve into the water, flooding the grow beds and draining into the fish tank. The beneficial bacteria from the worm castings will naturally infuse the grow beds as a result.

As discussed in Chapter 13, you can also gather worm castings from the bottom of a worm bin and create worm tea.

Black Soldier Flies

Black soldier flies are very beneficial because of their ability to consume food waste and the high-protein feed their larvae provide for reptiles and fish.

Unlike pest flies, the black soldier fly doesn't have mouthparts once it becomes an adult. Adult black soldier flies only live 5 days. It's nearly impossible to get an infestation of black soldier flies because they aren't adults for long and they hate being inside. The larval form of black soldier fly is the more interesting thing for an aquaponic gardener.

Black Soldier Fly Larvae

The larvae or grubs of the black soldier fly are high in calcium and are sold as reptile food under the name Phoenix Worms. They contain high levels of protein and fat and a high concentrations of nutrients.

They can compost decaying waste before it starts to rot, which reduces the greenhouse gas created by food waste in landfills and compost bins. A population of black soldier fly larvae can consume up to 3 pounds of waste per square foot each day, reducing the volume of the waste by up to 95 percent. The waste you put into a black soldier fly larvae bin will come out as high-protein, high-fat, high-nutrition grubs.

DID YOU KNOW ...

Black soldier flies are useful in forensic pathology because they are so predictable in their habits and lifestyle. When you see those fancy CSI detectives on TV studying bugs, they are probably studying black soldier flies.

Harvesting the Larvae

When black soldier fly larvae are done growing, they stop eating for about a week. Their mouthparts transform into climbing tools and they climb upwards, seeking a dry place to transform into the next stage of their existence.

When you have a properly designed bin, the mature larvae harvest themselves, climbing up a shallow incline and dropping into a drawer or trough below. You can purchase a black soldier fly larvae bin such as the BioPod. There are also DIY designs available online.

Attracting Black Soldier Flies

If you live in a warm climate, all you need to do is set up a bin. The female black soldier fly is looking for a textured surface suspended over rotting material for her eggs. A short roll of corrugated cardboard stuffed into a tuna fish can and fastened to the lid covering the compost bin would be ideal. Black soldier flies in the area will find your bin and populate it.

Dr. Radu Popa and Dr. Terry Green of Oregon State University have developed a black soldier fly nursery design that allows people to nurture a black soldier fly colony inside in colder climates. Their website (dipterra.com) contains a wealth of information on how to cultivate and care for black soldier flies for processing organic wastes. See Appendix B for more information.

This simple chest in Hawaii is used to convert household food scraps, including milk and meat, into high-protein black soldier fly larvae for feeding fish. The larvae harvest themselves into the two drawers (see detail).

(Photo courtesy of Raychel Watkins)

Honeybees

Humans have kept bees for thousands of years for their honey and to improve the yield of crops. Urban beekeeping has become increasingly acceptable, with cities like Paris; Berlin; London; Tokyo; Philadelphia; and Washington, D.C., explicitly legalizing beekeeping.

Honeybee colonies have been collapsing at an alarming rate in the past decade, with bee populations plummeting by as much as 90 percent in some areas. Adding a small bee colony to your household garden will improve not only your garden but also the gardens of your neighbors.

Bees generally keep to themselves unless you threaten them. Bees fly straight, so if you place the hive so the bees have to fly up to leave your yard, they may never even come in contact with your neighbors. If you want to learn more, I recommend you visit bushfarms.com, the website for Michael Bush, author of *The Practical Beekeeper*. See Appendix B for more information.

GREEN TIP

Honeybees need water in warm weather. Suburban and urban beekeepers are advised to provide well-aged (chlorine-free) water for their bees. An aquaponic garden provides a great source of chlorine-free water for bees. But bees don't like water to be too close to their hive. If you have a beehive, put it about 20 feet away from the fish tank or sump from which the bees might try to drink.

Chickens, Ducks, and Quail

Chickens, ducks, and quail can introduce rich diversity to food you get from your garden. You do have to be careful, however. Birds are warm-blooded animals, so they frequently harbor *E. coli* and salmonella bacteria in their intestines. You will need to keep your birds away from your aquaponic garden to prevent these dangerous bacteria from contaminating it.

It is illegal to feed an animal grubs that have fed on that same kind of animal. Keeping a different sort of animal, like chickens, allows you to feed grubs that consume the fish waste to the birds, and then feed the grubs that consume the chicken waste to the fish.

Chickens can be kept in a rolling cage or chicken tractor that lets them forage on different parts of your property. Chickens particularly like dandelion leaves.

Shellfish

Shellfish are scavengers and can help keep your tanks clean. They can also be fun to eat—either for you or for your fish, depending on their size. Since they are crustaceans, they don't go through the complicated transformations insects do. They simply hatch from an egg, grow big, and die. There are three types of freshwater shellfish you can add to an aquaponic system: scuds, shrimp, and crayfish.

Scuds or Gammarus

Scuds or gammarus are shrimp-like crustaceans only a fraction of an inch long. They eat waste products in your system and make the nutrients water soluble.

Trout particularly love scuds. However, in some gardens, the scuds can become so numerous that they start feeding on the plant roots and the foam of floating rafts.

Freshwater Shrimp and Crayfish

Shrimp and crayfish can be grown in aquaponic systems either in sump tanks or under floating rafts where they can help clean up sludge that can develop in floating raft grow beds and sump tanks.

Marmorkrebs are a strain of crayfish some aquaponic gardeners favor because each individual can reproduce by itself—there's no need to worry about maintaining balanced populations of male and female animals. But some localities have banned, fearing the potential of an invasive wild population.

The Least You Need to Know

- You can use worms to create compost tea for your garden, and worms will thrive in media grow beds.
- Black soldier fly larvae can compost a wide range of foods and make an excellent food for fish, reptiles, and birds.
- Adding chickens, ducks, or quail to your garden ecosystem can improve the diversity of your diet and the biological diversity of your home food production system.
- Shellfish like scuds, shrimp, and crayfish will eat the sludge that can develop in floating rafts and sump tanks. Some gardeners even raise crayfish and shrimp for food.

Taking Care of Your Fish

In This Chapter

- What to know about caring for your fish
- Treating sick fish
- Dealing with dead or dying fish
- Have your fish and eat it, too

Most people haven't had the opportunity to raise large fish that could be used for food. And despite the popularity of fishing as a hobby, some of us don't have a clue how to turn a living fish into a meal.

If you are considering breeding fish or raising fish on a large scale, I highly recommend you seek formal training or expert consultants. But this chapter provides basic instructions on fish that should be sufficient for a backyard gardener.

The Basics of Fish Life

You've cycled your system, and you've selected the type of fish you wanted to raise. You've applied for a permit, if required. You've done a bit of research and know what your fish are able to eat. You have most likely identified a store or hatchery that can provide you sizeable fingerlings.

If your fish are unlikely to breed, sigh with relief and skip to the next section. But if your fish are breeders, let's talk about the breeding process and its consequences.

The Birds and the Bees of Fish

Fish can be either live-bearers or egg-layers. Some, like salmon, spawn infrequently. Others, like tilapia, breed early and often.

If your fish are live-bearers, the pregnant fish will begin to swell as the young grow within her. They will remain inside until they are large enough to survive on their own—usually a month after the eggs are fertilized. Guppies are an example of a live-bearing fish.

There are different kinds of egg-layers. Some fish scatter their eggs, some spawn in a nest that they then guard, and still others collect the eggs in their mouths. The egg-scattering fish usually come from rivers and streams, where creating a nest or gathering the eggs after spawning simply isn't an option. Because these fish can't protect or nurture their spawn, they never developed the instinct to avoid eating their own spawn. One small fish is like another, and for a carnivorous or omnivorous fish, little fishies are food, first and foremost.

A net cage allows fingerlings to share the same water as your larger fish but avoid becoming a meal. This cage is improvised from a pool noodle, a mesh laundry bag, and a circle of flooded hose.

The nest-building fish will fight to protect their nest and the fry (tiny baby fish) that emerge. However, only the parents will protect young of the species. The rest of the fish will snap up the eggs, fry, and fingerlings for dinner, given a chance.

The mouth-brooders are almost like live-bearers. They will hold the eggs and tiny fish inside their mouths until the fry are large enough to survive. Female fish who *brood* their young in their mouths will be unable to eat during that time, so they tend to be smaller over time than the males.

DEFINITION

Brood means to protect eggs. A hen broods eggs by sitting on them in a nest; a fish broods eggs by holding them in its mouth.

Feeding Baby Fish

Baby fish (fry or fingerlings) can only eat small food. However, they need to feed frequently, and they also need to eat a large amount of food—as much as 30 percent of their body weight each day when they first emerge.

If you have a new tank and have purchased fry, you may need to feed them powdered flakes as often as eight times a day. You should not feed the fish more than they can consume in three to five minutes.

Some omnivorous fish will breed and feed successfully in shallow tanks covered in duckweed. For fry that eat duckweed, they always have a source of food close by, which can reduce your effort significantly.

If you are purchasing fry to save money, consider the value of your time and the fragility of such tiny fish in a new tank. I recommend a new aquaponic gardener purchase large fingerlings that can make do with inexpensive pond food fed to them once or twice a day. I would also recommend starting with a fish that is well known in aquaponic circles. There are several active aquaponic forums on the internet, and the people on the forums are willing to share lessons from their mistakes. They will be able to recommend foods and techniques for your fish of choice, and this kind of information may already exist in the archives of the site, making finding advice as simple as searching the web. I list some aquaponics forums in Appendix B.

Preventing Fish from Breeding

Some folks select a fish because it breeds easily. Tilapia and bluegill are in this category (see Chapter 15 for more on both). In nature these prolific breeders serve a distinct purpose—their eggs and fingerlings make delicious food for carnivorous fish higher up the food chain.

But in an unbalanced system that lacks predators, the younger fish overpopulate the space, leaving less space and food for the mature fish. The competition for resources stunts all the fish, leaving you with many fish that are small. If your plan is to eat the fish when they mature, a school of stunted fish can be a problem.

If you only stock male fish, you won't have to worry about breeding. Depending on your species of choice, there are various natural and unnatural ways to end up with predominantly male fish. But even if you think your school of fish is all male, you may come in one morning and find baby fish. It's just not that easy to tell male fish and female fish apart or guarantee that all the fish in a batch are actually male.

Physically crowding your fish can reduce breeding behavior and aggression. I think of it as the fish equivalent of being in an elevator—they mostly stay quiet and mind their own business. You can physically crowd your fish and maintain healthy stocking densities by corralling the fish in a mesh cage within the fish tank.

If your fish are mouth-brooders, like tilapia, the eggs can fall through the bottom of the netting. Even if these eggs are successfully fertilized, the female will be unable to reach the eggs to gather them in her mouth, and they will fail to develop.

If you want to use mesh cages to physically crowd your fish and prevent successful reproduction, make sure the gaps in the mesh are large enough to let the eggs fall through. The eggs will become part of the biological waste stream fertilizing your garden. If you have an omnivorous bottom feeder in the tank, the eggs will be a tasty addition to their diet.

When Fish Are Sick

Fish can fall ill just like any other animal. If this happens, you need to take care that the remedy is nontoxic. Even if you don't plan to eat your fish, the water you medicate will be drawn up into the plants. Luckily, there are a few things you can do to help out a sick fish that don't involve toxic chemicals.

DID YOU KNOW ...

Disease outbreaks in aquaculture have caused significant loss. For example, the global shrimp industry lost $5 billion in 1992 from a single viral outbreak. One prominent tilapia supplier protects his fish by meeting fish-hauling trucks a mile away from his facility, maintaining strict quarantine protocols, and following thorough disinfection procedures.

Here are some recommendations for avoiding problems in the first place:

- Get your fish from a reputable dealer who can certify the fish are free of parasites and disease.

- Never dump water from new fish into your tank.

- Quarantine new fish until you are certain they are not diseased.

- Don't put too many fish in your system. Even though you might physically crowd your fish to prevent aggressive behavior, make sure you start off with no more than one fish for every cubic foot of grow bed volume. A cubic foot is 7½ gallons or 30 liters.

- Don't overfeed your fish.

- Measure your water chemistry frequently and treat any problems before they kill your fish.

- Protect your fish from predators, sharp edges, and their own ability to escape uncovered tanks.

If your fish become ill despite all your precautions, here are some remedies for illness.

Salt

Salt is sometimes referred to as the aspirin of aquaculture. Salt can treat many external parasites and infections. It is also effective for nitrite poisoning and reducing stress when you are transporting or handling your fish. Use pool salt, rock salt, or sea salt. Do not use iodized table salt.

GREEN TIP

How can you tell if a fish is stressed? It won't take long before you're able to recognize casual, happy behavior. When your fish are skittish, swimming funny, or just not acting normal, you'll be able to tell something is wrong.

There are various ways to use salt. You can add a tiny amount of salt to a fish tank indefinitely to prevent nitrite poisoning. A bit more will protect against parasites and fungal infection. You can put sick fish in a moderate solution for 30 minutes or in a strong solution for 15 seconds.

Recommended Amounts of Salt to Treat Fish

Illness	Time	Weight per 100 Gallons
Nitrite poisoning	Indefinite	0.3 oz
Parasites	Indefinite	13.5 oz
Transport and handling stress	Indefinite (for holding tanks)	13.5–135 oz or 0.85–8.5 lbs
Parasites	30 minutes or until fish show signs of stress	8.5–25 lbs
External parasites in new fish stocks	15 seconds	25 lbs

When newbies complain about dying and diseased fish on aquaponics forums, you will often see experienced aquaponic gardeners recommend adding 6 kilograms of salt per 1,000 liters of water to treat the sick fish, equivalent to about 5 pounds per 100 gallons. This is an amount recommended to calm fish after transport and handling stress. Unfortunately, this much salt can kill plants that don't tolerate salt, like strawberries.

GREEN TIP

When treating your fish, use pure salt that doesn't have additives like iodine or anti-caking chemicals. One of the cheapest alternatives is the salt sold to soften water in filtration systems. This salt is usually 99.6 percent pure and evaporated using only sun and wind. A 40-pound bag can cost less than $6.

The salt solution can also be created in a small tank that is not connected to your aquaponics system. This allows you to use high concentrations of salt for a short time to kill bacteria and parasites that might survive prolonged exposure to a weaker solution.

Hospital Tank

There are times when you want to treat a fish but may not want to add salt to your system. A hospital tank can be made from a 20-gallon plastic tub. Fill the tub with water from your main tank. This will keep the pH, ammonia, nitrite, and nitrate levels constant to reduce stress on your fish. Next, add an air stone to keep the water oxygenated and moving. Finally, add the recommended amount of salt for the amount of water you have in the tub.

Once all the salt crystals have dissolved, you can place your fish in the hospital tank for the recommended amount of time, making sure the air stone is in a position to add oxygen.

To reduce stress on your fish, you can create a basket or net cage. This would be most helpful if you plan to treat the fish periodically, as might be the case for newly purchased fingerlings. The new fish would remain in the basket or net cage during the week, endure a short dip in the hospital tank, and return to the main tank. I've used a pool noodle (extruded closed cell foam) to keep the cage floating and form the upper rim of the cage. This also served to protect the small fingerlings from their larger tank mates.

Potassium Permanganate

Another effective antiseptic treatment is potassium permanganate ($KMnO_4$) or Condy's Crystals. This compound was first marketed as a disinfectant in the 1800s by London chemist Henry Condy. In subsequent decades, Condy's Crystals were widely used to treat fungal infections in humans and to disinfect water supplies. People used to gargle with a solution of Condy's Crystals to cure a sore throat.

If you can get the crystalline form of potassium permanganate (available online), add ½ teaspoon to 250 gallons of water. Since the crystals themselves can burn the skin of humans and fish, it's a good idea to wear gloves and mix the crystals with water in a bucket before adding them to the system.

Potassium permanganate turns water bright purple, but the color will go away within a day when exposed to sunlight. A weak solution of potassium permanganate can also be used on your plants to treat various fungus conditions.

When Fish Die

Sometimes fish die, despite the best attempts to cure them. Even when you don't think you're attached to your fish, it can be distressing. If you've named the fish and developed a real fondness for them, it can be heartbreaking.

Not Dead ... Yet

Sometimes you find a fish that is still alive, but so badly damaged or ulcerated that it's clear it can't recover. I've read that fish don't have the same kind of nervous system that mammals have. This is supposed to be why it isn't inhumane to steam a lobster while it's still alive.

However, it isn't a great idea to leave a dying fish in the tank. If it has parasites or an infection, the ailment could be transmitted to your other fish. Even if the fish is merely dying of old age or physical damage, a newly dead fish will sink to the bottom of the tank and start decomposing, increasing ammonia levels to potentially toxic levels.

If you wish to put the fish out if its misery, there are a few recommended techniques. If you don't feel able to do any of these, you might want to net the fish into a floating cage so you can easily retrieve it when it's actually dead. The swift, humane techniques are as follows:

- Use a sharp knife to cut off the fish's head.

- Put the fish in a small volume of water to which you've added a lethal dose of clove oil (25 drops per liter).

- Hit the fish hard with a blunt object on the back just behind the eyes. A hammer or wrench works well.

Fish advocates say it is cruel to boil, freeze, or suffocate a fish. The boiling and freezing create a phase change of the liquid in the fish's flesh, rupturing the fish's internal organs. Suffocation is an unpleasant death, which your fish will demonstrate by flopping around in a desperate attempt to get back into the water. According to the Humane Slaughter Association, live chilling in ice water is also deemed inhumane.

Diagnosing the Problem

It's a good idea to identify the cause of death while you still have the evidence before you. If you find a dry, stiff, but unbitten fish out of water, there still may be hope. Put it in the water and run oxygenated water through its mouth and over the gills. Koi-keepers often keep a bottle of steroids on hand to help revive expensive fish that are teetering on the brink of death after jumping out of the pond.

If there are strange-looking marks, bumps, or patches on the fish, you are likely dealing with parasites or fungal infections. You can take a picture of these and post them on aquaponics forums to get confirmation. It may be a good idea to give your remaining fish a quick salt dip while you are awaiting confirmation of the problem.

If you see no physical cause of death, test your water. Is the ammonia high? Is the pH the same as it has been for previous tests? Is the temperature in the range that is comfortable for your fish? If the water is not right, fix it to protect your other fish.

If you can't see any marks of disease on the fish and your water is fine, your fish may have suffered physical injury. Other fish may have attacked the fish, or you may have something in your tank that caused the fish to damage itself.

SOUNDS FISHY

It's pleasant to leave your tank open, but an open tank allows your fish to jump out and allows predators to grab your fish for a quick meal. If a raccoon can get a fish, he will eat it like a corncob. Cranes will snag koi if the lip of an open pond is less than 24 inches above the surface of the water.

What to Do with the Remains

Relatively few people feel comfortable eating a fish from their system unless they killed it themselves on purpose, but raccoons, cats, and bears might not be so picky. It's a good idea to dispose of your dead fish in a hygienic and socially acceptable manner. Some possible options are as follows:

- Bury the remains. Fish can be great fertilizer for your soil garden. The Pilgrim settlers in Massachusetts allegedly learned to fertilize their corn crops by placing a small fish at the bottom of the planting hole. If you do this, make sure the burial site is protected from dogs and other animals.

- If you have a compost tumbler, compost the remains. Add plenty of organic material to form a heated compost pile. Turn the compost and water it daily to help break down the remains in the compost pile effectively.

- Put the fish remains in your black soldier fly larvae container. Black soldier fly larvae will eat just about anything. There should be no problem feeding the larvae to the fish later. After all, most fish eat fish of their own species, so they won't recognize that any of the larvae protein originally came from a former tank mate. But if the idea makes you queasy or if local legislation prohibits feeding an animal a bug that fed on that sort of animal, you can always feed the black soldier fly from that bin to another type of animal, like chickens or ducks. See Chapter 16 for more about black soldier fly larvae.

- If the fish merely died, you might have an animal or flock that would happily feed on the remains in lieu of their normal feed.

- You can simply wrap the remains up the way you would with any meat gone bad and put it in the trash.

Cleaning Your System

In the worst case, you may discover the dead fish has contaminated your entire system to a degree that other fish in the tank are threatened. If you suspect this could be the case, send a sample of the dead fish to a reputable organization that can test your fish and verify your concern. Your local college biology department or department of natural resources should be able to point you in the right direction. While you're waiting for an answer, don't rush to disinfect your system. If the test indicates you will need to disinfect your system, see if the testing organization can tell you the least intrusive method that is appropriate.

Your grow beds should be full of the gentle, slow-growing bacteria that convert ammonia to nitrate. Aggressive measures to disinfect your system may be unnecessary and even harmful. Additionally, cleansing your system may kill any worms you might have added to your grow beds. But there are a few options that are minimally invasive to your system if your worst fears are confirmed by laboratory tests on your dead fish:

- Add salt to your system, or use salt baths or dips. This will protect your fish despite the presence of the contamination.

- Disinfect your system with potassium permanganate, as discussed earlier in this chapter.

Several of the following measures presume the contamination is so severe that you've had to get rid of your fish:

- After removing the diseased fish, put the water coming into your fish tank through an ultraviolet sterilizer. Over time, this will kill the harmful bacteria in your fish water without bothering the beneficial bacteria and worms in your grow beds.

- Disinfect your system with food-grade hydrogen peroxide. Simply immerse and scrub down everything with the stuff.

> **SOUNDS FISHY**
>
> Cleaning a tank with chemicals like bleach and baking soda, which are very alkaline, can leave residues that could harm your future fish and plants. Use more neutral chemicals like salt, potassium permanganate, or food-grade hydrogen peroxide.

Eating Your Fish

In the best possible world, the only dead fish you will see are the ones you dispatch in preparation for eating them. If you are an experienced fisherman, you already know how to do this. But in case you are clueless and would still like a fish dinner, here are a few tips on how to proceed.

Catching Fish

Your fish are in the proverbial barrel. You wouldn't think it would be hard to catch them, but fish can be downright canny at avoiding capture. These tips help make the task easier:

- Make sure you have a sufficiently large net. If your tank has a flat bottom, I recommend a large-mesh net with a flat edge. The large mesh size will allow water to pass through your net easily, and the flat bottom will prevent your fish from escaping the net. If you can catch a good-sized fish on the first try, it will be less stressful for everyone.

- Make sure you have enough light to see the fish. If you can see which fish you're trying to catch and have a bit of patience, you're less likely to come up empty-handed.

- Be prepared to quickly toss back in any fish you don't plan to cook immediately. This ordeal will stress them, and you don't want to prolong their stress.

Some folks catch their fish a week or so before they plan to eat them. The fish are placed in a separate tank where they are left unfed to purge the fish flesh of odors and flavors from the fish feed. Mature fish can go for several days without needing to eat.

Dispatching Fish

Now you've got your fish. How to kill it?

Most folks use a blunt object to hit the fish on the head, quickly killing them. If you can hold your fish in place, you can whack it in the brain, which is on the top of its head right behind the eyes. If you're not sure the fish is actually dead, roll it about in your hands. If the blow was effective, the eyes won't move as you roll the fish. To ensure a humane death, you can also simply cut off the fish's head.

Cleaning Fish

The method you use to clean your fish will depend on how you plan to cook the fish and the kind of fish you are cleaning. A popular video on YouTube shows marine biologist John Kimble learning how to clean a perch in 10 seconds from legendary fisherman Costa. Costa makes a slice on either side of the dorsal fin along the length of the fish. Then he quickly slips all the nonedible parts off the outside of the perch. If this method of cleaning fish works for your type of fish, the traditionally messy chore of cleaning fish will be a snap. This method works best for long, slender fish rather than short, pan-shaped fish. It also wouldn't work well for catfish.

If you need to clean a fish using the traditional method, cover an outside table with newspaper. Place the fish on the paper. With a dull knife or inverted spoon, scrape the fish from the tail toward the head with short strokes. The scales should fly off if you are using adequate pressure. Be careful around the fins, as these can puncture you. Scaling a fish under water will prevent the scattered scales from creating a huge mess.

To gut the fish, place the fish on its back. Insert a sharp fish knife in the hole on the fish's bottom side near the tail (the anus) and slice up toward the head with a shallow cut. You want to slice through the skin and initial layer of flesh, but avoid puncturing the gut containing partially digested food. Spread the abdominal cavity open and pull out the entrails.

To remove the head, cut the fish on either side behind the gills and snap off the head. This will maximize the amount of flesh left on the fish.

Filleting Fish

There are methods of filleting fish that remove the skin, entrails, head, and bones, eliminating the need to clean the fish. If you have access to YouTube, there are numerous videos that show how this is done. I like to see how chefs fillet fish, since they are practiced at doing this for a picky customer in an environment where waste is unacceptable and time is of the essence.

Here are the basic steps:

1. Using a fillet knife, cut behind the gill down to the spine.

2. Turn the fillet knife parallel to the spine. Slice down the length of the fish along the spine.

3. Place the bulk of the fish to the side while you complete the fillet you've just cut off the main body.

4. Place the fillet so the meat side is up. Poke a hole in the tail portion of the fillet so you can get a firm grasp on the fillet.

5. Put your thumb into the hole you've cut into the tail.

6. Remove the skin from the fillet by slicing down through the fish flesh next to your thumb. Once you have cut through the fillet to the skin, turn the knife blade away from your thumb. Slice along the inside of the skin, just above the surface of the cutting board.

7. Trim away any residual bone, fin, or gut and discard.

8. Bring the bulk of the fish back onto the board with the spine side up.

9. Holding the fish by the head, cut just barely through the spine.

10. Turn the knife and slice carefully along the length of the fish, just deep enough to remove the spine and bones. And the end of the fish, cut downward to remove the tail.

11. Cut off the head. Discard the bones and head.

12. Remove the skin from this second fillet in the same manner as you did the first time.

SOUNDS FISHY

Never use a dull knife to kill or fillet your fish. Dull knives are far more dangerous that sharp knives. Ideally, purchase a flexible knife designed specifically for cutting fillets. Never use your fillet knife to cut fishing line or rope, or to cut through fish skin and bones, as this will dull the blade.

If you scale the fish before filleting it, you don't have to skin the fillet. The skin on the fillet will crisp up nicely and make the cooked fish look and taste great.

Some fish have a double rib cage that can leave small pin bones in the flesh. You can squeeze the flesh of the fish and make these pin bones stick out enough to remove them with tweezers, or you can let each individual diner pick the bones out themselves.

Cooking Fish

There are many ways to cook fish. The rule of thumb is to cook fish for only 10 minutes per inch of thickness. If you steam fish, it will cook even more quickly. Whether baking, steaming, grilling, or microwaving, you will know the fish is done when the flesh is no longer translucent and flakes easily. When in doubt, take the fish off the heat a bit early and allow the residual heat in the fish to complete the cooking.

Don't marinate fish for more than 30 minutes. Acids in the marinade break down the delicate fish protein. Don't overcook fish either, as this will make the fish hard and rubbery. It's always best to undercook fish slightly and allow the heat in the fish to finish the cooking process after you've taken the fish off the stove.

Canning fish is another option, particularly if you have a lot of tiny fish. This will allow you to preserve your fish for a time in the year when you might not be so keen on netting something out of the tank. It also allows you to use small fish more effectively, since you can leave the flesh on the bones, which become edible as a result of the canning process. (See Chapter 15 for a recipe for canning fish.)

The Least You Need to Know

- Breeding fish can quickly overpopulate your tank and stunt the growth of all your fish.
- Salt is a great remedy for most fish ailments.
- A hospital tank can allow you to treat fish without adding salt to your plants' water.
- Kill a fish humanely by hitting it in the head with a blunt object or cutting off its head. Allowing the fish to suffocate or endure prolonged distress is considered inhumane.
- Fish will cook in about 10 minutes per inch of flesh thickness. When in doubt, you can remove the fish from the heat and allow the residual heat to complete the cooking.

Beyond the Basics

You've got your tanks, your plants, and your fish. What more could you want? Quite a bit, actually. Chapter 18 talks about different greenhouses, including inexpensive seasonal structures you can put up only when you need them. Chapter 19 covers insulation and ways to heat or cool your garden. Chapter 20 discusses how to automate tasks in your garden like feeding fish, adding water, and turning on fans when it gets too hot. Chapter 21 talks about ways you can reduce power and collect rainwater, which is useful in emergencies or if you want to put a garden in a remote location. Chapter 22 talks about basic maintenance tasks you'll need to do over time. The last two chapters discuss situations where aquaponics or aquaculture is integrated into schools and other communities to make life better and provide plans for making your own system if you are handy with tools.

Extend Your Growing Season with a Greenhouse

Chapter 18

In This Chapter

- Why you might want a greenhouse
- Features of permanent greenhouses
- Hoop houses and row covers
- The foundation and other construction considerations
- Do-it-yourself plan for a PVC hoop house

You've seen greenhouses in advertisements and catalogs. If you're like me, you probably figure greenhouses are for rich people. But I've been surprised to find that a greenhouse can actually be surprisingly affordable, whether it's a permanent addition to your property or a temporary structure you put up in the winter.

Greenhouse Pros and Cons

A greenhouse is a structure covered in plastic or glass where a gardener can control humidity and temperature to cultivate plants. There are a number of benefits from having some kind of greenhouse whether your primary garden is inside or outside.

When your garden or fish tank is inside, a greenhouse allows you to extend your garden outside and take advantage of sunlight. If your garden is outside, a greenhouse extends your growing season and protects a core portion of your garden from birds, raccoons, and other large animals.

Greenhouses may be a glass-covered addition permanently attached to your home or a freestanding structure. They can have a traditional shed-like appearance, can be sturdy geodesic domes, or can be inexpensive hoop houses. Whatever shape a greenhouse takes, it will protect your garden from the rain and dust that can disrupt the ecological balance of your system.

A greenhouse also protects your garden from wind damage and allows you to collect heat from the sun. There can be problems with a greenhouse, though, including overheating in the middle of summer, keeping wind from pollinating your plants, and deflecting rain you might need to top up your fish tank. As you can see, the same things that make a greenhouse an asset to your garden can also be problems.

GREEN TIP

Position a greenhouse on the side of your home or yard that gets sun and away from shade. This will allow the greenhouse to get the most sunlight throughout the entire day.

The Greenhouse Effect: Both Good and Bad

The greenhouse effect is caused when sunlight enters a closed space through glass or plastic windows. Light hits the air and surfaces inside the greenhouse and changes from light to heat. Heat energy can't get back out through the glass or plastic and just bounces around inside the space.

In the cool days of spring and fall, a greenhouse keeps your garden nice and warm. Depending on where you live, a greenhouse can help your garden survive through the winter. But a greenhouse can turn into an oven in the height of summer.

A Greenhouse Can Use a Lot of Energy

When you grow outside, you can take advantage of sunlight. Depending on the size of your garden and your local electricity costs, this can be a substantial savings. But if you heat or cool your greenhouse, you can end up spending a lot more money than you save on the lights you didn't have to buy.

Glass and plastic walls are not good for insulation, so your heater or air conditioner will run almost continually. It's almost like trying to heat or cool the outdoors.

Greenhouses Aren't Free

Even the simplest greenhouse will cost money. A permanent greenhouse can easily cost tens of thousands of dollars, particularly if you live in a place where a greenhouse must meet strict building codes. On the other hand, there are greenhouse options that are inexpensive and might not require building permits. Let's talk about the different kinds of greenhouses.

Permanent Greenhouses

I love a well-designed, permanent greenhouse. A permanent greenhouse is build to last for years and is often built from materials that complement your home. Such a greenhouse won't be cheap, but it can be an investment that can increase your property value, if done properly.

A permanent greenhouse can last for decades. This Victorian-style greenhouse has a powder-coated steel structure and should last for generations. I particularly like the cold frames along the front for winter vegetables.

(Photo courtesy of victoriangreenhouses.com)

Permanent greenhouses created by reputable businesses can be purchased with a wide variety of tools and fittings. Some common accessories include the following:

- Fans to both vent your garden and circulate the air for plant health

- Shade cloth to block excess sun

- Automatic window-openers

- Irrigation and misting systems designed for particular plants, like orchids

- Rain gutters and collection systems

- Window and door options to accommodate special requirements, like wheelchair accessibility

Even when you don't find the required accessories in stores, you may find communities of individuals who are invested in particular greenhouse models and who have posted tips and tricks online.

Some greenhouses are even designed to be added directly to the side of a home. This can make a greenhouse more convenient in winter by eliminating the need to go outside to enter the greenhouse. A greenhouse built onto the side of a home can also benefit from the heat or air-conditioning used to keep the home comfortable for the family, reducing heating and cooling needs.

If you aren't ready to invest in a permanent greenhouse, you might want to at least look at a greenhouse catalog. They are full of great ideas you might want to consider if you do decide to put up some kind of greenhouse.

DID YOU KNOW ...

Greenhouses were developed during the Renaissance in Italy to allow citrus trees to survive cold European winters. This was inspired by the discovery that eating citrus fruit prevents scurvy. The ability to make windows from glass was the technological breakthrough that made these early greenhouses possible.

Hobby Greenhouses

Hobby greenhouses are the utilitarian cousins of formal greenhouses. They are usually sold as kits in local stores.

These hobby greenhouses can be significantly less expensive than custom-made greenhouses with the same footprint. The kit comes with everything you need pre-cut to the proper dimensions. You can check out user reviews of hobby greenhouses before you buy to help you decide if a particular greenhouse will meet your needs. Some popular hobby greenhouses have enthusiastic owners who share ideas online for updating the hobby greenhouses.

A backyard greenhouse sold by Harbor Freight. Custom fencing and trim was added by the owner.

(Photo courtesy of Pat Chiu)

Geodesic Domes

Geodesic domes are ball-shaped buildings created from triangular sections. Domes are very stable and don't have flat edges that catch in high winds.

Geodesic domes were popularized in the mid-1900s by Buckminster Fuller, an American inventor and architect. Geodesic domes soon became popular in the western United States for gardens and temporary dwellings. Their futuristic design makes an unmistakable statement about environmental awareness, an association first established when Fuller designed the geodesic Biosphere for the 1967 International and Universal Exposition in Montreal.

Designs for geodesic domes are readily available online, and they can be made from inexpensive electrical metallic tubing (EMT) covered with construction film that has been stabilized to stand up under the ultraviolet (UV) radiation in regular sunlight. Kits are available for domes as large as 32 feet in diameter. These kits can include geothermal heating and cooling, as well as water tanks that serve as thermal batteries.

Hoop Houses

Hoop houses are bent hoops covered with plastic or vinyl that can extend for hundreds of feet. These structures can provide most of the benefits of traditional greenhouses over a vast area.

Hoop houses reduce water loss from evaporation and keep crops warm. Hoop houses extend the growing season the equivalent of moving a farm 500 miles closer to the equator. Using polyester row covers (mini hoop houses) inside a larger hoop house provides further protection and warmth.

Hoop houses are often made from polyvinyl chloride (PVC) pipe. Hoop houses built for use in farming often use heavy metal tubing, like the chain link fence top rail tubing that can be purchased at most hardware stores. Tools for bending metal tubing can be purchased for less than $100 from online gardening websites such as Johnny's Selected Seeds; see Appendix B for details.

Traditional hoop houses are formed from arched hoops. The arches are usually semicircles, meaning the width of a hoop house will usually be roughly twice the height.

High Tunnels

High tunnels are hoop houses that are tall enough (10 feet or taller) for a gardener to walk around without stooping. The height of the high-tunnel hoop houses allows warm air to rise above the level of the plants. During cool weather, plastic or vinyl covers enclose the tunnels. As the weather gets warm, the plastic or vinyl is rolled up to allow cooler air into the tunnels.

GREEN TIP

High tunnels capture solar energy to create favorable conditions for growing vegetables, berries, and other specialty crops in climates and at times of the year in which it would otherwise be impossible to grow these crops. In 2010 the U.S. Department of Agriculture helped fund over 2,400 seasonal high tunnels to encourage farmers to adopt this technology.

Maine farmer and author Eliot Coleman evolved the basic high tunnel design into a moveable high tunnel by adding bracing and skids. This allows the tunnel to be moved from a crop that no longer needs cover to an adjacent plot that does need either protective plastic or shade cloth.

Low Tunnels

Low tunnels are short hoop houses, just tall enough to let a gardener get in to work with the plants. The smaller area gets warmer in winter because the same amount of sunlight is heating a smaller space, and the heat can't rise too much above the level of the plants.

The downside of a low tunnel is the fact that it is low—typically too short for an adult to stand up. The width of a low tunnel will also be shorter than the width of a high tunnel. But a low tunnel doesn't use as much material, so it can be more affordable than a high tunnel.

Row Covers

Row covers are nonwoven textiles spread over crops that hold in warmth like a blanket, used to protect crops in open fields and inside hoop houses. Row covers are made from ultra-lightweight fabric supported by very short hoops. The nonwoven fabric allows sunlight and rain to get to the plant, but keeps the plant warm and protects it from wind. Protected plants can remain frost-free even when outside temperatures dip a few degrees below freezing.

The combination of row covers with either high or low tunnels protects the plants from pests as well. In an aquaponics system, the row covers also help retain the warmth in the water circulating through the grow beds. Warmer water in winter means happier fish.

These row covers and low tunnels help produce a bountiful garden in this West Virginia farm.
(Photo courtesy of Slant Vie Farm)

EMT Hoop Houses

Electrical metallic tubing (EMT) used as conduit for electrical wires can be bent to exactly the form you want, whether round or more like a traditional barn or house shape. EMT comes in 10-foot lengths, like PVC pipe, and isn't much more expensive than PVC.

The pipe bender for bending EMT is surprisingly inexpensive—less than $50. Bending tools are sold wherever electrical supplies are sold, so you won't have to pay for shipping. PVC will become brittle and break due to UV radiation, but EMT will hold its shape and stand up to the elements year after year.

It is possible to construct an EMT hoop house for less than $100, all with components from local hardware stores. While no EMT hoop house can compete with a classic greenhouse for style, it is an option you may not have considered that is both affordable and durable.

> **DID YOU KNOW ...**
>
> You can put up EMT hoop houses inside a larger greenhouse to provide targeted heating and cooling. This not only saves energy because you don't have to heat or cool the entire large greenhouse, but also allows a farmer to maintain different environments to grow cold- and warm-weather crops at the same time.

Construction Considerations

A formal greenhouse is a substantial building that must conform to local building codes. Depending on where you live, you may also have homeowner community covenants to consider. It's always best to inquire about these requirements before you buy a greenhouse or build your structure.

For the hoop houses and temporary hobby greenhouses, all you should need is a bit of flat ground. Still, it's wise to check with your community association to make sure you comply with existing covenants and building codes. In my neighborhood, for example, I'm not allowed to build any structure that is taller than the 5-foot-tall brick wall behind my home. The rest of this section refers to temporary structures like hobby greenhouses and hoop houses.

Foundation

A strong wind could carry your greenhouse away if you don't anchor it properly. One way to do this is bury posts in the ground and attach your structure to the posts. Alternately, you can use reinforcing bars found in the concrete section of a hardware store and form hooked stakes. These hooked stakes can be hammered into the ground with the hook capturing the lower edge of your structure. With an aquaponic garden, you can also use the weight of the water, media, and grow beds to help anchor the greenhouse.

A wooden frame used as part of your greenhouse will be useful for fastening your greenhouse covering. And if you attach this wood frame to your posts or stakes, it will further strengthen your structure to withstand wind.

Remember to avoid using pressure-treated lumber, since the chemicals used to treat wood can damage the soil in your garden. It's best to use simple kiln-dried lumber and then protect it with nontoxic, water-based preservatives.

Forming Hoops

Whether using PVC or EMT, hoop bending is best done with two people. In the case of PVC, you'll want one person at each end of the flexible pipe to bend it to shape. With EMT, a second person can keep the pipe from rotating during the bending, ensuring the final shape is a hoop and not a spiral.

PVC pipes will naturally bend to a rounded shape when you fasten them to a central ridgepole that forms the top spine of the greenhouse and bend the other ends of the pipes to fit into the foundation. Alternately, you can pound lengths of reinforcement bar (rebar) into the ground on either side of your intended structure and bend a single piece of PVC to slide over the rebar.

EMT hoops must be bent to shape ahead of time. Determine your desired shape and use an EMT bender to obtain the proper shape. Because EMT is metal, you can tweak the final angles, but I like to draw my desired angle(s) on a piece of scrap wood that can stand up by itself next to the EMT as I'm bending it so I can bend the angle right the first time.

I recommend you make a few practice bends on scrap EMT first to get a feel for how the bender works. Soon you'll be bending consistent angles that look like they were made in a factory.

GREEN TIP

You'll want to modify your greenhouse as the seasons change. When the weather warms up, roll up the plastic sheeting at the sides of the hoop houses. During the warmest part of the summer, I often take the plastic completely off my hoop house and replace it with shade cloth. When the weather gets cool in the fall, it's time to replace the plastic on the hoop houses.

DIY PVC Hoop House

A hoop house is easy to build if you have moderate DIY skills. It's best if you have at least two people working together on this project.

This PVC hoop house is inspired by the greenhouse designs published by the North Carolina Cooperative Extension Service and the Washington State University Extension. Original designs for each of these two greenhouses can be found at www.bae.ncsu.edu/programs/extension/publicat/postharv/green/small_greenhouse.pdf and cru.cahe.wsu.edu/CEPublications/em015/em015.pdf.

The final greenhouse will be 11 feet wide and about 6½ feet tall. You can make this house as long as you want by adding additional hoops at the end, but the instructions here will give you a house that is 15 feet long. The PVC pipes are cut so the assembled house can be covered with sheeting that is 20 feet wide.

Supplies:

(2) ¾" PVC S×S×S T-fittings

(2) ¾" PVC S×S couplings

(4) ¾" PVC S×S×S×S crosses

(12) 18" lengths of rebar

(2) 7' lengths of ½" EMT pipe

(16) 9' lengths of ¾" PVC pipe

(5) 34½" lengths of ¾" PVC pipe

(2) 12' lengths of 2×6 lumber, treated with water-based preservatives

(4) 6' lengths of 2×4 lumber for door side posts

(2) 32" lengths of 2×4 lumber for door lintels

(8) 5' lengths of 2×4 lumber for braces

(12) ¼"×4" bolts and matching wing nuts

1 box 3" self-tapping decking screws

1 roll 6 mil clear plastic, 20'×50', UV treated

1 can white latex paint (can be spray paint)

2 balls of twine, 210-lb tensile strength

Tools:

Permanent marker

Scissors

Miter saw

Hacksaw or pipe cutter

Drill with screw and $\frac{7}{8}$" drill bits

Hammer

Newspaper to protect ground during painting

Prepare the base of your greenhouse:

1. Mark the corners of your 11' by 15' greenhouse area. (You can make sure it's a rectangle by ensuring the diagonals are the same length.)

2. To extend the life of your greenhouse, paint the 12' length of 2×6 lumber with a nontoxic, water-based preservative. Also, paint all the PVC pipe with the latex paint since untreated PVC will make the plastic film fall apart.

3. Drill two 1"-diameter holes in each 2×6 board 6" from the each end. These will hold the double PVC hoops at each end of the greenhouse.

4. Drive lengths of rebar into the ground through the inside hole at each end of the 2×6 base boards. The rebar pieces should be pounded into the ground until only $4\frac{1}{2}$" protrudes above the 2×6 board.

5. Tie a string between each outside corner to show where the sides of the greenhouse will lie. Pound a piece of rebar a foot into the ground every 3 feet along the sidewall line. Each piece of rebar should stick 6" out of the ground.

Install the end walls and door:

6. Temporarily remove the 2×6 from the ground. Using the 3" self-tapping screws, screw two door side posts to the flat side of each 2×6 board so the inside dimension of the door is about 29" and the door is centered around the middle of the 2×6. Screw the 32" lintel to the top of the door side posts. (If you plan to use a regular door, adjust these measurements to fit the door you plan to use. You will have to cut 8" to 9" off a regular door to fit this hoop house.)

7. Cut the ends of the 5' 2×4s so the resulting pieces will fit as diagonal braces. Replace the 2×6 and door frame in place. Screw four braces in place to stabilize the door frame upright above the 2×6.

8. Place the wall framing at each end of the greenhouse area, with the door upright. Screw the other four braces so they hold each wall assembly upright.

Install the hoops:

9. Assemble the hoops by connecting two 9' lengths of PVC with either the crosses, the tees, or the couplings. Place one tee and one coupling hoop at each end of the greenhouse.

10. With one person on each end of the PVC hoop, bend each cross hoop so the ends can be slid over opposite pieces of rebar.

11. With the inside hoops in place, connect the crosses using the 32½" pieces of PVC pipe. This forms the ridgepole.

12. Slide the lengths of ½" EMT pipe inside the ridgepole.

13. Bend the tee hoops so opposing ends slide over the rebar protruding through the ends of the greenhouse. Push the hoop down through the hole in the 2×6 so it touches the ground.

14. Connect the tee hoops to the ridgepole.

Install the plastic cover:

15. Spread the plastic sheeting over the hoops. Cut to size, leaving about 6" of overlap at each end of the hoop house.

16. Bend the coupling hoops so opposing ends fit into the outside holes drilled into the 2×6s. Drill six holes through the double PVC hoops in each end wall, spaced about 3' apart.

17. Cut plastic sheeting so it will amply fit over each end wall. Secure the sheeting to the wooden door with staples. Cut the sheeting where the door is so you can get inside.

18. Pull the plastic taut through the gap between the double PVC loops. Push the 4" bolts through the holes in the double loops and spin on the wing nuts, securing the double loops together. The plastic sheeting for the roof and end walls should be securely held between the double loops.

19. Criss-cross the twine over the hoop house sheeting material, tying the twine at the bottoms of the hoops on the rebar. The twine should be tight enough to prevent the wind from ripping the plastic, but loose enough so you can pull the plastic up to allow the greenhouse to vent in warm weather.

20. Install a door of your choice, which could be as simple as a flap of plastic.

The Least You Need to Know

- A greenhouse can let you plant earlier in spring and keep your plants alive in the late fall when frost would damage an unprotected garden.
- Sunlight enters a greenhouse and becomes heat, which is trapped beneath the glass or plastic. This can be great when it is cool outside—but bad when it's already hot.
- Permanent greenhouses come with many accessories and can add value to your property, but they can also be expensive.
- Hoop houses and row covers can provide garden protection and cost much less than a formal greenhouse.

Heating and Cooling Your Garden

In This Chapter

- The value of insulation
- Options for heating your garden
- Using the sun and other options to heat your garden
- Options for cooling your garden
- Subterranean heating and cooling

A few of us don't need to heat or cool our gardens. Either your indoor facility is already temperature controlled or you live in a fabulous year-round climate. Most of us, though, will want to change the temperature that our garden would otherwise naturally experience. Maybe we want to grow tomatoes in the dead of winter or lettuce in the heat of summer. Or maybe there's a killing frost or heat wave coming our way, and we want our fish and plants to survive.

There are many ways to control the temperature of your garden. This chapter will give you an overview of your options.

Insulation Keeps Heat and Cold in Your Garden

Whether you're trying to heat during cool months or chill the garden during warm months, you want to keep your garden at the desired temperature. Insulation will help keep your garden cool in the summer and warm in the winter.

All materials have a value called thermal resistance, or R. When you go to the store and look for insulation, the material will often be labeled R-3, R-8, or something like that, where the higher the number, the better the insulation is at maintaining temperatures.

If you have multiple layers, you can add the R-value for each layer. The thicker the layer, the greater the insulation value. It's similar to how a thick blanket keeps you warm better than a thin blanket. For example, straw bales make good insulation even though the R-value of a single inch of straw baling is not much more than 1. The insulation value comes because bales are usually many inches thick.

The following table gives you the R-value for a variety of common materials you might use to keep heat inside your garden greenhouse.

Insulation Value of Common Materials (1-Inch Thickness)

Material	Thermal Resistance (R)	Insulation Value
Glass	R-0.1	None
Brick	R-0.2	Poor
Still air	R-0.6 to R-0.9	Slight
Snow	R-1	Slight
Wood	R-0.7 to R-1.4	Slight
Reflective film	R-1 to R-5	Varies
Straw bale (per inch)	R-1.5	Good for entire bale
Dry cardboard	R-3 to R-4	Good
Fiberglass batting	R-3 to R-4	Good
Expanded Polystyrene Foam (EPS)	R-4	Good
Extruded Polystyrene Foam (XPS)	R-5	Good
Foil-faced polyisocyanurate	R-6	Very good
Spray foam insulation	R-4 to R-8	Very good

Whether you are heating during winter or cooling during summer, you want to have good insulation.

Standard Heat Sources

If your garden is indoors and you need to heat your garden or the fish tank, always use standard appliances. Do not experiment with DIY techniques that could degrade the air quality of your home or business. These standard methods are well understood. You can buy the equipment at your local stores. Because these appliances are used in so many different situations, the unit prices of these appliances are pretty low, even if the cost of the energy that powers them isn't.

If your garden is outside in some kind of greenhouse, a standard heater may not be your best option. A cold snap could leave you with a massive bill for electricity or propane. Also, the environment in an outdoor greenhouse is likely to be very moist during the winter, which can be a particular problem for electrical appliances.

SOUNDS FISHY

Using water and electricity together can be dangerous. Make sure you use ground fault current interrupter (GFCI) receptacles in your aquaponic garden. GFCI electrical receptacles will trip off in case water gets into the electrical workings of the appliances.

Electric Space Heaters

Electric space heaters warm the air. These appliances create heat by passing current through metal or ceramic, creating heat.

In the most common type of electric space heater, a fan blows air over the heated material. These kinds of heaters are called forced air heaters. They are popular because they make you feel warm immediately, but these high-heat appliances can be dangerous if not handled properly. To avoid getting burned or causing a fire, follow these tips:

- Keep the space heater away from flammable objects.

- Place the heater on the floor to keep it from falling off a higher platform.

- Make sure the cords are not frayed, and don't hide them under rugs or other flooring.

- Keep children, pets, and yourself at least a foot away from the top and front of a heater.

- Keep water away from the electrical cords except where they are specifically designed to be immersed in water.

In an electric radiator, the heat warms oil or water inside a metal container. The metal transfers the heat to the surrounding air, which naturally rises to be replaced by cold air. Because these radiators operate at relatively low temperature, they are considered safer than forced air heaters.

Any modern electric space heater will have a thermostat that controls when it comes on. Most have safety features to turn the power off if the heater tips over.

Propane and Pellet Heaters

Propane heat is another option for enclosed spaces where people live. Propane heaters are often used in boats, where they provide safe heat in the wet, enclosed environment found in a boat.

A propane boat heater is a good option for an indoor garden or a small greenhouse. The moisture in your garden will not cause a propane heater to malfunction catastrophically. However, propane heaters can consume the oxygen in an environment if they are not properly designed, so always use a propane heater that has been properly certified and use the heater according to the manufacturer's specifications. As long as you have a properly installed, certified propane heater, you should be safe using one inside, but be sure to read the manufacturer's instructions to be certain.

If you have a larger greenhouse or indoor space, there are heavy-duty propane heaters available. There are also a number of pellet stove options on the market that burn wood or paper pellets. I lump pellet stoves in with propane heaters since they also use combustion to create heat.

Pellet stoves are attractive because they burn a renewable resource. Modern pellet stoves can be self-igniting and can turn themselves on and off based on thermostat control. Gravity or an auger feeds more pellets into the burn box as required, allowing a pellet stove to function unattended.

Because modern pellet stoves are efficient and use renewable biomass to create heat, your local government may offer tax credits to offset the cost to purchase and install pellet stoves.

Electric Water Heaters

Plants can die in an unusual cold snap, but it is the health of the fish that motivates most aquaponics gardeners to add heat to their system. The most efficient way to ensure your fish tank is warm is to heat the water directly.

Electric water heaters for aquariums are high-wattage devices. But because electric water heaters operate in water, the heater itself never gets very hot. On the other hand, the cord and power outlet may overheat due to the electricity passing through them on the way to the water heater. It is wise to use a GFCI receptacle that will trip off if the current draw becomes too great.

Because the water in your fish tank circulates through the roots of your plants, your plant roots will be sitting in warm water, which will produce fast plant growth. If you heat the water in your garden, insulate your grow beds and fish tank to reduce the amount of heat lost.

> **DID YOU KNOW ...**
>
> You can recycle the heat you've created with other appliances to help heat your garden. You can pass heated water from other sources (dishwashers, grow light cooling water) through pipes coiled in reservoirs that feed into your fish tanks. This allows you to heat your fish tank with energy that would otherwise get dumped down the drain.

Solar Heaters

As discussed in Chapter 18, an outside garden in a greenhouse is already heated by the sun. But you can boost your garden heat gain during the day with solar water and air heaters. Solar heat is also a safe way to add heat to an indoor space. Systems can either be bought or built.

You can also use rain barrels located inside the greenhouse to store solar heat. The rain barrels should be painted black on one side and white on the other. The black side should face the sun in winter because black absorbs heat. In summer, the white side should be turned to the sun, to reflect the sun's energy away from the barrel. This will keep water inside the barrel relatively cool.

Water Heaters

Solar water heaters allow the sun to heat water enclosed in dark tubes. The heated water rises, causing the water to circulate to tubing inside a reservoir tank. The water transfers the heat energy to the reservoir tank and becomes cool. The cooled water returns to the solar water heater to begin the cycle again.

You can also use a solar heater to warm a water tank that isn't connected to your fish tank. The sun will heat the tank during the day. When temperatures drop at night, the heat energy will radiate to the rest of your garden, moderating the temperature inside your garden. Separating a heater like this from your other tanks allows you to use copper tubing and a pump to circulate the water between the tank and the solar heater.

SOUNDS FISHY

If you build some kind of solar water heater to warm your fish tank, make sure you do not put coiled copper pipe into your fish tank. Copper can be toxic to fish, and the typical pH range of your garden will cause the surface of the copper pipe to dissolve into your fish water.

Air Heaters

Solar air heaters work using the same principles as a greenhouse. But in the case of a solar air heater, the inside of the enclosed volume is painted matte black to maximize the solar gain. A fan circulates the air through the collector into the space to be heated. Solar air heaters are a favorite project for DIY folks who want a way to warm up a winter workshop.

There are numerous designs for building the solar collectors that gather the sun's energy. Common collectors include empty boxes, soda cans, aluminum soffits, aluminum downspouts, and aluminum screens.

It turns out that black aluminum screen collectors perform surprisingly well. Testing performed by hobbyists associated with Build It Solar and the Annamalai University have demonstrated that wire mesh screen collectors heat air better than solid metal plates, cans, or tubes. A screen collector is also the easiest kind of solar collector to build since it isn't much more than a simple empty box.

A solar air heater isn't the most efficient way to heat your garden. But a home-built solar collector is inexpensive, is easy to build, and can make the air temperature very comfortable on cold but sunny days.

Rocket Mass Heaters

Rocket mass heaters are wood stoves in which the stove exhaust is routed through a thermal mass. The thermal mass captures a significant amount of heat energy before allowing the exhaust gases to escape up the flue.

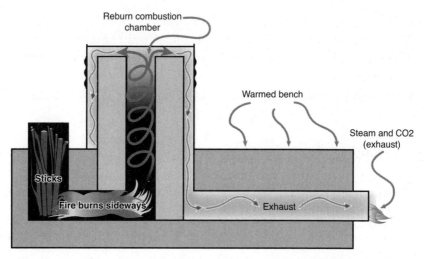

Reburn combustion chamber

Warmed bench

Steam and CO2 (exhaust)

Sticks

Fire burns sideways

Exhaust

This diagram of a rocket mass heater shows how heat from the fire is used to heat a bench built into a home. In a garden, the exhaust from a rocket stove can be buried under a grow bed or in the soil.

(Adapted with permission from illustration created by Paul Wheaton, permies.com)

GREEN TIP

Folks who use rocket mass stoves claim they can heat their homes with only 20 percent of the wood required for a traditional wood stove.

Rocket mass heaters probably aren't covered by your local building codes. However, most governments are much more lenient about what you do in your garden than they are about what you do to your home. Installing a rocket mass heater in your yard or greenhouse should be an option in any jurisdiction that allows outside barbecue pits.

I wouldn't use a rocket mass heater as my only method of heating a garden, but it can be useful when the electricity is out or the sky has been persistently overcast.

Thermal Mass and Raised Beds

Thermal mass can capture significant heat to moderate temperatures in a winter garden, and raised beds allow cold air to flow away from your plants.

A rock or brick wall on the side of your garden opposite the sun can absorb heat energy in the day and release it at night. An ideal example if this would be a greenhouse built against the side of a brick or stone home. The darker the rock, the more solar energy will turn into heat.

In summer the stone wall will absorb less heat because the sun is higher in the sky, keeping your garden from getting terribly hot.

Cooling Your Garden

As we move into summer, our main concern will be keeping the garden cool. This is particularly important if you are raising a cold-water fish like trout.

There aren't as many options for cooling a garden as there are for adding heat, but following are a few.

Using Shade Cloth

The easiest way to cool down a garden is to shade it from the sun. Shade cloth or shade fabric is widely available in home improvement stores and online. It is primarily used to shade patios. There are numerous accessories available to customize the cloth, including grommets, butterfly clips, wood fasteners, and lacing cord. The cloths come with differing amounts of sun-blocking capacity, and some block the ultraviolet rays that can cause sunburn in humans.

I like to keep a length of shade cloth on hand that I can use to shade my garden during the heat of summer. I drape the cloth over the hoops that support my winter greenhouse. Another option is light shade netting that you stretch over low hoops to provide both shade and protection from birds and bugs.

Using Water to Cool the Air

A swamp cooler can be an effective and inexpensive way to cool a space in dry climates. Air is blown through a rotating drum that continually dips itself in a shallow pool of water. As the water on the drum evaporates, heat energy is removed from the air. Evaporation can be so effective at removing heat energy from water that it's possible to use this effect to make ice in the hot desert.

Even in humid climates, you can drop the local temperature a few degrees by spraying a fine mist into the air.

This aquaponics gardener has installed a used swamp cooler in the greenhouse.
Swamp coolers work well in dry climates.
(Photo courtesy of Pat Chiu)

Using the Earth to Cool the Water

The ground can store a large amount of energy without significant changes in temperature. Long after summer has faded into fall, the ground 10 feet below you is only beginning to warm up. If your fish tank is partially or entirely buried in the ground, this slow movement of temperature in the ground will keep the water cool in summer and relatively warm in the winter.

DID YOU KNOW ...

The temperature 30 feet below the surface is constant year round. This is why the temperature in caves seems cool in summer and warm in winter.

If you can submerge your fish tank in the ground, you can keep the water cooler in summer than an equivalent aboveground tank.

Some parts of the country use this geothermal energy to warm schools and other large buildings. You can install a small geothermal closed-loop system with a backhoe if you have the space and the desire. The lengths of high-density polyethylene loop piping are draped over one another like a flattened slinky and will last 200 years. A depth of just 5 feet will provide significant heating and cooling over the course of the year.

Subterranean Systems

Following the oil crisis of 1973, the U.S. patent office was flooded with applications for new ways to save energy. Since most patents are only valid for 17 years, these technologies are now freely available for anyone to use.

An underground heat exchange system (UHES) pumps moist, hot air through narrow tunnels in the ground. The moist air cools and the water condenses out of the air, cooling the air even more. The dry air that comes out of the ground can be as much as 30 degrees cooler than it was when it went into the ground. During the winter, the heat energy stored in the ground during the summer warms the dry, cold air, which is able to absorb the moisture from the ground, coming out as moist, warm air.

A quick online search shows at least four patents granted for subterranean heating and cooling systems. This method of heating in winter and cooling in summer was included in an integrated agriculture system developed in China and republished by the United Nations Food and Agriculture Organization (FAO). This isn't fringe science.

Most systems in the United States use corrugated drainage pipe to form the narrow tunnels. Tubing is buried in several layers, with the tunnels spaced at least 1 to 2 feet apart. If the installation is not done properly, the drainage pipe can be crushed, blocking airflow through the crushed pipes. Screens are recommended to prevent the tunnels from becoming homes for rodents.

In the Chinese system, they used unglazed clay pipe to form tunnels buried a couple of feet below the surface. Hollow concrete blocks could be used in lieu of clay pipe if clay pipe is unavailable.

If you find the possibility of an underground heat exchange system appealing, you can find geodesic dome greenhouse kits that include underground heating and cooling as part of the basic design.

The Least You Need to Know

- Good insulation helps keep your garden cool in summer and warm in winter.
- Be careful when using electricity. Keep your gear in good repair, read the manufacturer's instructions for proper use, and follow safety precautions.
- There are several nonelectrical ways to heat your garden using the sun and materials like wood pellets or firewood.
- In dry climates, you can cool your garden using evaporation. You can also use shade cloth to cool your garden.
- Installing a subterranean heat exchange system under your garden will keep your garden cool in summer and relatively warm in winter.

Automating Your Garden

In This Chapter

- What automation is and how it can help
- Getting information with measurement systems
- Automating temperature control
- Replacing lost water
- Automating fish feeding
- Getting help from other people

Most standard garden chores are already eliminated in an aquaponic garden. You don't have to fertilize. You don't have to water. You don't have to weed. As easy as it is to tend an aquaponic garden, there are opportunities to make it even more carefree.

Most of the discussion in this chapter presumes you have a greenhouse structure where temperature can be influenced by fans or vents. However, automated fish feeders and water top-up can help even when you don't have a greenhouse.

Why Automate?

As fun as it is to work in an aquaponics garden, there are times when you may have to leave your garden unattended for a significant length of time. But how will your unattended garden adapt to extreme weather? How will you add water to replace evaporation? And how will you feed your fish while you're gone? *Automation* can improve the growth rate of your fish and crops by preventing them from suffering extremes of weather and keeping their water and feed levels optimal.

> **DEFINITION**
>
> **Automation** is the use of machines and control systems to optimize productivity. The goal of automation is to increase productivity and quality beyond that possible with current human labor.

Measurement Systems

In order to perform the proper action, you need information. Measurement systems in your garden provide you the information your automation needs to act.

Sensors inputs you may need include temperature, humidity, light, and pH. Automation can use these inputs to turn devices on and off, or cancel a scheduled event if conditions are not right.

An indoor garden will likely exist in a temperature-controlled situation. When this is the case, it is usually sufficient to know the amount of time that has elapsed. In this case, you can use simple timers to automate your garden. If you want to do something more elaborate, there are systems that will help monitor your indoor garden and allow you to vary conditions based on the particular needs of your plants.

A few automatic measurement systems have been developed for gardens. Gardenbot.org talks about the garden robot Andrew Frueh created to automate watering his garden, with understandable information about programming *Arduino microcontrollers* and solenoid valves. Bitponics is a garden monitoring and control system that successfully completed a Kickstarter fundraising campaign in 2012. The target market is hydroponic gardeners, but it can be easily adapted to aquaponics. Aquaponics enthusiast Rob Torcellini of Bigelow Brook Farms (you saw his Torcellini siphon break in Chapter 7) has created the IX series of timers that provides great control over the length of time your device is on. These timers also allow the device to control power on based on temperature probes, which measure temperature and send that information to an automation system to control fans, solenoids, or window openers.

> **DEFINITION**
>
> **Arduino microcontrollers** are hobby computer boards that can be programmed to automate a garden. **Solenoids** are water valves you can open and close using electrical commands.

In an outdoor garden, the sun will rise and set no matter what your timer says. Many operations can still be controlled based on time, but the critical measurement in an outdoor garden is temperature.

You will want to be able to turn on fans or open vents when the temperature rises above the desired level. During the winter, you will want to be able to turn on heaters based on the temperature of the garden. If you are using solar or geothermal heaters, you will want to know that turning on the fan will actually blow warm air into the garden.

You may want to install lights that turn on when sunlight is inadequate or if you're growing out-of-season plants that are sensitive to the duration of sunlight over a day.

Even if you aren't forced to be away from your garden for days on end, automation can take care of many important garden tasks on a routine basis, freeing you from concern about the effect of unusual temperatures on your garden, the need to add water to your system, or worry about feeding fish.

If you aren't yet at a point where you want to buy fancy equipment, you can set timers to turn equipment on and off based on the expected conditions. This kind of mechanization can be adequate for controlling temperature—after all, one would expect summer temperatures to be hot after the sun rises and winter temperatures to be cool at night. But there are other decisions where you'll want to take temperature into consideration.

Keeping an Eye on Temperature

Other than time itself, temperature is the main measurement you care about as a gardener. By knowing the temperature, I can control fans and vents properly. The temperature can also inform my decision to feed my fish, since fish won't feed when they (and the water in which they are swimming) are either too hot or too cold.

If I know the temperature and have an appropriate bit of automation gear, I can make things turn on or off in response to the temperature. You can do this to either control tasks, like feeding fish, or to control the temperature itself, like opening vents or turning on fans.

Fans

A fan can be useful even if you aren't trying to control temperature. The breeze created by the fan circulates oxygen and carbon dioxide through your garden and helps pollinate your plants.

If temperature control is your aim, a fan can gently push the warm air back down towards your plants in cool weather. In warm weather, the fan can blow hot air out of the garden entirely, pulling cool air in at the base of the greenhouse.

When you have an underground heating and cooling system (see Chapter 19), the fan can be turned on when temperatures are high in summer, forcing the hot, moist air into the ground where it is cooled and dehydrated. The recommended flow rate should allow the entire volume of the greenhouse to circulate under the ground five times an hour to achieve maximum efficiency.

In winter the fan can turn on to either pump cold, dry air down into the now-warm, moist earth, or you can have a solar heater with a fan that turns on when the sun has sufficiently warmed the heater.

Shades and Vents

Shades reduce the extent to which the sun heats up your garden, and vents allow hot air to escape, cooling your garden. But it's usually not practical for you to adjust shade cloth and vents more than once a day, if that. Shades and vents that automatically open and close in response to garden conditions are great. Let's take a look at some options.

Automatic vent openers. Vent openers that are powered using gas-charged cylinders can be inexpensive. The gas expands when it is warm and contracts when it gets cool. Unfortunately, reviews from users are mixed. Some think they work great, but others complain that the gas cylinder openers either didn't work or stopped working earlier than expected.

A more expensive but reliable option is a motorized vent opening system that is connected either to a timer or to a temperature-activated control system. Check out your options, paying attention to whether you could open or close the vent manually in case of a power outage or the materials used in the device. For example, some motors contain mercury to help determine temperature, which you may want to avoid.

Vents allow air to escape, but they may not be sufficient by themselves to moderate temperature. In the heat of summer, using a shade cloth can help enormously.

Automatic shades. Most of us won't need to automate our shade cloth. We'll just notice the fish tank temperature climbing over a period of several days and pull the shade cloth over our greenhouse structure for the duration of summer. But if you have the luxury of a high-end setup, you can get shade cloth on rollers or louvers that close when the temperature in the garden gets too high or even when the sun is too bright, based on readings from a light meter.

> **DID YOU KNOW ...**
>
> Hydroponic growers use electrical conductivity sensors to determine the concentration of nutrients. Electrical conductivity sensors measure the salts in hydroponic nutrient solutions, not the nutrients themselves. The fish-based nutrients in an aquaponic system don't contain salts, so they will not show up on hydroponic sensors. Make sure you buy measurement devices that will actually work with an aquaponic garden.

Adding Water

Your aquaponic garden is very water thrifty, but plants always have to evaporate water from their leaves in order to draw water up through their roots. This means you will always need to add a small amount of water to your garden to replace these losses.

You won't need to add much water to an aquaponic system, and there's no need to schedule regular watering. You just need to keep the tank or sump topped up.

My favorite way to automate water is to use a mechanical valve with pressurized water from either a water barrel or a hose running to city water. If you're in an arid climate, you can find float valves used with swamp coolers. Or you can do the job with a stock tank float valve, which is available online or at your local agricultural supply store. Either the swamp cooler valve or the stock tank float valve can be acquired for under $30.

A fancy automation system can use a solenoid valve to add water when a sensor says the water level is low, but most of us can get by with a mechanical water timer. A mechanical water timer is a simple timer device you screw onto your hose that turns itself off when it counts down to zero.

If you notice your tank getting low, you would only need to turn the timer dial so hose water flows into your system for the amount of time you set (5 to 10 minutes). You don't have to worry about flooding your system by accidentally leaving the water on, or having to wait around for 5 to 10 minutes just to turn off the spigot.

Automatic Fish Feeders

Automating food delivery to your fish can be tricky business. On the one hand, it allows your fish to get their food reliably on their preferred schedule. On the other hand, automatic feeding can lead to overfeeding. A broken feeder could leave the fish unfed without anyone noticing.

Commercial Feeders for Large Fish Tanks

If your system is roughly 250 gallons (1,000 liters) or greater, you will be interested in a pond feeder. A number of options have been developed for koi pond owners and can be found online. You should research your options and read reviews before purchasing one.

If you want to feed your fish continuously, you may be interested in a belt feeder. This is a mechanical device that slowly advances the belt during the course of the day. As the fish food reaches the edge of the belt, it tumbles down into the fish tank. The belt feeder approach minimizes the time you need to spend fussing with food while potentially allowing the fish to eat all day long for maximized growth. If the weather forecast calls for temperatures that will be too cold or too hot for your fish, you can just reduce or eliminate the food you lay out on the belt for the day.

Commercial feeders can cost a few hundred dollars but are designed to work reliably for years of use. This belt feeder uses a mechanical timer to move the belt, dumping feed into the water gradually over the course of the day.

Another type of commercial feeder vibrates to shake food into the tank. The times when fish are to be fed and the duration of the shaking must be programmed into a computer-based timer. This kind of feeder is more expensive, but it can operate when the gardener can't visit the fish tank on a daily basis.

DIY Fish Feeders

If you really want an automatic or timer-activated feeder and can't find anything of quality in your price range, consider building your own.

For a small aquarium-sized fish tank, you can use an electric 24-hour timer to drop fish food into the water once a day. To do this, drill two holes in the side of a pill bottle and another hole through the top of the lid near an edge to hold a straw. Put some epoxy on the holes in the side of the bottle and stick it to the dial of the timer. After the epoxy has cured, remove the lid, add fish food, and replace the lid. Place the timer over the fish tank so food can drop into the tank from the straw when the face of the timer rotates. Each day the straw fills with feed when the lid of the bottle is facing up. When the lid of the bottle faces down, the feed in the straw falls into the tank.

For a larger tank, you can build a funneled container for your feed. A wood auger rests at the bottom of the funnel, allowing feed to fall into the spaces in the auger blade. A motor turns on, turning the auger and pushing the food out through a pipe into the fish tank. Rob Torcellini of Bigelow Brook Farms has a detailed video on YouTube showing his auger-based feeder (go to tinyurl.com/DIYfeeder). His feeder comes complete with a button so he can add additional feedings if he's in the garden and wants to give his fish a treat.

GREEN TIP

Make a habit of feeding your fish a bit when you visit your garden. If you do this, they will be excited to see your coming, even if your garden is mostly automated.

Controlling Feed Rates Using Water Temperature

Rob Torcellini has also created an automation routine that determines the timing and rate of feed based on temperature. As demand for such a product grows, it is certain that Rob or someone else will develop a consumer product to adjust feed rate based on environmental factors.

The key to temperature-controlled feeding is determining the optimal temperature range for your fish. Keep a log of how much food your fish eat and the water temperature. Before long, you'll know the temperature range where they are eager to feed.

When the temperature is in the optimal range, fish often like to be fed at both dawn and dusk. When temperatures are higher than optimal but still in a range where the fish eat, the fish would be fed only in the morning—the coolest part of the day. As temperatures drop below optimal, the fish would be fed only at dusk, after the sun has had all day to warm the water.

Getting Someone Else to Do the Job

If you are just looking for some way to automate fish feeding and minor chores during a vacation or business trip, you can sometimes find someone willing to do these chores for a bit of cash.

A phone and a friend can often get important jobs done when you can't be around. If you have a larger garden or facility, you may be able to find interns who are interested in learning about aquaponics and who would be willing to do such tasks as part of their learning experience.

I have also seen businesses that offer garden maintenance. One exciting service is offered by Smart Gardener, where employees use the Smart Gardener website tools to keep track of the required chores in each subscriber's garden. This service allows you to eat food grown on your own property without having to do any of the actual gardening yourself. In 2012 this service was not yet available in my area, but they were expanding quickly. See Appendix B for details.

Getting someone else to help you with your garden chores might not seem like automation, but for many of us, people will always be easier to work with than machines.

The Least You Need to Know

- You can use automation in your garden to optimize productivity and lessen your daily chore load.
- Using temperature sensors to turn on fans and open vents can keep your garden comfortable in hot weather.
- You need only a mechanical float valve to keep your water levels topped up.

- You can automate feeding your fish, but be careful not to feed fish when their water is either too hot or too cold.

- In a pinch, you can "automate" your garden by hiring someone else to do chores when you have to be away from your garden.

When You Can't Use Public Electricity or Water

In This Chapter

- Benefits of going off-grid
- Collecting rainwater
- Generating and storing your own electricity
- Naturally powered pumps

For aquaponics you need water—and you need to pump that water between the fish tank and the grow beds. We'll explore some of the options you have to keep your system going when you can't rely on the utility company for your electricity and water. Even if you plan to use public utilities, emergencies happen. In 2012, a fierce summer storm hit the Midwestern and Mid-Atlantic United States where I live and killed over 20 people. Three million people lost power as a result, and the temperature was over 100 degrees in my town each day of the extended power outage. Major outages like this occur every couple of years.

You might also want to reduce your dependence on public utilities to reduce your power use. Going green appeals to many people, and an increasing number are trying to go off-grid.

Finally, your ideal garden location might not be close to public utilities. You might have a large yard with a perfect garden location that is far from your house, or you might be gardening in a community garden that doesn't have electricity and water.

First I'll talk about collecting water, then I'll talk about generating your own electricity. Finally, I'll discuss water pumps that require very little electricity.

Harvesting Water

If you live in an area that gets rain, you should be able to collect enough water to run your aquaponic system. Though you can harvest a small amount of rainwater without a structure, most of the following suggestions presume you are planning to put up at least a simple hoop house (see Chapter 18). The rain you can get from the covered volume of a greenhouse or hoop house is significant. Rainwater harvesting allows you to collect rainwater during storms, then sparingly use that water across the dry days until it rains again.

Most localities allow collection of rainwater, though the quantity may be limited in dry regions. If you have 100 square feet of collection area, you can get as much as 62 gallons (or 230 liters) for every inch of rain that falls. Depending on your water needs, you may choose to store the water in rain barrels or cisterns.

Rain Barrels

Rain barrels are literally barrels that hold rain and are usually designed to hold 40 to 80 gallons of water. Rain barrels are relatively inexpensive and can cost less than $50 each if you make them yourself. Local governments often encourage homeowners to install rain barrels. When local homeowners store rainwater, it reduces storm runoff coming into central water processing plants. In a city where 10,000 households install a rain barrel, the storm surge experienced at the water plant can be reduced by as much as a 500,000 gallons. Capturing those half-million gallons of water before it hits the water plant may prevent flooding that could send raw sewage into local waterways.

DID YOU KNOW ...

It used to be illegal to collect rainwater in some western states. However, most states have relented and now allow rainwater collection in barrels. Check with your local government to find out if there are restrictions on how you connect a rain barrels to the roof of your home or greenhouse. You may even find that your local government holds rain barrel workshops or offers discounts, now that more local governments are coming to understand the benefits of citizen rainwater collection.

To direct water from your gutter to your rain barrel, install a simple diverter. The diverter will send the water coming down your rainspout over to your rain barrel until your rain barrel gets full. Once your rain barrel is full, the water will continue down the downspout to your drainage system.

If you are collecting water from your roof, you should use a first-flush diverter. This will prevent loose tar, dust, sticks, and leaves from getting into your rain barrel. Ready-made diverters can be purchased for $30 to $50, or there are DIY designs available on the internet.

Cisterns

If you live in a really dry climate, you might need to store more water to get you through dry spells. An underground cistern is a sturdy container designed to hold a large amount of water. Local governments will often allow a much larger cistern volume than rain barrel volume. To keep a cistern from freezing in winter, a cistern should be buried below the frost line.

My favorite example of a cistern collection system is found at the Old Point Loma Lighthouse near San Diego. There's a large concrete basin there to collect rainwater. In the early days of this historic lighthouse, the lighthouse keeper's family was surrounded by saltwater and 10 miles away from the nearest neighbors. Rainwater collection was critical to their survival, since abandoning the lighthouse wasn't an option in a dry year.

Installation of a cistern involves significant expense. The tank itself is large and must be able to withstand the load of the ground around and above it. Installation involves major earth-moving equipment. A modern cistern will also involve various devices to ensure water quality, like ultraviolet (UV) sterilization and other filtration equipment.

On the other hand, the volume of the cistern allows you to extend water availability across long periods without rain. If your climate has a single rainy season followed by many dry months each year, a cistern may be a reasonable investment.

Collecting Rain Without a Roof

In wet climates, you can simply put a large funnel on top of your rain barrel. The RainSaucer is a commercial option that does not require a roofed structure and is both food safe and UV resistant. The amount of rain captured will be small compared to a roof system, but it may be enough for your needs if you live in a wet climate. Go to rainsaucers.com for more information.

Harvesting Energy

Now you have your water. How can you get the power to run air pumps, water pumps, and fans?

The answer in an earlier age was human power or animal power. When there was a person or animal, there was power. Traditional windmills would also provide power as long as there was wind.

Modern technology allows us to harvest energy from wind, streams, and sunlight and store it in batteries. In this section I'll talk about collecting energy from sunlight and wind, as well as the kind of batteries you'll need to store that energy.

Solar Panels

Electricity is very much like water. To understand electrical terms, you can think of similar attributes of water. Some examples are given in the following table.

Comparing Electrical Terms to Water Terms

Physical Property	Electrical Term	Water-Related Term	Water Example
Potential energy	Volts	Pressure	Pounds per square inch (psi)
Current	Amperes or amps	Flow rate (gallons per minute)	Gallons per hour (gph)
Resistance	Ohms	Drag	Drag increasing as pipe diameter decreases or when something is stuck in the pipe
Power	Watt	Pressurized flow	Water shooting out of a fire hose

A solar panel will produce a certain amount of electrical power under standard conditions. For electricity this power is usually described in terms of watts. Luckily, that is the same unit used to describe power consumption. For example, my water pump consumes 100 watts each hour and my air pump consumes less than 5 watts per hour. Unfortunately, my pumps will consume those 105 watts per hour whether the sun is bright or covered by clouds. My solar panels can only convert the light that falls on them.

There are a variety of tools to help you calculate the number of solar panels you'll need to produce the power you consume. One good online tool is sunsoglobal.com/calculator.html.

You usually need solar panels that can generate about 5 to 10 times as much electricity per hour as your pumps consume. That's because the sunlight falling on your solar panels is rarely as bright as the direct lights manufacturers use for their measurements. Also, your pumps are sometimes running when it's dark outside.

If you do decide to go with solar, you'll need the solar panels themselves, batteries to store the power, and a charge controller to feed the proper amount of electricity to the batteries.

Harnessing Wind to Generate Electricity

Whenever you can get something turning, you can use that rotation to generate energy. This is the fundamental principle behind a gas generator, but it can work with a waterwheel or a wind turbine.

You connect the rotating part to a permanent magnet direct current (DC) motor. To convert wind energy into rotation, you can either use a traditional windmill or you can have a vertical set of blades that rotate no matter which direction the wind is coming from.

You'll want to evaluate how much wind your location gets. If your average wind speed is more than 12 miles per hour, wind is a great resource. In the United States, these higher wind speeds are found in the center of the country, from North Dakota to Texas. Unfortunately, the coastal regions that are most densely populated have weaker wind resources. Where I live, in the southeastern United States, average wind speed is less than 9 miles an hour. This explains why you don't see wind turbines in some parts of the country.

Using Batteries to Store Energy

You'll need a bank of batteries to store your electrical power. This is true whether you are creating your own electricity or simply looking to store electrical energy from the utility company in case of an emergency.

Batteries are usually labeled with the number of amp hours (Ah) they will support at a particular voltage. You can figure the number of Ah by multiplying the number of watts your equipment uses by the number of hours you might need to operate without wind or sun. Then multiply that number by 3, since you will never want to fully discharge a battery, and they are less effective during times when it is cold.

Once you know the number of watt-hours you need, divide that number by the voltage of the battery you are thinking of buying to get amp hours.

For example, if I need 40 watts per hour, usually use my equipment for 15 hours a day, and want to be able to run my system in cold weather for 4 days without power using 12-volt batteries (batteries come in 12, 24, or 48 voltages), I'd need 600 Ah worth of batteries:

> 40 watts × 15 hours per day = 600 watt hours per day
>
> ÷ 12 volts = 50 Ah per day
>
> × 4 days = 200 Ah (used)
>
> × safety factor of 3 = 600 Ah (battery capacity required)

You can also use a battery-bank-sizing calculator, like the one at wholesalesolar.com/battery_sizing.html.

You'll want to get deep cycle batteries since these are energy storage batteries rather than start-your-motor batteries. Lead acid batteries are inexpensive, but will wear out quickly when used for this kind of purpose.

SOUNDS FISHY

If the power goes out and your pumps stop, your fish can die of suffocation very quickly, particularly in hot weather. You can keep as many as 3 pounds of fish per cubic foot of grow bed volume if your electricity won't fail. But if power outages are likely, I recommend you keep no more than 1 pound of fish per cubic foot of grow bed volume, and maybe even less than that.

Water Pumps That Don't Use Much Energy

If you live near a river or stream, you may be able to use gravity and the movement of water in the river or stream to pump water up to your garden. I love the ingenuity in these environmentally friendly mechanical devices. It certainly beats hauling water from the stream in a bucket.

Wind and muscle power have been used for thousands of years. The water-driven pumps were all invented around the dawn of the Industrial Revolution. The air-driven water pumping systems are new ways to use electrical air pumps to move water.

Wind and Manual Power for Pumps

Chain or rope pumps have been used for over 1,000 years. In the simplest designs, a loop of rope is turned by a wheel so it passes through water then up a pipe, dragging the water with it. To improve the efficiency of a rope pump, the rope can be knotted at intervals, or the rope can be fitted with discs to capture the water as the rope travels up the pipe. At the top of the pipe, the water is allowed to escape from a T-fitting near the top.

A modern version of the rope pump is used by about 4 million people in Africa, Asia, and Latin America, where modern technologies to improve food production are not affordable. The rope pump can be driven by hand or it can be connected to a wind-mill to drive the rope.

Nonelectric Water Pumps

The hydraulic ram pump was invented in 1796 in France by the Montgolfier brothers, who also invented the hot air balloon. Hydraulic ram pumps pump water high above the level of the stream or pump itself. Hydraulic ram pumps work well to pump water, but they are complicated, noisy, and spurt water, so they aren't practical for all situations.

Another nonelectric pump is the spiral waterwheel. The first spiral waterwheel was invented in Europe in 1746 but was mostly forgotten. Perhaps it was not as easy to market as the more compact and mechanical Montgolfier ram pump.

The spiral waterwheel was re-invented in 1979 by Peter Morgan, a pioneer in rural African water supply and sanitation. The waterwheel turns as the river or stream moves past paddles attached the wheel. A spiral of tubing is attached to the wheel, alternately taking in air and water. As the wheel turns, the weight of the water pressurizes the air, which forces water out the center of the wheel through a slip joint and up piping going uphill.

Rope pumps and spiral waterwheels could be adapted for use as emergency water pumps in larger aquaponic gardens when all power is lost for multiple days. But it is the idea behind the hydraulic ram pump that has been adapted to pump large amounts of water using pumped air using very little electricity.

Pumping Water with Air

The hydraulic ram pump uses naturally compressed air to move water. You can create your own compressed air with an air pump. Even though an air pump large enough to move hundreds of gallons of water requires electricity, it requires far less electricity than a water pump that could move hundreds of gallons of water.

GREEN TIP

You can improve the performance of most water pumps by submerging them in an additional 3 to 4 feet of water. This works particularly well with an air-powered water pump. In the case of an air-powered water pump, you might have to reduce the submergence if the air can't push its way out against the weight of the water.

Glenn Martinez of Olomana Gardens in Hawaii, and one of the first aquaponic gardeners to obtain organic certification, has developed a system for pumping water using air. The air pump system can either be used to pump water from a distant stream or to pump water in an aquaponic garden. With Glenn's pump, you don't need to have a moving stream. Though not as noisy as a ram pump, the air does lift water up from the sump or stream in batches rather than in the steady stream typical for electric water pumps.

In addition to using little energy, Glenn's air-powered water pump doesn't require rotating blades to work. That means the pump is almost impossible to clog. Most parts can be bought from your local hardware store, though you might need to buy the swing check valve from a specialty store like Aquatic Ecosystems (aquaticeco. com).

Detail of Glenn Martinez' air-powered water pump. The water enters through a swing check valve and air blows down a 2-inch pipe. The check valve closes, forcing the air and water into the 1-inch pipe, where the air lifts the water to the top of the pipe and into the grow bed.

The Least You Need to Know

- Power and water can be disrupted for a variety of reasons and power can be off for several days, so it's valuable to be able to provide your own.
- Rainwater collection is legal in most areas and can provide water for your garden and reduce sewage overflows associated with stormwater runoff.
- It is possible to use solar and wind energy to power a system. You can reduce costs by minimizing power requirements.
- Simple water pumps that can be driven manually or by wind power are used by millions in the developing world. An air-powered water pump can also reduce the amount of power required if you want to go off-grid.

Maintaining Your Garden

In This Chapter

- Routine daily maintenance
- Weekly and monthly tasks
- Recommended seasonal tasks
- How to refresh clogged grow beds

Maintaining your aquaponic garden is easy. Spending a couple of minutes in your garden daily will be enough to handle most maintenance. Plan on taking a bit more time on the weekends, and tackling a couple of major garden projects during the year. That's all you'll need to have a delightful and productive garden with healthy fish. In this chapter I cover everything that needs to be done on a daily, weekly, monthly, and seasonal basis.

Daily Tasks

There are three things you should do every day. You'll need to check your water level and temperature, feed your fish, and check your plants.

You may need to add water to your fish tank, and the temperature will tell you if your fish will be willing to eat—unless they're too cold or too hot, your fish always like to eat. A daily check of your plants will help you know how close they are to harvest and whether there are any pests you need to deal with.

Checking the Water

Each day you should look at the sump tank or fish tank and make sure the water level is okay. If the water level is low, add water. Also check the water temperature.

It's a good idea to have a bucket full of water that you use to top off your tank. Letting water from the tap sit in a bucket allows any chlorine in your water to evaporate out of the water. Chlorine is bad for your fish and can interfere with the growth of your plants.

Letting a bucket of water sit for at least a day before adding it to your system also allows the temperature to match your garden. Since the outside temperature can be a very different temperature than the water in the fish tank, I like to add the water to the grow beds instead.

> **SOUNDS FISHY**
>
> Fish won't eat if their water temperature is too high or too low. Once you learn the temperature limits of your fish, you can simply look at the water temperature thermometer and know if the fish will eat that day. Typical ranges for various fish can be found in Chapter 15. Your fish can go without eating for several days, particularly during cold weather. It's better to underfeed than overfeed.

Feeding Your Fish

For the first few days after you get your fish, spend some time to see how much food your fish can eat in five minutes. If there's anything the fish haven't eaten in five minutes, scoop it out of the tank and discard it. After a while, you'll know how much food your fish eat. Most fish like to eat in the morning and in the evening, though small fingerlings may need to eat several times a day.

Automatic fish feeders are tempting, but some can easily dump too much food into your tank. This extra food will rot, raising the ammonia to levels that are toxic for your fish. If you are interested in automated fish feeding, see Chapter 20.

Checking Your Plants

Take a few moments to see if your plants need any care. It's unusual to have weeds, but if you see any, pull them up. If your plants are ready for harvest, this is a great time to reap the bounty. If certain plants are maturing, it's a good time to think about how you will prepare them.

Check for pests. The initial remedy is to take a hose and spray off any bugs you may see. If the pests are animals or birds, you may need nets or fencing to keep the pests away. Chapter 13 covers a number of organic remedies that you should be able to assemble from items in your home. It is wise to stock one or two of the more exotic remedies, just in case.

Weekly Tasks

On a weekly basis, you should do the following tasks:

- Tidy up your plants by pinching off unwanted growth and discarding dead leaves.
- Check your plumbing to make sure everything is working properly.
- Check your pH, ammonia, nitrite, and nitrate.

The process for testing your water was covered in detail in Chapter 10. The pH test takes only a minute. The nitrite test, the ammonia test, and the nitrate test each take a little bit more than five minutes and can be done simultaneously.

If your nitrate levels are above 40 parts per million (ppm), it's time to consider adding more plants or more grow beds. If you won't be able to add more plants to your system and nitrate levels are higher than 80 ppm, you can reduce the levels by performing a 25 percent water change. The extra nitrate-rich water is great to use on any other plants you might have around your home.

If your plants are looking funny, review the pH and consult Chapter 14 for information on what you might need to add to correct plant growth problems caused by nutrient deficiencies.

Monthly Tasks

On a monthly basis, make sure your pump is clean and check your hoses, tank walls, and pump for potential problems. Set a time each month to plan what you'll need to do the following month. This is particularly important if you will need to buy any supplies or seeds.

Cleaning Your System

Each month you want to make sure that everything is still working well. I like to keep a crochet hook, a toothbrush, and a bristle brush available to maintain my system. Here's what you'll want to check:

- **All of your hoses into your grow beds.** Is there any algae growth that you want to remove? A toothbrush is a great tool for this. If your plumbing is polyvinyl chloride (PVC) pipe, you can flush out the pipes with water from a hose.

- **All of your standpipes or siphons.** I find a crochet hook a useful tool to pull my bells off my siphons. Check that everything is flowing well, and see if there are any obstructions in the standpipes or roots growing in through the media guard.

- **Your tanks.** It is not necessary or even recommended to scrub down the tank walls. However, you should turn off your air pump and let the water settle so you can see everything in your tank—you might find that something has fallen into the tank. This is also a good time to get a good look at your fish.

- **Your pump.** If you have any reason to think your pump might be clogged, this is the time to turn it off, remove it from the water, open it up, and make sure everything is clean.

It's a good idea to keep spares of critical components, like water pumps (shown here), air pumps, and air stones. I usually remove the plastic mesh filter and let the outer casing keep out big pieces. Let your grow beds filter the smaller debris out of the water.

Planning Your Next Set of Plants

Once you know your nitrate levels and see how your plants have been growing, sit down at the beginning of each month and plan what plants you'll need to start or buy in the coming month. Also think about what seedlings you want to plant in the next month, if you like to grow your plants from seed. Go to the store and purchase any seeds or seedlings you want.

Since you can easily reposition your plants in an aquaponic garden, this is also a good time to see if any of your plants needs to be repositioned. Move your tall plants to the side of your garden away from sunlight, ensuring that your shorter plants get the sunlight they need to thrive.

Purchasing Supplies

While tending your garden, odds and ends will occur to you. You could buy anything you need as soon as you think about it, but I find it useful to have a shopping day where I purchase any unusual supplies I found myself wanting during the prior month. An exception would be any remedies you need for pest control—I would get those as soon as you suspect a problem.

Seasonal Tasks

When the seasons change, you'll change the kind of plants you're growing (for example, winter crops instead of cool-weather crops). If you have a greenhouse of some sort (see Chapter 18), now is the time to either hunker down for a cooler season or get ready for warm weather.

Winter

During the winter you're unlikely to be active in the garden. This quiet time is perfect for planning next year's garden. Here are some suggested tasks:

- Plan any material additions to your aquaponic system. This includes new grow beds, trellises, or additional fish tanks.

- Sketch out which plants you will add in what sections of your garden. Do this by month as well as by square foot. Remember that you can rearrange your plants during the season if you need to.

- Determine what fish you need to purchase for the coming season. Investigate appropriate vendors, and make sure you've budgeted for the needs of your new fish.

- Renew or acquire licenses for the fish you have or want. In most fisheries departments, licenses expire at the end of December.

- If you're starting your plants from seed, purchase your seeds, prepare your growing medium, and get those seeds started.

- Organize your seeds based on what happened in your garden the previous year. Note which plans works well and which didn't.

Wintertime is a great season, and with luck you may be able to have enough warmth in your garden and enough sunlight to continue growing a few crops. Even if you're not growing new crops, you may find that hearty crops such as carrots, spinach, kale, and beets can safely remain in place.

DID YOU KNOW ...

Carrots and kale grown during the fall and left in place during winter will become sweet—a real winter treat.

Spring

It's exciting to see the first buds of spring popping up above the ground. Make sure you know when the last frost date is projected to occur in your area. Your aquaponic garden may be warmer than the soil gardens in your area, but you won't want to put any tender plants in your garden until you're sure that any chance of frost is past. Here are some tasks to attend to:

- Directly seed any plants that can be planted in your garden before the last frost of the winter. Beets and spinach are in this category.

- Monitor the temperature in your tank. If you use a heater to keep your winter garden warm, think about turning it off.

- Plant the seedlings that you've either purchased or started indoors.

- Build any vertical supports or trellises that you need. If you wait until the plants start climbing, it will be too late.

- Check the levels of ammonia, nitrite, and nitrate in your system. See Chapter 10 if you need to jumpstart your nitrogen cycle again. Adding seaweed extract will provide many key nutrients for your plants.

- Buy fish. Spring is when the fish wagon starts rolling again and it's safe for online distributors to resume shipping fish.

Summer

Since I use a hoop house, which is a temporary type of greenhouse, summer is the time when I take down the walls and make sure air can flow freely. Here are a few other tasks you may want to do at this time:

- Summer heat increases water evaporation. Establish a routine for adding water to your tank. Consider buying a float valve to automatically fill up your tanks.

- If the summer sun is particularly intense in your area, acquire shade cloth. I use the frame of my hoop house to support the shade cloth over my garden.

- Summer is when you will harvest the bulk of your crop. Find ways to eat, share, or preserve your produce.

- Harvest some of your edible fish if they are big enough to be eaten. You can either eat your fish now or preserve your fish by canning, freezing, or smoking.

- Reinstall waterproof covers over your grow beds if end of summer brings a rainy season in your area. Torrential rains can significantly disrupt the pH of your water, which can hurt your fish.

Check your system periodically so you know what you'll need to replace, like this shredded plastic roofing.

Fall

Fall is a time to plant a second round of cool-weather crops. It is also the time to prepare your garden for the winter, whatever that means in your area. Here are some suggested tasks:

- If you have a greenhouse, enclose it before the weather gets too cold. It's not at all fun to work outside when the weather gets nippy.

- Take down any grow towers or unprotected grow beds before the first frost of the season.

- Pull up any annual plants that have finished bearing. Prepare your grow beds for any crops that you plan to leave in the garden during winter.

Renewing Your Grow Beds

If you use media beds in your system, they may need to be cleaned out after several years of service. There's no need to sterilize your media unless there's been some kind of disease—just remove the rocks from the grow bed to rinse out excess sand, silt, and organic debris. These same rocks are then placed back in the grow bed.

Here is a suggested process for renewing a grow bed:

1. Remove the plants from your grow bed. Lay them to the side with plastic on the roots to keep them moist.

2. Place a large tarp on the ground.

3. Shovel the media from your bed onto the tarp.

4. Rinse out your grow bed.

5. Repair any damage to the grow bed, standpipe, or siphon.

6. Rinse your media. If possible, use water that has been sitting out for a day or two in a rain barrel to eliminate chlorine that could damage the bacteria in your bed.

7. Put your media guard back in place. Place a security rock on top so it doesn't shift as you refill your grow bed.

8. Replace your rocks in the grow bed.

Depending on what kind of plants were in your grow bed, renewing it could take as little as an afternoon. However, if you were growing big plants, such as papaya trees or banana trees, this could be a more difficult and time-consuming task.

In the case of infection or disease, you can sterilize the media by rinsing with hydrogen peroxide or bleach. Don't do this unless absolutely necessary, since this sterilization process will kill the beneficial bacteria and worms in the system. If you have to do this, rinse off the peroxide or bleach afterward with plain water and let the media dry on the tarp for another day or two before putting it back in your grow bed.

The Least You Need to Know

- Check your water every day. If the water is at a temperature where your fish are willing to eat, go ahead and feed your fish.
- Check your water chemistry every week.
- Take time each month to purchase seeds, plants, or supplies you might need.
- As each season changes, review and schedule tasks for the new season.
- Media-filled grow beds may need to be cleaned out after a few years.

Integrated Aquaponic Systems

Chapter 23

In This Chapter

- Integrating aquaponics into an abundant lifestyle
- Integration in a rural village in Africa
- Integration in a retirement community in the United States
- Integrating aquaponics with teaching science

There are two ways to think about integrating aquaponics with other systems in your home. The first is an engineering approach to integration: what can we do to make aquaponics and other tasks more efficient? The second is a lifestyle approach to integration: what can we do to include aquaponics in a way that makes life more enjoyable and abundant?

While I was working on this book, two people approached me to discuss integrated agriculture. Dirk Bouma, from Engineers without Borders, had just come back from spending time at a demonstration village where he was integrating aquaculture and agriculture near Porto Novo, Benin, a country in West Africa. Dirk and his friends wanted to see what I was doing with aquaculture in the small yard behind my townhome.

Joanie, an older woman who recently moved to a retirement community, was looking to use aquaponics to provide an outlet for retired seniors to showcase their skills, mentor youth, and grow decent tomatoes for their dinner table.

I also had the chance to meet some people who are integrating aquaponics into school settings to teach the rising generation.

This chapter discusses how aquaponics can be integrated into a lifestyle to achieve important goals for both individuals and communities.

Life on the Edge

Many in Africa and Asia suffer from lack of clean water and adequate food. Embracing sustainable practices in these communities is a matter of life and death.

Songhai (songhai.com) is a private voluntary organization that seeks to empower individuals and communities to develop resilient, integrated communities linking agriculture, industry, and services. Named after one of the greatest African empires of history, Songhai is trying to develop green rural cities to make rural settlements economically viable.

Songhai has set up 10 model villages in West Africa, from Sierra Leone to Congo. These model villages demonstrate how integrated agriculture can improve food production to benefit everyone. There are several elements to their village system.

DID YOU KNOW ...

As of 2007, more than 50 percent of the world's population lives in cities. The United Nations expects that over 60 percent of the world will live in cities by 2030. Unfortunately, few cities could feed their inhabitants in a crisis. Most cities have only a two-day reserve of food supplies.

Central Fishpond

The Songhai villages use a central pond to raise fish and produce nutrient-rich water for the surrounding fields. Even though this sort of system isn't exactly the soil-less kind of system I have in my backyard, it is very much like the integrated aquaculture practiced in China, and anciently in Egypt and Mexico, that many look to as the first aquaponic systems. The Songhai village raises tilapia, carp, and catfish. But they haven't stopped at merely using fish with their crops.

Quail and Other Birds

The village also raises quail and other fowl for meat and eggs. Quail are quiet birds that produce an unusually large amount of meat and eggs compared to the amount of feed they eat. The villagers also raise chickens and ducks, creating a diversity of meat and eggs.

The birds, however, aren't merely useful for the food they produce. The villagers collect the bird droppings to enrich the compost piles.

Waste Streams

The industrialized western world embraced the toilet when it was invented in the late 1800s, but a village living on the edge can ill afford the costs of discarding human waste. The waste products from the Songhai communal latrine are used to power a bio-digester. The liquid coming out of the latrine flows past lush hyacinths and other water plants that absorb nutrients and purify the water that comes from the latrine.

The solid wastes such as extra plant matter and human and animal feces are added to a bio-digester. The waste decomposes, producing flammable methane gas that is used for heat and combustion. Songhai produces 80 percent of its electrical power using the methane from plant trimmings and fecal waste.

Songhai uses black soldier fly larvae to further reduce waste products from the village. These larvae can also be used to feed fish and birds.

The water hyacinths that grow near the latrines are used to help feed pigs. The choice of pigs is also interesting. Pigs breed easily and grow fast; as a result, a pound of pork requires fewer resources to produce than a pound of beef, lamb, or goat.

Water Tower

Songhai has a water tower to provide pressurized water. Locating the water in the center of the village reduces the time and energy women and children need to spend on collecting water. The water tower allows for centralized purification of drinking water supplies, preventing premature deaths.

The women and children don't need to spend much time on the traditional task of collecting water because of the water tower, and the bio-digester eliminates much of the need to gather wood for cook fires. This extra time is used for education, which is always associated with an improved standard of living in this part of the world.

It's not likely that you or I will have the kind of complete, ecologically integrated system possible in the Songhai village, but there are elements of this wider vision that might be appropriate in a system you create for yourself and your family.

Integrated Agriculture for Communities of Choice

Western communities often have sufficient financial resources to procure clean water and food—but even money sometimes can't buy decent tomatoes.

Joanie is a great example of mature America. She has spent her long life in a wide range of pursuits, mastering skills as diverse as farming and counseling.

Joanie recently moved into a retirement community. She likes the staff and fellow residents, but the food quality was lacking. Joanie's past experience in 4-H, an agricultural youth development organization, led her to believe something could be done. Her research led her to aquaponics, and we had a chance to meet. I've worked with Joanie to develop a vision for how aquaponics could be integrated into her community.

Building a Geodesic Dome

A geodesic dome is stable and resistant to wind. Joanie and her colleagues are leaning towards constructing a large dome for the main section of their garden. The eventual structure may have standard hoop house extensions for rainwater collection, but a well-constructed dome at the heart of the agricultural complex would be functional and unique.

GREEN TIP

You can build your own geodesic dome. Math teacher Tara Landry put together a website that explains how to build them at desertdomes.com. Tara makes geodesic domes for the annual Burning Man festival in the Nevada desert.

Integrating Automation

Joanie has access to numerous experts who are now retired. Her community can build on that expertise to create projects building on these expert skills.

Her retired colleagues have developed agriculture, plumbing, water testing, and gardening skills over their long lives. Once the retirement community's systems were created, they could be automated. Automation using the techniques covered in

Chapter 20 can use social media to allow the surrounding community to interact with the garden.

Adding Other Animals

Joanie plans to use her 4-H experience to mentor young people. Rabbits, chickens, and quail are fun and useful to raise in their own right, and make a great project for young people. But these animals and their by-products could be integrated with fish and plants in an aquaponics ecosystem, as they were in the African village.

Rabbit pellets are great feed for composting worms. The rabbits would also be able to feed on the excess harvest from the aquaponic garden. The fish and birds could eat the black soldier fly larvae that feed on other wastes. Eggshells would provide calcium for the aquaponic system.

Harvesting Energy

Depending on where the retirement home is located, the garden might need to be kept warm in winter. Reducing the cost of heating the garden would definitely be useful. It's simple to harvest heat using solar air heaters and solar water heaters. Construction is easy and could serve as yet another opportunity for mentorship between the retirement community and youth and others in the neighborhood who want to learn how to use solar energy to reduce heating bills. A rocket mass heater in the garden can provide heat when the sun isn't sufficient.

Using geothermal heat to heat and cool the greenhouse might not be possible if the garden is placed on a preexisting surface. But in locations where it makes sense to include it in this kind of demonstration facility, a functioning geothermal system can provide a model of how to use geothermal energy to reduce dependence on fossil fuels.

Integrating Air, Water, and Soil Gardening

Many crops such as basil, lettuce, chives, and lettuce can grow just fine in towers, where the plant roots mostly hang in air. A pergola behind the greenhouse could be used to support additional plants during the summer, providing welcome shade while surrounded by aromatic plants and herbs.

Within the greenhouse proper, the water from the fish tank could flow first into gravel grow beds and then to a swirl filter to collect any residual solids before flowing into floating rafts. The gentle sound of flowing water is uniquely soothing.

Wicking beds outside the greenhouse would allow gardeners used to soil gardening to continue using their hobby without learning new techniques. Those soil gardens in the wicking beds would enjoy many of the benefits of aquaponics, require no watering and getting nutrients from the fish water.

Encouraging Community Celebrations

Starting seeds and celebrating harvests are wonderful opportunities for communities to gather—communities often stage such events for their members. But in the case of a garden farm, the celebrations take on a vital meaning. Spring sowing and fall harvest are both great times to gather and celebrate life.

Few of us can return to a simple small town life, but we can create cooperative communities in our new lives, wherever we may find ourselves.

Adding Agriculture to Technology Education

Integrating aquaponics into education can improve a student's grasp of math and science. Aquaponics provides many opportunities to apply math and science to something tangible—not to mention edible. I've recently had a chance to talk with several individuals who are integrating aquaponics into the classroom environment to help students learn.

DID YOU KNOW ...

A recent survey in the UK of young adults (16 to 23 years old) showed half didn't know milk comes from a dairy cow. A third didn't know eggs come from chickens. Another survey in Australia showed one in five children in the sixth grade think pasta comes from an animal.

International Aquaponics in Yokohama

In 2011 a magnitude 9.0 earthquake set off a tsunami that devastated much of northeast Japan. The tsunami contaminated vast areas of ground with saltwater.

Around this time, Aragon St. Charles of Japan Aquaponics worked with the Yokohama International School to integrate aquaponics into the curriculum. The teachers at all grade levels of the school integrated school's aquaponic garden into their curriculum.

The aquaponic garden at the Yokohama International School is helping the students understand how plants and fish work together to produce food and how a wide variety of school topics are tangible and relevant.

Aquaponics in a High School Honors Program

When I first met Dr. Kevin Savage, it was clear he was passionate about his students. Dr. Savage teaches at Cincinnati Hills Christian Academy, a private school where it's cool to be smart.

Dr. Savage uses aquaponics to teach advanced students about chemistry and environmental science, pulling in aspects of physics and biology. As the students approach the end of their high school education, they get to do independent research. Doing high-level research projects generally requires advanced degrees, but Dr. Savage is able to develop a wide array of research topics for his students using aquaponics.

I remember school research projects when I was a student. Mostly we were just repeating experiments that had already been done years ago. But with aquaponics, Dr. Savage has an opportunity to guide his students in doing research that hasn't been done yet. Their published results will break new ground—very cool to be able to do at the high-school level.

"HOT STEAM Drives You MAD"

Glenn Martinez of Hawaii will tell you he is a certified NQW—no qualifications whatsoever. Yet he is a life-long farmer and one of the first to earn organic certification for an aquaponics farm.

At a recent conference, Glenn talked about hands-on training, making a difference, and adding agriculture to the traditional math and science curriculum, known as Science, Technology, Engineering, and Math (STEM). His title was "HOT STEAM drives you MAD," which stands for "hands-on training in science, technology, engineering, agriculture, and math drives you to make a difference."

Glenn has traveled throughout the countries in the western Pacific teaching how to build effective aquaponic farms that can feed communities and run off as little as 40 watts of power. One recent system was created at Tuloy Foundation in Alabang, Philippines, a school that serves 800 street children and helps them gain the skills to become productive members of society. The Tuloy system has attracted attention from a wide range of visitors, including the vice president of the Philippines.

When Glenn leaves one of his air-powered water pump systems behind, he leaves an army of students who understand the pump and can assemble it from the individual plumbing parts. Growing plants and living animals give immediate feedback, and that feedback has a direct impact on what and when the students eat, making this one of the most relevant kinds of education imaginable.

The Least You Need to Know

- Integration of the multiple available technologies will depend on the needs of each individual or group.
- Integrating fish, plants, composting, animals, and waste processing can make a rural village almost fully self-sufficient.
- Integrating aquaponics into a retirement home can open up opportunities for growth and mentoring.
- Integrating aquaponics into a school curriculum can help teachers demonstrate math, biology, chemistry, physics, and environmental science—and large systems can feed the students as well.

Do-It-Yourself Systems

Chapter 24

In This Chapter

- Creating a small indoor aquaponic garden
- Building a medium-sized aquaponic garden
- Information on free online plans for barrels and IBC totes

Although there are many prebuilt systems out there, I didn't want to leave you without giving you a couple of complete plans for making your own system. I feel the best way to learn is by doing, and these plans are relatively inexpensive. If you do it yourself, you should already have the tools and skills for these projects. These are projects you can do by yourself, although having an assistant is always helpful.

The first set of plans is for a small 10-gallon system you can put together for about $100. This small system would work well in a classroom or home setting, and allow you to grow some kitchen herbs and a few other plants, with a couple of fish in the tank. The second set of plans is for a larger 100-gallon system you can put together for about $400. This plan would allow you to have over a dozen edible fish and grow a respectable crop.

At the end of this chapter there's also a list of the other DIY plans in the book and the chapters where you can find them, as well as information on a few of my favorite online sources of DIY inspiration.

A 10-Gallon System for About $100

This small aquarium-based system can be created from parts you can buy at local pet, home, and hardware stores. It's a great little aquaponic system for a sunny window at home or in a classroom.

Supplies:

1 sturdy plastic bin at least 6" deep ($10)

Enough ¾" river rocks to fill the plastic bin (3 of the bags commonly sold at hardware stores—$10)

1 wire shelving unit (23"×13"×30"—$20)

1 glass 10-gallon fish tank ($15 at pet store)

1 media guard (Chapter 5, made from 3" PVC pipe)

1 inexpensive bulkhead fitting (Chapter 5, using PVC conduit connectors and #18 O-rings)

1 Coanda drain with 2" lengths of PVC (Chapter 7, made from ¾" PVC and a 45° elbow)

1 Affnan-style standpipe (Chapter 7, made from ¾" plumbing pieces)

1 bag zip ties (roughly ¼" wide)

1 glass jar from 15-oz jar of olives ($3)

1 black vinyl tubing to fit water pump ($5)

(1) 200-gallon per hour water pump ($30)

1 air stone ($1)

(1) ¼" vinyl air tubing ($2)

1 air check valve ($2)

1 small air pump ($7)

Tools:

Permanent marker

1" spade drill bit and drill

Wire cutter (most pliers can also cut wires)

Miter saw (to cut PVC pipe for media guard and plumbing)

Scissors

1. Place the rocks in the plastic bin. Rinse the rocks until the water runs clear. Set the rocks aside to dry.

Assemble the main components:

2. Assemble the wire shelving unit according to instructions.

3. Place the fish tank on the middle shelf.

4. Place the plastic bin on the top shelf.

Drill the hole in the plastic bin:

5. Put the media guard in a corner of the bin. Mark the center of the bin under the media guard. This is where you will drill through the bin.

6. Remove the media guard.

7. Use the spade drill bit to cut a hole in the corner of the bin on the mark you've made. You may be able to cut the hole by hand using the bit alone to reduce the probability of the bit ripping the bin. If you must use the drill, put a piece of scrap wood under the drill bit to reduce tearing.

Cut the shelf so the plumbing will fit:

8. Place the bin on the shelf. Identify which wire in the shelf you will need to cut so the plumbing can go through the shelf.

9. Cut the wire in the top of the shelf with wire cutters.

Assemble the bulkhead, drain, and standpipe:

10. Assemble the bulkhead fitting in the hole through the bin. I like to stick the male conduit connector through the hole, slide the O-ring over the male pipe threads, and then screw on the female conduit fitting.

11. Stick the Coanda drain into the bottom of the bulkhead fitting.

12. Stick the Affnan-style standpipe into the top of the bulkhead fitting. The standpipe should be shorter than the edge of your bin. If necessary, cut the PVC pipe connecting the fittings to the bulkhead so there is no extra space.

13. Close the zip tie so it is a bigger than the threaded part of the olive jar. It's better to err on the side of leaving the zip tie too large.

14. Slide the zip tie over the standpipe. Make sure the olive jar fits on the zip tie, supported at two points on the round part of the zip tie and also by the tail. Adjust the zip tie if necessary. Clip off the excess on the zip tie, leaving about an inch of a tail.

15. Slide the media guard over the olive jar. Push the tail of the zip tie inside the media guard if it is sticking out.

Assemble the water pump and tubing:

16. Connect the black vinyl tube to the water pump. If the water pump has a foam filter pad inside, remove it. Turn any flow rate dial to the maximum setting.

17. Place the water pump in the aquarium.

18. Run the black vinyl tube up to the grow bed. Fasten the tube with zip ties so it will securely empty into the grow bed.

Assemble the air pump, tubing, and air stone:

19. Push the air stone onto the ¼" tubing. Clip a small segment of the tubing for later use.

20. Push the ¼" tubing onto the check valve. Make sure the check valve is facing the right way.

21. Push the other end of the short length of tubing on the opposite end of the check valve.

22. Push the free bit of short tubing onto the air pump.

23. Put the air stone into the fish tank.

Add media and water. Turn system on:

24. Add the rinsed stones to the grow bed.

25. Add water to the system.

26. Turn on the pumps.

You'll want to let the water circulate for a day before planting to let the chlorine evaporate. This system is only large enough for one or two small fish. Purchase a freshwater aquarium test kit and see how the measurements change over time.

> **DID YOU KNOW ...**
>
> If the sound of water bothers you when you're trying to sleep, you can get a timer to turn the pump off at night. But leave the air pump going so the oxygen level stays high for the fish.

A 100-Gallon System for About $400

This stock tank system uses Rubbermaid stock tanks, available at agricultural stores. If you can't find Rubbermaid stock tanks, you can use one of the wooden grow beds from Chapter 4 and a surplus bathtub. A bathtub holds about 80 gallons.

If you want to use lightweight clay balls or expanded shale, you'll need about 350 liters or 100 gallons. River rock or gravel is the least expensive and is what is listed in these instructions.

Supplies:

(2) 10' kiln-dried 2×6 planks ($6.50 each)

(2) 50-gallon Rubbermaid stock tanks ($75 each)

(1) 100-gallon Rubbermaid stock tank ($80)

(1) 1×3 board ($2)

(1) 2×3 board ($2.50)

(12) 8"×8"×16" concrete blocks ($2.50 each)

2 inexpensive bulkhead fittings (Chapter 5)

2 Coanda drains with 2" lengths of PVC (Chapter 7)

2 Affnan-style standpipes (Chapter 7)

2 bell assemblies (Chapter 7, made from 2" PVC pipe and a 2" PVC cap)

2 media guards (Chapter 5)

(1) 25' ⅝" drinking water hose ($30)

2 female hose fittings ($2 each)

(1) 400-gallon-per-hour water pump ($50)

1 plastic hose splitter ($5)

1 roll synthetic twine ($3)

1 air stone ($1)

(1) ¼" vinyl air tubing ($2)

1 air check valve ($2)

1 small air pump ($7)

13 cubic feet of rocks from quarry to fill plastic bin ($20)

Tools:

Permanent marker

1" spade drill bit, ¼" bit, and drill

Miter saw (to cut lumber and PVC pipe for plumbing)

Scissors

Prepare the support lumber:

1. Place the two 2×6 planks on the ground about 4" apart.

2. Place one of the 50-gallon grow beds on the planks, bottom side down. Mark where the bottom of the grow bed hits the planks. This is where you'll be cutting.

3. Move the grow bed over about 4' and mark the planks again. (It's okay to rearrange the planks if you see a way to reduce waste.)

4. Cut the planks with the miter saw. Set aside.

5. Trim the 2×6 scrap pieces so they are 16" long.

6. Trim the 1×3 and 2×3 into as many 16" pieces as you can.

SOUNDS FISHY

Remember to put a heavy system like this on a strong floor. The best places to put this would be in a basement, a garage, or outside on a level bit of ground or hardtop.

Position the fish tank and grow bed supports:

7. Place the 100-gallon tank in the center of your space.

8. Create two stacks of three concrete blocks each on either side of the tank.

9. Create two more stacks of three concrete blocks about 20" away from each of the stacks that are next to the fish tank. These columns of blocks will support your grow beds.

10. Place the 2×6 planks across the concrete block stacks.

11. Shim the planks with the 16"-long boards you cut in Steps 5 and 6.

Cut the holes in the grow beds:

12. Turn the 50-gallon stock tanks upside down. Locate a good place for the standpipe in the middle near one end.

13. Put the 1" spade bit in the drill. Carefully drill a 1" hole into the bottom of each 50-gallon stock tank.

Assemble the bulkheads, Coanda drains, and standpipes in the beds:

14. Assemble the bulkhead fittings (instructions in Chapter 5) in the hole through the bin. I like to stick the male conduit connector through the hole, slide the O-ring over the male pipe threads, and then screw on the female conduit fitting.

15. Stick the Coanda drains (instructions in Chapter 7) into the bottom of the bulkhead fittings.

16. Stick the Affnan-style standpipes (instructions in Chapter 7) into the top of the bulkhead fitting. I find a $5\frac{1}{2}$" PVC pipe is a good length for connecting the fittings to the bulkhead.

17. Position the 50-gallon stock tanks on the planks so the water will drain into the fish tank. These will be your grow beds.

18. Place the PVC bell assemblies (instructions in Chapter 7) over the standpipes.

19. Slide the media guards (instructions in Chapter 5) over the bells.

Assemble the water pump and tubing:

20. Cut the drinking water hose about 2' away from the male fitting. Cut two more lengths about 7' long.

21. Attach the cut end of the short hose to the pump. If the pump has a foam filter pad inside, remove it.

22. Attach the hose splitter to the male end of the hose connected to the pump.

23. Connect the female hose fittings to the each of the 7' hose sections.

24. Connect the 7' hose sections to the hose splitter. Make sure the splitter levers are turned so water will come out.

Connect the hose to the tank and grow beds:

25. Use the twine to connect the hose splitter to the fish tank.

26. Use the twine to fasten the hoses so they will add water to the far end of each grow bed. You want the water coming in at the opposite side of the grow bed from where it will drain out. It should be sufficient to tie the hose along the side of the grow bed.

Assemble the air pump, tubing, and air stone:

27. Push the air stone onto the ¼" tubing. Clip a small segment of the tubing for later use.

28. Push the ¼" tubing onto the check valve. Make sure the check valve is facing so air can come out of the air pump.

29. Push the other end of the short length of tubing on the opposite end of the check valve.

30. Push the free bit of short tubing onto the air pump.

31. Put the air stone into the fish tank.

Add media and water. Turn system on:

32. Rinse the stones one bucket at a time and add the rinsed stones to the grow beds. When finished, discard the dirty rinse water.

33. Add water to the system.

34. Turn on the pumps.

35. Adjust the levers on the hose splitter to reduce the flow rate if necessary. If the flow rate is too high, your siphon won't break.

You'll want to let the water circulate for a day before planting to let the chlorine evaporate. This system is large enough for about 15 fish, assuming they grow to weigh a pound when they are mature. Purchase a freshwater aquarium test kit and see how the measurements change over time.

DID YOU KNOW ...

You can increase the number of grow beds by adding fish tank volume. Rubbermaid stock tanks also come in 150- and 300-gallon sizes, and the 300-gallon stock tanks can sometimes be purchased through Ace Hardware stores, saving you shipping.

Where to Find Other DIY Plans in This Book

There are a variety of other DIY plans scattered through the book. You can find them at the end of the chapter where they appear. For the exact page number, you can also check out the index to the book.

Chapter	Description
4	3×5 wooden grow bed
5	PVC media guard
5	Inexpensive bulkhead fitting
5	PVC standpipe and drain
5	Solids lifting overflow for drain in the bottom of a fish tank
5	Solids lifting overflow for drain in the side of a fish tank
7	Inexpensive 15-minute timer

continues

continued

Chapter	Description
7	Affnan bell siphon and Coanda drain pipe
8	PVC tower
8	Pergola
9	Nutrient film technique tube from fence post
9	Swirl filter
18	PVC hoop house

Online DIY Plans and More

The vast amount of information available on the internet is amazing, and it is constantly growing. However, there are a few sources for DIY plans and videos I want to particularly mention. Be sure to check the resources in Appendix B as well.

Joel Malcolm and the folks at Backyard Aquaponics put together a great manual with information about making systems out of intermediate bulk container (IBC) totes. They've now turned the manual into a website to make it even easier to get you the latest information. The website is ibcofaquaponics.com, where you can also find the original manual for download.

Rob Torcellini of Bigelow Brook Farm is continually working on new projects related to aquaponics. I highly recommend you check out his popular YouTube channel, youtube.com/web4deb. His videos are entertaining and informative, and he's received over 2 million views.

Travis Hughey put together plans for making an aquaponic system using 55-gallon barrels. His plans have been used by countless people in the past decade, and he has installed systems around the world. Check out Travis's website at fastonline.org.

You will find the plans for his Barrel-Ponics system by clicking on Technology and Aquaponics. I created the shortened URL tinyurl.com/BarrelPonics, which will take you straight to the smaller version of Travis Hughey's free plans.

Finally, when I first started asking friends what they thought a new aquaponic gardener would need to know, almost all said "Tell them to come to the forums!" There are several vibrant online communities dedicated to aquaponic gardening. You'll find a wealth of information, and a lot of friendly people.

Best wishes as you move ahead with aquaponics!

The Least You Need to Know

- It's relatively easy to put together a small 10-gallon aquaponics system for an apartment or school class.
- A larger 100-gallon system isn't much more complicated that a 10-gallon system—the pieces are just bigger.
- You can always buy parts from someone else, but this book contains plans you can follow if you're handy with tools.
- Free online plans are available and well worth checking out.

Glossary

acid   Acids break down organic compounds. Water is considered acidic when it has a ph level below 7.0. Stomach acid, lemon juice, and vinegar are examples of acids.

aerobic   Requiring or having abundant air.

Affnan bell siphon   A bell siphon where the standpipe has a funnel-like top to increase the amount of water priming the siphon when the water begins flowing over the top of the standpipe.

Affnan-style standpipe   A standpipe with a funnel-like top used in an Affnan bell siphon.

aggregate   Coarse material that includes crushed rock or gravel.

air lift   When air bubbles lift water so it can rise from the fish tank into the grow bed or vertical tower where you are growing your plants.

air pump outlet   A port on the side of the air pump from which high-pressure air is pushed.

alkaline   Alkaline water has a ph above 7.0. Alkaline water contains earth metals and salts and can be corrosive. Baking soda, bleach, and soap are alkaline.

ammonia   A form of nitrogen exhaled by fish and produced by organic waste, like fish poop and rotting food. Ammonia can be toxic to fish.

anaerobic   Dead zones caused by lack of oxygen that harbor bacteria and release harmful toxins.

annual   An annual plant that germinates, flowers, sets seed, and then dies within a year.

aphid   Soft-bodied, sap-sucking insects that may be white, yellow, black, or green.

aquaculture   The cultivation of aquatic animals and plants in a controlled environment.

aquaponic gardening   Gardening using an aquaponics system, where the water from your fish tank irrigates your plants and then drains back into your fish tank.

aquaponics   Gardening where the plants are grown without soil (either floating in water or in an inert medium irrigated by water) and the nutrients come from keeping fish in the water tank (aquaculture).

Arduino microcontrollers   Hobby computer boards that can be programmed to automate a garden.

automation   The use of machines and control systems to optimize productivity. The goal of automation is to increase productivity and quality beyond what's possible with human labor.

auto-siphon   A siphon that automatically drains a container when the fluid level rises to the lip of the overflow. Auto-siphons require no electricity or moving parts.

bacteria   Naturally occurring microscopic organisms, both good and bad.

ballast   An electrical device that supplies and controls the high voltage that HID lights require.

bell siphon or bell auto-siphon   An auto-siphon where a bell or jar is placed over a standpipe to quickly drain water from the media bed when the water level reaches the top of the standpipe.

biological filter   A container filled with inert material that hosts nitrifying bacteria to convert ammonia into nitrate.

bolt   When a plant begins to produce a stalk, flowers, and seeds. The leaves of leafy vegetables like lettuce and spinach become bitter when the plant bolts.

brassica   Plants in the mustard family, collectively known as cabbages. They are very nutritious and contain many antioxidants.

broadcast   To scatter seed during sowing. Radio and television transmissions were named broadcasts because of the well-understood agricultural image.

brood   To protect eggs. A fish broods by holding her eggs in her mouth.

broodstock   Mature fish used for spawning and the production of young.

buffer   Additive that resists changes in pH when small quantities of an acid or alkali are added.

bulbing   Formation of a bulbous root, such as for a beet.

calcium Silvery-white soft alkaline earth metal that is necessary for plant growth.

calcium carbonate Found naturally in chalk, limestone, and marble and is used to buffer pH.

carnivore An organism that feeds mainly or exclusively on animal tissue.

certified organic Products certified to meet strict standards for growing, processing, storing, packaging, and shipping that minimizes use of synthetic chemicals. Requirements vary from country to country.

check valve A fixture you attach between two tubes or pipes to ensure that flow goes in only one direction.

chloramine Combination of ammonia and chlorine usually used as a disinfectant and water treatment.

chlorine A powerful bleaching and disinfecting agent used to produce safe drinking water.

chlorosis A condition in which leaves do not produce enough chlorophyll, resulting in pale, yellow leaves. Often caused by a lack of iron.

constant height in fish tank, pump in sump tank (CHIFT PIST) *See* constant height, one pump (CHOP).

constant height, one pump (CHOP) An aquaponic system with a pump in the sump where the water in the fish tank stays at a constant height.

cisterns Containers for storing large amounts of water underground that are usually located below the frost line.

clay Naturally occurring material consisting of fine-grained minerals that hardens when fired or dried.

Coanda drain A drainpipe where the lowest leg is connected using a 45-degree connector. The gentle 45-degree bend causes the water to mound up inside the connector, starting the siphon action.

coir A natural fiber extracted from coconut husks.

cold frame An unheated, bottomless box on the ground with a glass cover that is used for protecting crops during the winter.

cold-season crops Crops that can survive freezing and continue to grow when the temperature is above freezing.

compact fluorescent lights (CFL)   Fluorescent bulbs that have been twisted to reduce the size of the bulb for the same light output.

compost   Decomposed organic matter. Decomposition can be sped up by using composting worms and black soldier fly larvae.

compost tea   Water rich in beneficial bacteria that has been formed by steeping a bag of compost in aerated water for several days.

composting worms   Worms that are particularly suited to feeding on decaying organic matter. The most common type of composting worm is *Eisenia fetida*, known by the common names redworm, brandling worm, panfish worm, trout worm, tiger worm, red wiggler worm, and red Californian earthworm.

cool-season crops   Crops that prefer to grow at temperatures between 50° and 75°F. They can tolerate light frost but will be harmed by a prolonged freeze. Temperatures above 75° cause these crops to bolt and taste bitter.

cotyledons   A part of the seed that becomes the first leaves after the seed germinates. Also known as seed leaves, they don't look like the true leaves that form later.

cross-pollination   A process where pollen is delivered from one flowering plant to another.

cycling   The process of introducing ammonia to an aquaponic system to produce a robust colony of nitrosifying and nitrifying bacteria. A fully cycled system is one where all the ammonia and nitrate are transformed into nitrate.

damping off   Condition created by fungus-related diseases that can kill seeds before they germinate.

deadheading   Cutting flower heads or new growth off the plants.

dechlorinate   To remove chlorine.

deep water culture (DWC)   A technique in hydroponics and aquaponics where the plants are supported over grow beds filled with water. The grow beds should ideally be 12 inches deep.

deficiency   A lack or shortage.

determinate   Plants that stop growing at maturity and put their energy into producing fruit.

detritus   Waste or rotting matter.

diffuser   Something that breaks up the airflow in an air line so that you get a cloud of tiny bubbles instead of large individual bubbles.

dissolved oxygen (DO)   A measure of oxygen dissolved in or carried in a given media.

drain   To suck water out of a media bed using gravity or a siphon to allow air to reach plant roots.

ebb and flow   *See* flood and drain.

egg-layers   Fish that lay eggs.

expanded clay   Clay pellets fired in a kiln that expand into porous balls.

expanded polystyrene (EPS)   Foam board made of pre-expanded polystyrene beads. Also known as bead board, it is inexpensive but will break easily.

extruded polystyrene (XPS)   Durable foam sheeting suitable for use in a wet environment.

fingerlings   Young fish that are approximately the size of a human finger.

flood   To fill the media bed with water.

flood and drain   The process of adding and emptying fish water in a media-filled grow bed.

flood tank   A reservoir located above the media beds used to hold water to flood the beds.

flood valve   A flapper valve that opens when the flood tank is full, allowing the water in the flood tank to rush into the media beds.

fluorescent lights   Bulbs that produce light by bouncing gas off metal powder inside the bulb.

food desert   An area with limited access to affordable fresh food, resulting in malnutrition and obesity among residents.

food grade   Components designed for safely coming in contact with foodstuff.

fry   Baby fish that have just emerged from the egg.

fungicide   Chemical compounds used to kill or inhibit fungal spores or fungi.

geodesic domes   Round structures created from many individual triangle sections. Dome greenhouses are resistant to wind damage because there are no large flat sections for the wind to catch.

germinate   The process in which a plant sprouts from a seed and begins to grow.

germination percentage (or rate)   The percentage of seeds in a packet or group of seeds that are expected to germinate.

gravel   Rock fragments.

greenhouse   A large structure covered with glass or plastic that protects a garden. Greenhouses can be either freestanding or attached to another structure, such as a home.

grow bed   A watertight planter or container that holds plants in an aquaponic system.

grow lights   Special lights and fixtures that produce large amounts of light in colors plants use (white but with more red and blue than normal lights).

growing media   Substances, often rocks or similar material, placed in grow beds for anchoring roots and hosting nitrifying bacteria.

harden off   Preparing plants that have been grown indoors for introduction into the garden.

hardy crops   *See* cold-season crops.

heirloom   Variety of a plant that was commonly grown before the industrialization of agriculture. Usually pollinated by bees and birds rather than by hand.

high-intensity discharge (HID)   Lights that operate at much higher voltages than standard light bulbs.

high-pressure sodium (HPS)   High-intensity discharge (HID) bulbs that produce reddish light and are used for flowering plants.

high tunnels   Hoop houses that are tall enough for a gardener to walk around without bending.

hoop houses   Greenhouses made from hoops of PVC or metal tubing covered in plastic.

hot-season crops   Crops that thrive in temperatures above 80°F and can't tolerate cold conditions.

hybrid   Hybrid seed is produced by cross-pollinating two distinct and very uniform strains. The resulting offspring are vigorous, productive, and uniform and are therefore popular with commercial growers. These plants don't produce seed that reproduce their good qualities, so it isn't as useful to save their seeds.

hydroponics   A type of gardening where plants are grown without soil by adding nutrients to the water.

Hydroton   A brand of expanded clay/clay balls with high water storage capacity.

indeterminate   Plants that continue to grow, with the older branches and leaves withering to focus energy on the new growth.

indexing valve   Valve that shifts flow from an inlet to any of several outlets. An indexing valve requires some other device, like a repeat cycle timer, to interrupt the water flow briefly to trigger the mechanical shift between outlets.

intercrop   Planting a fast-growing crop in the vacant space between slow-maturing crops. Intercropping makes use of the fact that a plant doesn't need its full amount of space for its entire life, only for the final weeks when it is reaching maturity.

intermediate bulk container (IBC)   A container used to store and transport liquids.

interplant/interplanting   Growing two crops simultaneously in the same bed, taking advantage of mutually compatible features to get the highest yield from the smallest area.

irrigation   Artificial application of water to land or soils.

light expanded clay aggregate (LECA)   Generic term for Hydroton, which has been discontinued.

light-emitting diodes (LEDs)   Devices that convert electricity to light and without using mercury or high voltage.

lime   Calcium oxide that is extracted by heating limestone, coral, seashells, or chalk and used for buffering ph.

limestone   Rocks used for buffering pH.

live-bearers   Fish that keep the baby fish inside their bodies until they are old enough to swim on their own, like guppies and seahorses.

locavores   People who make a point of eating locally grown food to promote sustainability and green businesses.

loop siphon   A simple auto-siphon that uses a loop of tubing to quickly drain water from a media bed when the water level reaches the top of the loop.

low tunnels   Hoop houses that capture heat from the sun and hold the warm air down near crops.

lumen   The unit of measure for a quantity of light.

lux   The number of lumens per square meter.

media bed   A grow bed filled with some kind of material to support the plants. Rocks, stones, expanded clay pellets, expanded shale, and volcanic rock are popular forms of media used in aquaponic systems.

media guard   A shield around your drain or siphon to keep rocks out and allow you to inspect or clean your drain plumbing.

mercury   A heavy metal used in fluorescent lights that can cause numerous health problems.

metal halide (MH)   High-intensity discharge (HID) bulbs that produce bluish light, perfect for green, leafy plants.

micro-farm   An area approximately 1 acre where fresh food is grown for sale.

micro-farmer   A person who grows food on a micro-farm.

micro-greens   Shoots of standard salad plants that are unusually rich in flavor and vitamins.

neutral   Neutral water is neither acidic nor alkaline and has a pH of 7.

nitrate   A form of nitrogen that can be absorbed by plants to fuel conversion of sunlight into energy.

nitrification   The process by which aerobic bacteria convert the ammonia from fish waste into nitrate for plants.

nitrifying bacteria   Bacteria that convert nitrite into nitrate.

nitrite   A form of nitrogen between ammonia and nitrate that can cause brown blood disease in fish.

nitrobacter   Nitrifying bacteria, which oxidize nitrite into nitrate.

nitrogen   An important plant nutrient that is a key component of chlorophyll. The form of nitrogen used by plants is nitrate.

nitrogen cycle The process in which nitrogen is converted between various chemical forms.

nitrosifyers Bacteria that convert ammonia into nitrite.

nutrient A chemical that is used by a plant or organism to grow and thrive.

nutrient deficiency When nutrients are in limited supply or not available.

nutrient film technique (NFT) Growing plants with their roots in pipes or gutters with a small amount of water flowing along the bottom.

open pollination Pollination occurring through natural means, such as wind, birds, or insects.

oxygen A gas critical to healthy function of animals and plant roots. Oxygen is produced by plant leaves as a result of photosynthesis.

perennial A plant that lives for three seasons or more.

pergola An open, roof-like structure used to support plants, usually supported by four posts.

pH The measure of the acidity or alkalinity of a solution. Neutral pH is 7.0, with acids having lower pH and alkaline solutions having higher pH.

phosphorous Phosphorus is a primary nutrient and essential for photosynthesis and cell division. It helps produce strong roots, increases resistance to disease and is needed for respiration. In an aquaponic system, phosphorus is often added with seaweed extract.

photosynthesis The process by which plants exposed to sunlight create food from carbon dioxide and water. Oxygen is produced as a by-product of photosynthesis.

photosynthetically active radiation (PAR) A term used to describe the frequency and intensity range of light plants convert to energy, which is slightly different from the light visible to the human eye.

polyisocyanurate (ISO or PIR) A foam insulation material that can withstand temperatures up to 400°F (200°C). It contains compounds like cyanide and can irritate skin.

polyvinyl chloride (PVC) A plastic polymer.

potassium Abbreviated K, it is one of the three primary plant nutrients (along with nitrogen and phosphorus). It is the nutrient that promotes good root growth, so is especially recommended for root crops and seedlings.

ppm   Parts per million.

ppt   Parts per thousand.

pregerminate   A technique used to make direct sowing more reliable and speed up growth in cool weather by keeping the seed in a warm, damp environment.

pruning   Cutting off parts of a fruiting or woody plant to improve plant health or shape.

purge   The removal of impurities by cleansing.

rain barrels   Containers for storing rainwater above ground. Plastic 55-gallon barrels are often used for this purpose.

rainwater harvesting   Collecting rain for storage on your property, reducing the amount of water feeding into storm drains and providing free water for landscaping.

repeat cycle timer   A timer that repeats a pattern of on and off actions that can be as short as 10 seconds apiece, usually repeating the pattern every 40 minutes.

row cover   Nonwoven textiles spread over crops that hold in warmth like a blanket. It is used to protect crops in open fields and inside hoop houses.

salt   Mineral mainly composed of sodium chloride. It is useful for medicating fish but can inhibit growth in some plants.

S×S   A plumbing term that tells you what kind of piping you can attach on either side of a fitting.

seaweed extract   A solution made from seaweed, which is particularly rich in the key nutrients needed by plants, and one of the primary additives in aquaponic gardening.

self-pollinated   Plants that are able to fertilize their own flowers without cross-pollination from another individual.

semi-hardy crops   *See* cool-season crops.

silt   Particles, like sand and fish wastes, that collect at the bottom of an aquaponic grow bed and can, over time, clog a bed.

siphon   Plumbing that sucks water out of a container, such as a media bed.

solenoids   Water valves you can open and close using electrical commands.

solids lifting overflow (SLO)   A way to suck the organic matter off the bottom of a fish tank without the risk of draining the tank.

spawn Fish eggs, or the act of producing fish eggs.

species Biological classification for a group of organisms capable of interbreeding and producing fertile offspring.

standpipe A pipe that sets the maximum water level in a grow bed, allowing excess water that is pumped into the bed to go straight over the top of the standpipe and down the drain.

standpipe surround *See* media guard.

stigma The part of the plant that catches and traps pollen.

stoma A tiny pore found on leaves and stems that is used for gas exchange. The plural of stoma is stomata.

stormwater Water that originates during rain events.

suckers Shoots that emerge from the root or stem that will take energy from the plant but produce no edible fruit.

sump A low-lying place that receives drainage.

T-5 Straight fluorescent bulbs with a diameter of $\frac{5}{8}$ inch.

temperature probes Equipment that measures temperature and sends that information to an automation system to control fans, solenoids, or window openers.

tender crops *See* warm-season crops.

tendrils Special thread-like stems sent out by climbing plants that curl and coil around anything they touch, lifting a plant upwards.

T-fitting A plastic connector shaped like a T for joining three lines.

thinning The cutting or pinching back of leafy plants.

timer A device that turns power on and off and can be used to alternately flood and drain an aquaponic grow bed.

Torcellini siphon break A bell siphon that adds additional plumbing to ensure a bell siphon starts and breaks. It is useful in media beds larger than 20 cubic feet.

training Manipulating a plant to do something it would not naturally do, usually by fastening a plant to a trellis or other structure.

transpiration A form of evaporation plants use to cool themselves.

trellis   A vertical structure that supports plants that climb or produce long vines.

U siphon   A simple auto-siphon that uses a upside-down U bend created from PVC pipe on the outside of a grow bed to quickly drain water from a media bed when the water level reaches the top of the loop.

UV stabilized   A substance or object protected from long-term effects of light and ultraviolet (UV) exposure.

very tender crops   *See* hot-season crops.

vining   The process of a plant producing long stems that would naturally spread across the garden bed but can be trained to grow upward.

warm-season crops   Crops that grow best at temperatures between 70° and 85°F and don't grow well in colder or hotter conditions.

water deficiency   A lack of water such that the pump cannot push water from the sump or fish tank into the grow beds, causing plants to suffer.

wire cage   A cage that is used to support sprawling plants like tomatoes and cucumbers.

worm bin   A container that contains the earthworms used to convert kitchen waste into high-quality compost.

Resources

In this appendix you'll find online resources, books, and websites that offer great information, tips, and supplies for aquaponic gardening.

Aquaponic Forums

One of the best places to learn more about aquaponics is in the online communities. Each one has a slightly different flavor, though you'll find some folks are active on all of these sites.

Aquaponics Gardening Community

community.theaquaponicsource.com

A community created by Sylvia Bernstein of the Aquaponic Source and author of the book *Aquaponic Gardening*. The site has thousands of members from around the world, but it has more of an American feel.

Aquaponics HQ

aquaponicshq.com

A site created by Gary Donaldson, author of *The Urban Aquaponics Manual*. Gary is located in South Australia and is an advocate of integrating aquaponics with other animals, such as quail.

Backyard Aquaponics

backyardaquaponics.com/forum

A forum site created by Joel Malcolm, creator of the *Backyard Aquaponics Magazine*. Joel is located in Perth, in Western Australia.

Practical Aquaponics

aquaponics.net.au/forum

A forum created by Murray Hallam, who has created a popular series of aquaponics videos. Murray himself is located in Brisbane, on the east coast of Australia in Queensland.

Online Information

Visit the following websites and blogs for additional resources and innovative ideas for your aquaponic garden.

Aquaponics Association

aquaponicsassociation.org

The Aquaponics Association promotes the benefits of aquaponics through education and outreach. The big learning opportunity is at the annual conference held in September, but content and video from past conferences can be accessed through the main website.

Backyard Aquaponics

backyardaquaponics.com

The Backyard Aquaponics site has a wealth of information, including the free manual *IBCs of Aquaponics*, which showcases aquaponic systems designed around intermediate bulk containers.

Dave's Garden Freeze/Frost Dates

davesgarden.com/guides/freeze-frost-dates

Dave's Garden is a great site for general plant information. This link also offers specific information on your growing zone.

Faith and Sustainable Technologies (F.A.S.T.)

fastonline.org

Travis Hughey uses Barrel-Ponics as a core technology for his Christian outreach. Look under Technology and Aquaponics to find the free Barrel-Ponics manual.

Gaisma

gaisma.com

Gaisma is a website that provides sunrise, sunset, dusk, and dawn times for thousands of locations all over the world, as well as average amounts of sunlight and rainfall based on information from the National Aeronautics and Space Administration (NASA) and the National Oceanic and Atmospheric Association (NOAA).

Global Buckets

globalbuckets.org

A great website put together by teenagers Grant and Max Buster showing how you can grow in soil with minimal water use—a great way to use extra water from your aquaponic system to grow those few plants that do better in soil.

International Seed Saving Institute

seedsave.org

A good website if you are interested in seed-saving and learning about permaculture.

National Gardening Association

garden.org

This organization focuses on free education in education, health and wellness, environmental stewardship, community development, and home gardening.

Nelson + Pade

aquaponics.com

Website of aquaponic pioneers, Rebecca Nelson and John Pade, who operate out of Wisconsin.

The Veggie Lady

theveggielady.com

Great information on growing healthy, organic vegetables in your home garden.

Vegetable Gardener

vegetablegardener.com

If you're looking for answers on growing vegetables and herbs, this is the place for you. Go ahead and post your questions—there are many experts here to answer them.

Product Resources

I've gathered some product websites that offer excellent products and great service.

Aquaponic Lynx LLC

aquaponiclynx.com

Aleece Landis, also known as TCLynx, offers a wealth of aquaponics information on her site, as well as supplies and consultation.

Aquaponic Store

theaquaponicstore.com

Everything you need for aquaponics, including media, fish, components, complete systems, books, and DVDs.

Aquatic Eco-Systems, Inc.

aquaticeco.com

This site has all the hardware you need for aquaculture, aquariums, koi, and aquaponics.

Backyard Aquaponics Shop

backyardaquaponicsshop.com

A source for aquaponic supplies out of Perth, Australia, as well as the online magazine *Backyard Aquaponics*.

Bigelow Brooks Farm

Bigelowbrook.com

Rob Torcellini offers automated timers and expanded shale, among other things.

EarthBox

earthbox.com

A portable, contained gardening system that allows you to add a water-thrifty, soil-based component to your garden.

Garden Harvest Supply

gardenharvestsupply.com

This online company has diatomaceous earth as well as plant starts.

Gardener's Supply

gardeners.com

Gardener's Supply is an employee-owned company where you can get seed starting equipment and an amazing array of gardening tools and supplies.

Harbor Freight

harborfreight.com

Whether you go online or visit one of their stores, Harbor Freight is a source for affordable tools, submersible pumps, and greenhouses.

HydroFarm

hydrofarm.com

HydroFarm is a wholesaler, but you can use this website to find your local hydroponics supplier and comparison shop for pumps and grow beds.

Johnny's Selected Seeds

johnnyseeds.com

A website that carries not only a wide range of seeds but also supplies for creating hoop houses and row covers.

Koi Pond: Dispelling Myths About Concrete Ponds

aquarticles.com/articles/ponds/Hoover_Doug_Concrete_Ponds.html

This article by Doug Hoover provides an overview of how to create a fish-safe pond using concrete, which is inexpensive and more durable than rubber liners.

Practical Aquaponics Shop Factory
practicalaquaponics.shopfactory.com
A source for aquaponic supplies out of Brisbane, Australia. It's fun to look and see what kinds of innovations the folks at Practical Aquaponics are dreaming up.

Simply Arbors
simplyarbors.com
This site sells arbors and trellises in metal, wood, iron, and vinyl.

Simply Trellises
simplytrellises.com
Trellises, arbors, lattice, and planters—they've got a vast selection here.

Smart Gardener
smartgardener.com
This fabulous website takes all the hard work out of planning your garden, and it's free.

Books

If you're interested in expanding your interest in aquaponic gardening and related topics like pond construction, soil gardening, and food preservation, here are some recommended books.

Barber, Terry Anne. *Setup and Care of Garden Ponds.* Neptune City, NJ: TFH Publications, 2007.

Bernstein, Sylvia. *Aquaponic Gardening: A Step-By-Step Guide to Raising Vegetables and Fish Together.* Canada: New Society Publishers, 2011.

Cancler, Carole. *The Home Preserving Bible: A Living Free Guide.* Indianapolis: Alpha Books, 2012.

Coleman, Elliot. *The Winter Harvest Handbook: Year Round Vegetable Production Using Deep Organic Techniques and Unheated Greenhouses.* White River Junction, VT: Chelsea Green Publishers, 2009.

Jabbour, Niki. *The Year-Round Vegetable Gardener: How to Grow Your Own Food 365 Days a Year, No Matter Where You Live.* North Adams, MA: Storey, 2011.

Kraft, Sundari Elizabeth. *The Complete Idiot's Guide to Urban Homesteading.* New York: Alpha Books, 2011.

McLaughlin, Chris. *The Complete Idiot's Guide to Small-Space Gardening*. Indianapolis: Alpha Books, 2012.

———. *Vertical Vegetable Gardening: A Living Free Guide*. Indianapolis: Alpha Books, 2013.

Ortho Book Editorial Staff. *All About Building Waterfalls, Ponds, and Streams*. New York, NY: Meredith Books, 2006.

Nelson, Rebecca and John S. Pade. *Aquaponic Food Product—Raising Fish and Plants for Food and Profit*. Montello, WI: Nelson and Pade, Inc., 2008.

Smith, Edward C. *The Vegetable Gardener's Bible*. North Adams, MA: Storey, 2000.

Taylor, Lisa, and Seattle Tilth. *Your Small Farm in the City*. New York, NY: Black Dog & Leventhal Publishers, 2011.

Other Resources

Here's where you can find some wonderful sources for fish, worms and other helpful critters, and seeds. It's usually best to acquire fish from local vendors, but I include a few websites where you can buy fish for aquaponics.

Fish

Ausyfish

ausyfish.com

A source for Australian fish commonly used in aquaponics—but first make sure they are legal in your area.

Fish Wagon

fishwagon.com

A source for channel catfish, fathead minnows, grass carp, bluegill, hybrid bluegill, koi, and other pond fish. They usually make the rounds to agriculture stores in the Southeast, saving you shipping costs.

The Aquaponic Store

theaquaponicstore.com

A source for tilapia fingerlings as well as bluegill, channel catfish, and mosquito fish (Gambusia).

Tilapia Fingerlings

tilapiafingerlings.com

One of many good sources for tilapia fingerlings.

USA Koi

usakoi.com

An online source for prize koi.

Bees, Worms, and Black Soldier Flies

Bush Farms

bushfarms.com

Michael Bush, author of *The Practical Beekeeper*, covers most everything you need to know to raise bees on this website.

Compost Mania

compostmania.com

Here you can get black soldier fly larvae and BioPods for composting with black soldier fly larvae.

DipTerra

dipterra.com/products---services.html

Site for information and products for raising black soldier fly larvae for composting.

Garden Worms

gardenworms.com

A website for buying worms with tips on how to go green by Jim Shaw.

Uncle Jim's Worm Farm

unclejimswormfarm.com

Uncle Jim has been raising red wiggler worms, among others, for over 40 years.

Red Worm Composting

redwormcomposting.com

Bentley "Compost Guy" Christie's website contains information and products for red worm composting, including plans for DIY compost bins.

Seeds

Baker Creek Heirloom Seeds

rareseeds.com

Baker Creek in America's heartland near Springfield, Missouri, offers 1,400 heirloom varieties. All of the seeds they carry are open-pollinated and non-GMO (free of genetically modified organisms).

BBB Seed

bbbseed.com

This Boulder, Colorado, company has open-pollinated, non-GMO (free of genetically modified organisms) seeds available for veggies, wildflowers, and herbs.

Kitchen Garden Seeds

kitchengardenseeds.com

A Connecticut company with a dizzying array of seeds and growing tips.

The Natural Gardening Company

naturalgardening.com

Website for the oldest certified organic nursery in the United States.

Peaceful Valley

groworganic.com

This website offers seeds and fish-safe remedies to control pests.

Reimer Seeds

reimerseeds.com

These folks in Saint Leonard, Maryland, have more than 4,500 quality non-GMO (free of genetically modified organisms) vegetable, herb, and flower seeds for the home garden and market growers.

Renee's Garden

reneesgarden.com

A lovely site created by Renee Shepherd. Each seed packet has a watercolor portrait of the plant on the outside, and Renee sells varieties not always available from other vendors (like mâche).

Index

Symbols

A

H

X–Y–Z